EDUGORILLA PUBLICATION

AF426194

STUDY NOTES

UGC

COMPUTER SCIENCE
(PAPER – II)

VOLUME –6

Content Table

Unit No	Unit	Page No
10.	Artificial Intelligence (AI)	**2–176**

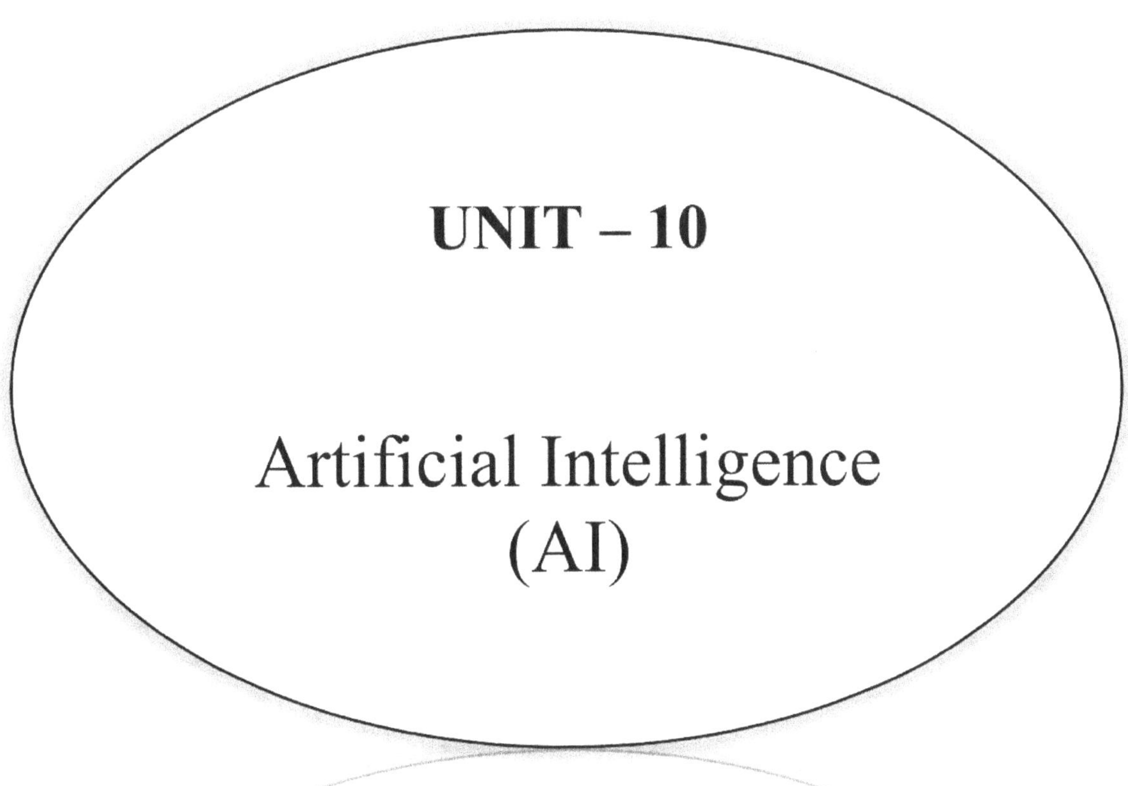

UNIT – 10

Artificial Intelligence
(AI)

Artificial Intelligence

In today's world, technology is growing very fast, and we are getting in touch withdifferent new technologies day by day.
Here, one of the booming technologies of computer science is Artificial Intelligence which is ready to create a new revolution in the world by making intelligent machines. The Artificial Intelligence is now all around us. It is currently working with a variety of subfields, ranging from general to specific, such as self-driving cars, playing chess, proving theorems, playing music, Painting, etc.
AI is one of the fascinating and universal fields of Computer science which has agreat scope in future. AI holds a tendency to cause a machine to work as a human.

Artificial Intelligence is composed of two words **Artificial** and **Intelligence**, where Artificial defines "man-made," and intelligence defines "thinking power", hence AI means "a man-made thinking power."

So, AI can be defined as:
"It is a branch of computer science by which we can create intelligent machines which can behave like a human, think like humans, and able to make decisions."

Artificial Intelligence exists when a machine can have human-based skills such as learning, reasoning, and solving problems
With Artificial Intelligence we do not need to preprogram a machine to do some work, despite that we can create a machine with programmed algorithms which can work with own intelligence, and that is the awesomeness of AI.
It is believed that AI is not a new technology, and some people says that as per Greek myth, there were Mechanical men in early days which can work and behave like humans.

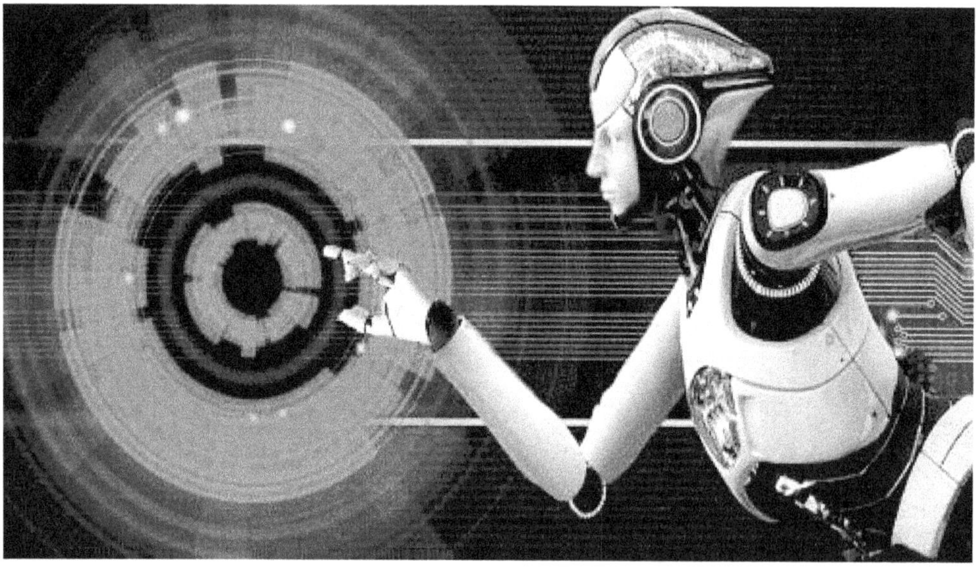

Why Artificial Intelligence?
Before Learning about Artificial Intelligence, we should know that what is the importance of AI and why should we learn it. Following are some main reasons to learn about AI:
- With the help of AI, we can create such software or devices which can solve real-world problems very easily and with accuracy such as health issues, marketing, traffic issues, etc.
- With the help of AI, we can create our personal virtual Assistant, such as Cortana, Google Assistant, Siri, etc.
- With the help of AI, we can build such Robots which can work in an environment where survival of humans can be at risk.
- AI opens a path for other new technologies, new devices, and new Opportunities.

Goals of Artificial Intelligence
Following are the main goals of Artificial Intelligence:
1) Replicate human intelligence
2) Solve Knowledge-intensive tasks
3) An intelligent connection of perception and action
4) Building a machine which can perform tasks that requires humanintelligence such as:
   - Proving a theorem
   - Playing chess

- Plan some surgical operation
- Driving a car in traffic

5) Creating some system which can exhibit intelligent behavior, learn new things by itself, demonstrate, explain, and can advise to its user.

Comprises to Artificial Intelligence

Artificial Intelligence is not just a part of computer science even it's so vast and requires lots of other factors which can contribute to it. To create the AI first we should know that how intelligence is composed, so the Intelligence is an intangible part of our brain which is a combination of **Reasoning, learning, problem-solving perception, language understanding, etc**.

To achieve the above factors for a machine or software Artificial Intelligence requires the following discipline:
- Mathematics
- Biology
- Psychology
- Sociology
- Computer Science
- Neurons Study
- Statistics

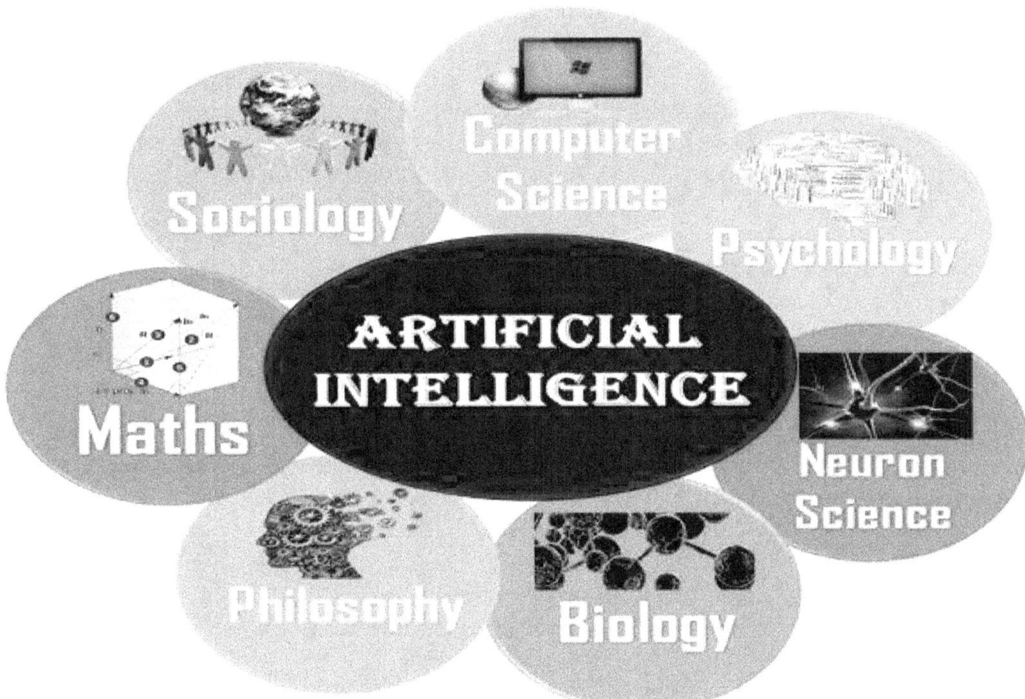

Advantages of Artificial Intelligence

Following are some main advantages of Artificial Intelligence:
- **High Accuracy with less errors:** AI machines or systems are prone to less errors and high accuracy as it takes decisions as per pre-experience or information.
- **High-Speed:** AI systems can be of very high-speed and fast decision making, because of that AI systems can beat a chess champion in the Chess game.
- **High reliability:** AI machines are highly reliable and can perform the same action multiple times with high accuracy.
- Useful for risky areas: AI machines can be helpful in situations such as defusing a bomb, exploring the ocean floor, where to employ a human can be risky.
- Digital Assistant: AI can be very useful to provide digital assistant to the users such as AI technology is currently used by various E-commerce websites to show the products as per customer requirement.
- **Useful as a public utility:** AI can be very useful for public utilities such as a self-driving car which can make our journey safer and hassle-free, facial recognition for security purpose, Natural language processing to communicate with the

human in human-language, etc.

Disadvantages of Artificial Intelligence

Every technology has some disadvantages, and the same goes for Artificial intelligence. Being so advantageous technology still, it has some disadvantages which we need to keep in our mind while creating an AI system. Following are the disadvantages of AI:

- High Cost: The hardware and software requirement of AI is very costly as it requires lots of maintenance to meet current world requirements.
- Can't think out of the box: Even we are making smarter machines with AI, but still they cannot work out of the box, as the robot will only do that work for which they are trained or programmed.
- No feelings and emotions: AI machines can be an outstanding performer, but still it does not have the feeling so it cannot make any kind of emotional attachment with human and may sometime be harmful for users if the proper care is not taken.
- Increase dependency on machines: With the increment of technology, people are getting more dependent on devices and hence they are losing their mental capabilities.
- No Original Creativity: As humans are so creative and can imagine some new ideas but still AI machines cannot beat this power of human intelligence and cannot be creative and imaginative.

5 Main Approaches to AI Learning

An algorithm is a kind of container. It provides a box for storing a method to solve a particular kind of a problem. Algorithms process data through a series of well- defined states. The states need not be deterministic, but the states are defined, nonetheless. The goal is to create an output that solves a problem. In some cases, the algorithm receives inputs that help define the output, but the focus is always on the output.

Algorithms must express the transitions between states using a well-defined and   Algorithms must express the transitions between states using a well-defined and formal language that the computer can understand. In processing the data and solving the problem, the algorithm defines, refines, and executes a function. The function is always specific to the kind of problem being addressed by the algorithm.

Each of the five tribes has a different technique and strategy for solving problems that result in unique algorithms. Combining these algorithms should lead eventually to the master algorithm that will be able to solve any given problem.

The following discussion provides an overview of the five main algorithmic techniques:

Symbolic reasoning

One of the earliest tribes, the symbolists, believed that knowledge could be obtained by operating on symbols (signs that stand for a certain meaning or event) and deriving rules from them. By putting together complex systems of rules, we could attain a logic deduction of the result we wanted to know, thus the symbolists shaped their algorithms to produce rules from data.

In symbolic reasoning, deduction expands the realm of human knowledge, while induction raises the level of human knowledge. Induction commonly opens new fields of exploration, while deduction explores those fields.

Connections modelled on the brain's neurons

The connectionists are perhaps the most famous of the five tribes. This tribe strives to reproduce the brain's functions by using silicon instead of neurons. Essentially, each of the neurons (created as an algorithm that models the real- world counterpart) solves a small piece of the problem and using many neurons in parallel solves the problem as a whole.

The use of backpropagation, or backward propagation of errors, seeks to determine the conditions under which errors are removed from networks built to resemble the human neurons by changing the weights (how much a particular input figures into the result) and biases (which features are selected) of the network. The goal is to continue changing the weights and biases until such time as the actual output matches the target output.

At this point, the artificial neuron fires and passes its solution along to the next *neuron in line. The solution created by just one neuron is only part of the whole solution. Each neuron passes information to the next neuron in line until the group of neurons creates a final output. Such a method proved the most effective in human-like tasks such as recognizing objects, understanding written and spoken language, and chatting with humans.*

Evolutionary algorithms that test variation

The evolutionaries rely on the principles of evolution to solve problems. In other words, this strategy is based on the survival of the fittest (removing any solutions that don't match the desired output). A fitness function determines the viability of each function in solving a problem. Using a tree structure, the solution method looks for the best solution based on function output.

The winner of each level of evolution gets to build the next-level functions. The idea is that the next level will get closer to solving the problem but may not solve it completely, which means that another level is needed. This particular tribe relies heavily on recursion and languages that strongly support recursion to solve problems. An interesting output of this strategy has been algorithms that evolve: One generation of algorithms actually builds the next generation.

Bayesian inference

A group of scientists, called Bayesians, perceived that uncertainty was the key aspect to keep an eye on and that learning wasn't assured but rather took place as a continuous updating of previous beliefs that grew more and more accurate.

This perception led the Bayesians to adopt statistical methods and, in particular, derivations from Bayes' theorem, which helps us to calculate probabilities under specific conditions (for instance, seeing a card of a certain seed, the starting value for a pseudo-random sequence, drawn from a deck after three other cards of same seed).

Systems that learn by analogy

The analogyzers use kernel machines to recognize patterns in data. By recognizing the pattern of one set of inputs and comparing it to the pattern of a known output, we can create a problem solution. The goal is to use similarity to determine the best solution to a problem. It's the kind of reasoning that determines that using a particular solution worked in a given circumstance at some previous time; therefore, using that solution for a similar set of circumstances should also work.

One of the most recognizable outputs from this tribe is recommender systems. For example, when we buy a product on Amazon, the recommender system comes up with other, related products that we might also want to buy.

The ultimate goal of machine learning is to combine the technologies and strategies embraced by the five tribes to create a single algorithm (the master algorithm) that can learn anything. Of course, achieving that goal is a long way off. Even so, scientists such as **Pedro Domingo's** are currently working toward that goal.

Programming without and with AI

The programming without and with AI is different in following ways:

Programming without AI	Programming with AI
A computer program without AI can answer the **specific** questions it is meant to solve.	A computer program with AI can answer the **generic** questionsit is meant to solve.
	AI programs can absorb new modifications by putting highly independent pieces of information together. Hence, we can modify even a minute piece of information of program without affecting its structure.
Modification in the program leads to change in itsstructure.	
Modification is not quick and easy. It may lead toaffecting the program adversely.	Quick and Easyprogram modification.

AI Technique

In the real world, the knowledge has some unwelcomed properties:

- Its volume is huge, next to unimaginable.
- It is not well-organized or well-formatted.
- It keeps changing constantly.

AI Technique is a manner to organize and use the knowledge efficiently in such a way that:

- It should be perceivable by the people who provide it.
- It should be easily modifiable to correct errors.
- It should be useful in many situations though it is incomplete or inaccurate.

AI techniques elevate the speed of execution of the complex program it is equipped with.

Applications of AI

AI has been dominant in various fields such as:

- Gaming – AI plays crucial role in strategic games such as chess, poker, tic- tac-toe, etc., where machine can think of large number of possible positions based on heuristic knowledge.
- Natural Language Processing – It is possible to interact with the computer that understands natural language spoken by humans.
- Expert Systems – There are some applications which integrate machine, software, and special information to impart reasoning and advising. They provide explanation and advice to the users.
- Vision Systems – These systems understand, interpret, and comprehend visual input on the computer. For example,
- A spying aero plane takes photographs, which are used to figure out spatial information or map of the areas.
- Doctors use clinical expert system to diagnose the patient.
- Police use computer software that can recognize the face of criminal with the stored portrait made by forensic artist.
- Speech Recognition – Some intelligent systems are capable of hearing and comprehending the language in terms of sentences and their meanings while a human talks to it. It can handle different accents, slang words, noise in the background, change in human's noise due to cold, etc.
- Handwriting Recognition – The handwriting recognition software reads the text written on paper by a pen or on screen by a stylus. It can recognize the shapes of the letters and convert it into editable text.
- Intelligent Robots – Robots are able to perform the tasks given by a human. They have sensors to detect physical data from the real world such as light, heat, temperature, movement, sound, bump, and pressure. They have efficient processors, multiple sensors, and huge memory, to exhibit intelligence. In addition, they are capable of learning from their mistakes, and they can adapt to the new environment.

History of AI

Here is the history of AI during 20th century:

Year	Milestone / Innovation
1923	Karel Čapek play named "Rossum's Universal Robots" (RUR) opens in London, first use of the word "robot" in English.
1943	Foundations for neural networks laid.
1945	Isaac Asimov, a Columbia University alumni, coined the term Robotics.
1950	Alan Turing introduced Turing Test for evaluation of intelligence and published Computing Machinery and Intelligence. Claude Shannon published Detailed Analysis of Chess Playing as a search.
1956	John McCarthy coined the term Artificial Intelligence. Demonstration of the first running AI program at Carnegie Mellon University.
1958	John McCarthy invents LISP programming language for AI.
1964	Danny Bobrow's dissertation at MIT showed that computers can understand natural language well enough to solve algebra wordproblems correctly.
1965	Joseph Weizenbaum at MIT built ELIZA, an interactive problem thatcarries on a dialogue in English.
1969	Scientists at Stanford Research Institute Developed Shakey, a robot, equipped with locomotion, perception, and problem solving.

| 1973 | The Assembly Robotics group at Edinburgh University built Freddy, the Famous Scottish Robot, capable of using vision to locate and assemblemodels. |

| 1979 | The first computer-controlled autonomous vehicle, Stanford Cart, wasbuilt. |

| 1985 | Harold Cohen created and demonstrated the drawing program, Aaron. |

1990 — Major advances in all areas of AI –
- Significant demonstrations in machine learning
- Case-based reasoning
- Multi-agent planning
- Scheduling
- Data mining, Web Crawler
- natural language understanding and translation
- Vision, Virtual Reality
- Games

| 1997 | The Deep Blue Chess Program beats the then world chess champion,Garry Kasparov. |

| 2000 | Interactive robot pets become commercially available. MIT displays Kismet, a robot with a face that expresses emotions. The robot Nomad explores remote regions of Antarctica and locates meteorites. |

Turing Test

A Turing Test is a method of inquiry in artificial intelligence (AI) for determining whether or not a computer is capable of thinking like a human being. The test is named after Alan Turing, the founder of the Turning Test and an English computer scientist, cryptanalyst, mathematician, and theoretical biologist.

Turing proposed that a computer can be said to possess artificial intelligence if it can mimic human responses under specific conditions. The original Turing Test requires three terminals, each of which is physically separated from the other two. One terminal is operated by a computer, while the other two are operated by humans.

During the test, one of the humans functions as the questioner, while the second human and the computer function as respondents. The questioner interrogates the respondents within a specific subject area, using a specified format and context. After a preset length of time or number of questions, the questioner is then asked to decide which respondent was human and which was a computer.

The test is repeated many times. If the questioner makes the correct determination in half of the test runs or less, the computer is considered to haveartificial intelligence because the questioner regards it as "just as human" as thehuman respondent.

History of the Turing Test

The test is named after Alan Turing, who pioneered machine learning during the 1940s and 1950s. Turing introduced the test in his 1950 paper called "ComputingMachinery and Intelligence" while at the University of Manchester.

In his paper, Turing proposed a twist on what is called "The Imitation Game." The Imitation Game involves no use of AI, but rather three human participants in three separate rooms. Each room is connected via a screen and keyboard, one containing a male, the other a female, and the other containing a male or femalejudge. The female tries to convince the judge that she is the male, and the judge tries to disseminate which is which.

Turing changes the concept of this game to include an AI, a human, and a human questioner. The questioner's job is then to decide which is the AI and which is thehuman. Science the formation of the test, many AI have been able to pass; one ofthe first is a program created by Joseph Weizenbaum called ELIZA.

Limitations of the Turing Test

The Turing Test has been criticized over the years, in particular because historically, the nature of the questioning had to be limited in order for a computer to exhibit human-like intelligence. For many years, a computer might only score high if the questioner formulated the queries, so they had "Yes" or "No" answers or pertained to a narrow field of knowledge.

When questions were open-ended and required conversational answers, it was less likely that the computer program could successfully fool the questioner. In addition, a program such as ELIZA could pass the Turing Test by manipulating symbols it does not understand fully. John Searle argued that this does not determine intelligence comparable to humans.
To many researchers, the question of whether or not a computer can pass a Turing Test has become irrelevant. Instead of focusing on how to convince someone they are conversing with a human and not a computer program, the real focus should be on how to make a human-machine interaction more intuitive and efficient. For example, by using a conversational interface.

Variations and alternatives to the Turing Test

There have been a number of variations to the Turing Test to make it more relevant. Such examples include:

- Reverse Turing Test- Where a human tries to convince a computer that it is not a computer. An example of this is a CAPTCHA.
- Total Turing Test- Where the questioner can also test perceptual abilities as well as the ability to manipulate objects.
- Minimum Intelligent Signal Test- Where only true/false and yes/no questions are given.
- Alternatives to Turing Tests were later developed because many see the Turing test to be flawed. These alternatives include tests such as:
- The Marcus Test- In which a program which can 'watch' a television show is tested by being asked meaningful questions about the show's content.
- The Lovelace Test 2.0- Which is a test made to detect AI through examining its ability to create art.
- Winograd Schema Challenge- Which is a test that asks multiple-choice questions in a specific format.

Features required for a machine to pass the Turing test:

- Natural language processing: NLP is required to communicate with Interrogator in general human language like English.
- Knowledge representation: To store and retrieve information during the test.
- Automated reasoning: To use the previously stored information for answering the questions.
- Machine learning: To adapt new changes and can detect generalized patterns.
- Vision (For total Turing test): To recognize the interrogator actions and other objects during a test.
- Motor Control (For total Turing test): To act upon objects if requested.

Agents in Artificial Intelligence (Rational Agent)

Artificial intelligence is defined as a study of rational agents. A rational agent could be anything which makes decisions, as a person, firm, machine, or software. It carries out an action with the best outcome after considering past and current percepts (agent's perceptual inputs at a given instance).

An AI system is composed of an **agent and its environment**. The agents act in their environment. The environment may contain other agents. An agent is anything that can be viewed as:

- perceiving its environment through **sensors** and
- acting upon that environment through **actuators**

Note: Every agent can perceive its own actions (but not always the effects)

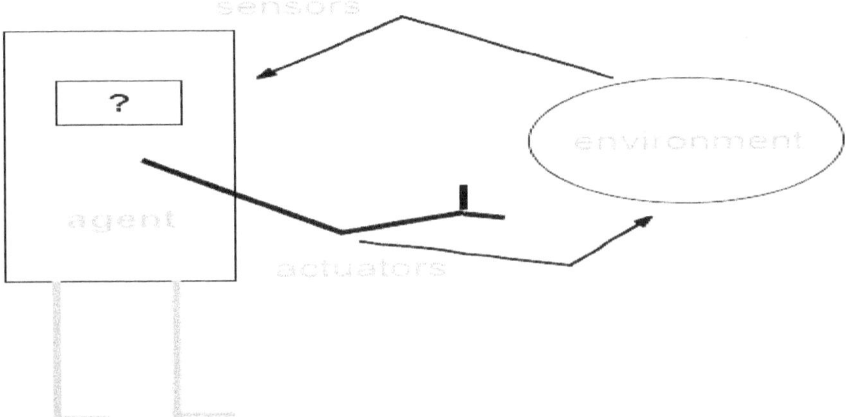

To understand the structure of Intelligent Agents, we should be familiar with Architecture and Agent Program. **Architecture** is the machinery that the agent executes on. It is a device with sensors and actuators, for example: a robotic car, a camera, a PC. **Agent program** is an implementation of an agent function. An **agent function** is a map from the percept sequence (history of all thatan agent has perceived till date) to an action.

Agent = Architecture + Agent Program

Examples of Agent:

A **software agent** has Keystrokes, file contents, received network packages whichact as sensors and displays on the screen, files, sent network packets acting as actuators.

A **Human agent** has eyes, ears, and other organs which act as sensors and hands,legs, mouth, and other body parts acting as actuators.

A **Robotic agent** has Cameras and infrared range finders which act as sensors andvarious motors acting as actuators.

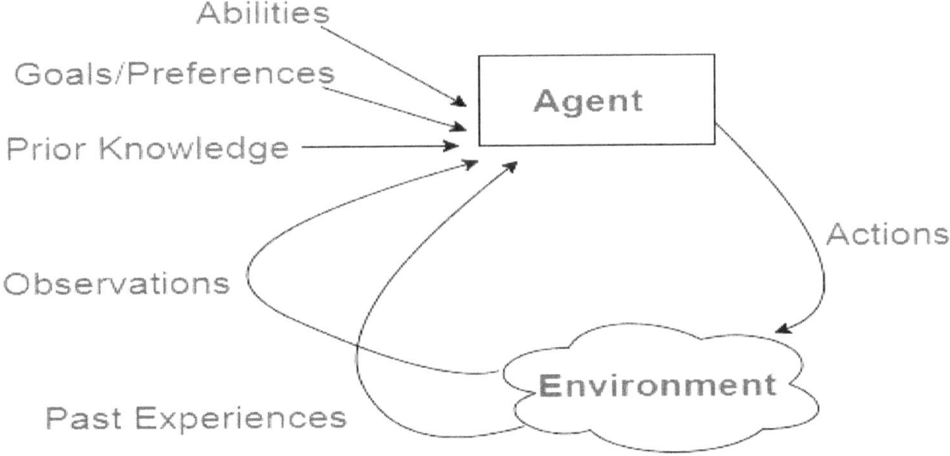

Types of Agents

Agents can be grouped into four classes based on their degree of perceived intelligence and capability:

- Simple Reflex Agents
- Model-Based Reflex Agents
- Goal-Based Agents
- Utility-Based Agents
- Learning Agent

Simple reflex agents

Simple reflex agents ignore the rest of the percept history and act only on the basis of the **current percept**. Percept history is the history of all that an agent has perceived till date. The agent function is based on the **condition-action rule**. A condition-action rule is a rule that maps a state i.e., condition to an action. If the condition is true, then the action is taken, else not.

This agent function only succeeds when the environment is fully observable. For simple reflex agents operating in partially observable environments, infinite loops are often unavoidable. It may be possible to escape from infinite loops if the agent can randomize its actions. Problems with Simple reflex agents are:

- Very limited intelligence.
- No knowledge of non-perceptual parts of state.
- Usually too big to generate and store.
- If there occurs any change in the environment, then the collection of rules needs to be updated.

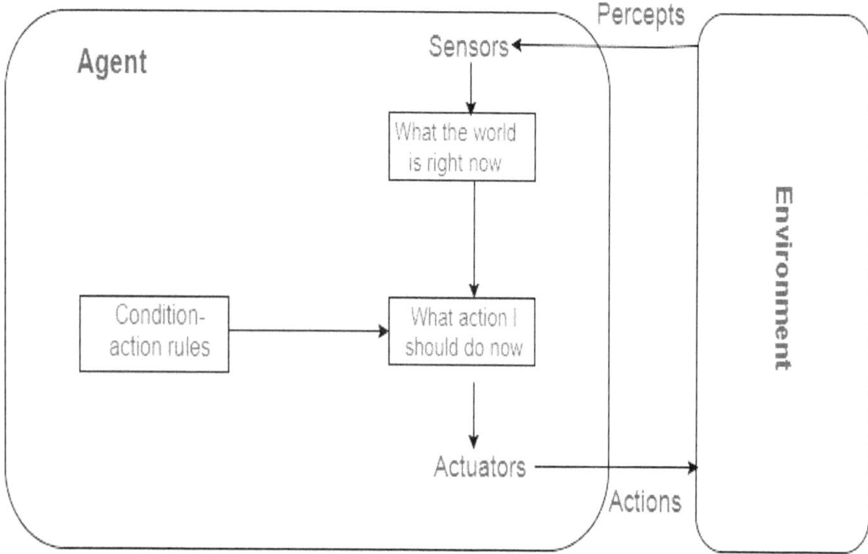

Model-based reflex agents

It works by finding a rule whose condition matches the current situation. A model-based agent can handle **partially observable environments** by use of model about the world. The agent has to keep track of **internal state** which is adjusted by each percept and that depends on the percept history.

The current state is stored inside the agent which maintains some kind of structure describing the part of the world which cannot be seen. Updating the state requires information about:

- how the world evolves in-dependently from the agent, and
- how the agent actions affect the world.

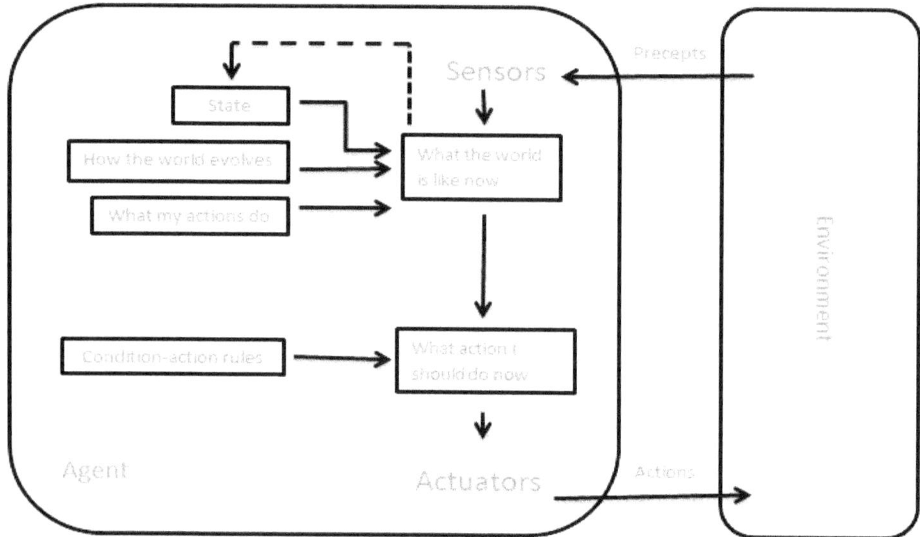

Goal-based agents

These kinds of agents take decision based on how far they are currently from their **goal** (description of desirable situations).

Their every action is intended to reduce its distance from the goal. This allows the agent a way to choose among multiple possibilities, selecting the one which reaches a goal state.

The knowledge that supports its decisions is represented explicitly and can be modified, which makes these agents more flexible. They usually require search and planning. The goal-based agent's behavior can easily be changed.

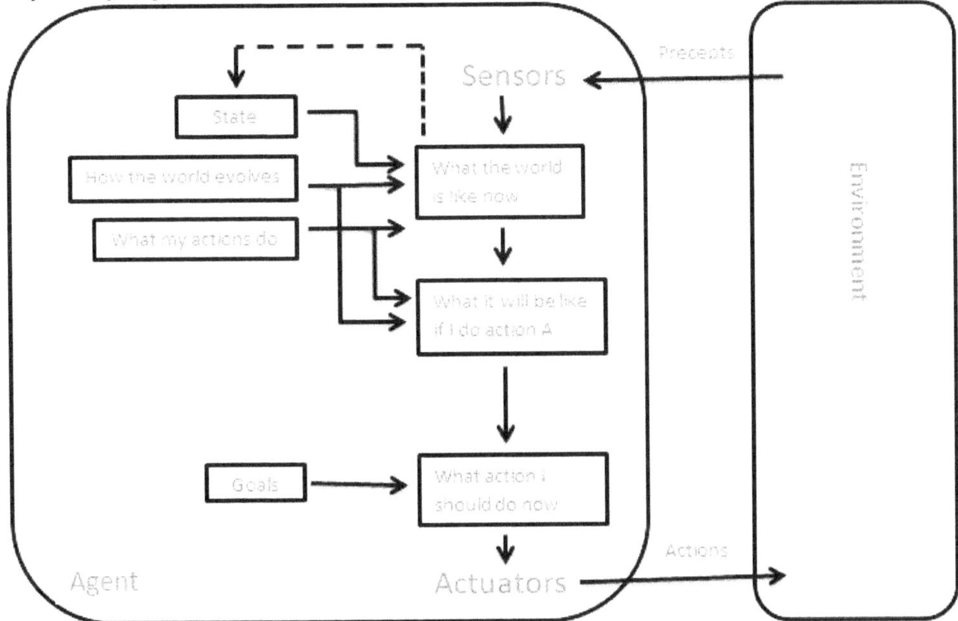

Utility-based agents

The agents which are developed having their end uses as building blocks are called utility-based agents. When there are multiple possible alternatives, then to decide which one is best, utility-based agents are used. They choose actions based on a **preference (utility)** for each state. Sometimes achieving the desired goal is not enough. We may look for a quicker, safer, cheaper trip to reach a destination.

Agent happiness should be taken into consideration. Utility describes how **"happy"** the agent is. Because of the uncertainty in the world, a utility agent chooses the action that maximizes the expected utility. A utility function maps a state onto a real number which describes the associated degree of happiness.

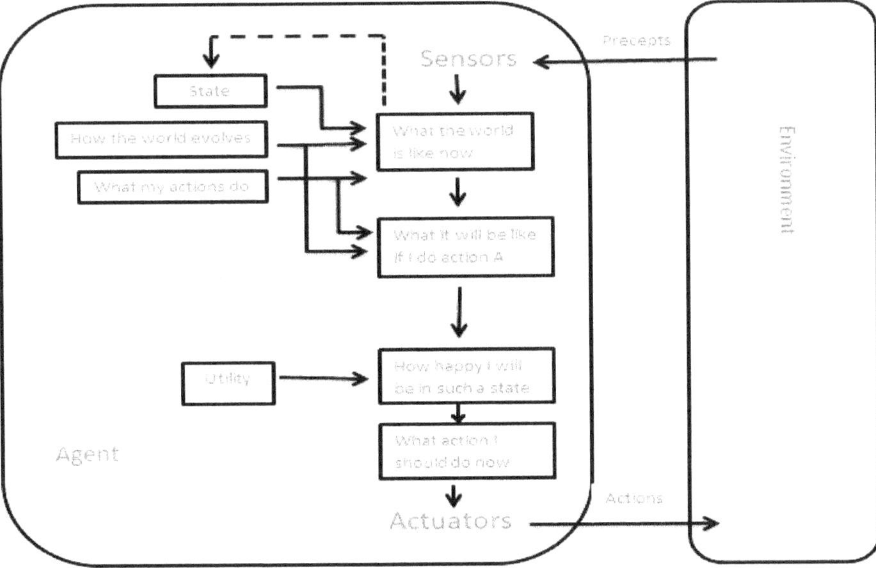

Learning Agent

A learning agent in AI is the type of agent which can learn from its pastexperiences, or it has learning capabilities. It starts to act with basic knowledge and then able to act and adapt automaticallythrough learning.

A learning agent has mainly four conceptual components, which are:

1) **Learning element:** It is responsible for making improvements by learningfrom the environment.

2) **Critic:** Learning element takes feedback from critic which describes howwell the agent is doing with respect to a fixed performance standard.

3) **Performance element:** It is responsible for selecting external action.

4) **Problem Generator:** This component is responsible for suggesting actions that will lead to new and informative experiences.

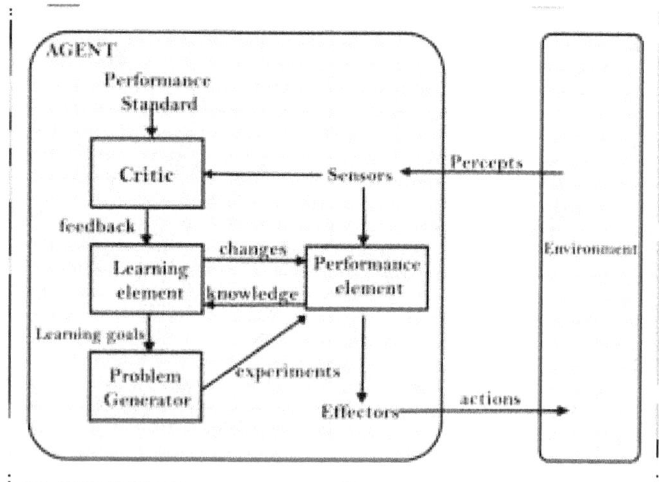

Heuristic Search

A Heuristic is a technique to solve a problem faster than classic methods, or to find an approximate solution when classic methods cannot. This is a kind of a shortcut as we often trade one of optimality, completeness, accuracy, or precisionfor speed. A Heuristic (or a heuristic function) takes a look at search algorithms.

At each branching step, it evaluates the available information and makes a decision on which branch to follow. It does so by ranking alternatives. The Heuristic is any device that is often effective but will not guarantee work in everycase. Heuristics refers to a non-optimal solution for experience-based techniques tosolve problems, learning, and discovery.

Heuristic Search Techniques

(a) **Direct Heuristic Search Techniques in AI:** Other names for these are Blind Search, Uninformed Search, and Blind Control Strategy. These aren't always possible since they demand much time or memory.They search the entire state space for a solution and use an arbitrary ordering of operations. Examples of these are Breadth First Search (BFS) and Depth First Search (DFS).

(b) **Weak Heuristic Search Techniques in AI:** Other names for these are Informed Search, Heuristic Search, and Heuristic Control Strategy. These are effective if applied correctly to the right types of tasks and usually demand domain-specific information. We need this extra informationto compute preference among child nodes to explore and expand. Each node hasa heuristic function associated with it. Examples are Best First Search (BFS) and A*.

Before moving on described certain techniques, first take a look at the ones wegenerally observe. Below, a few names.
- Best-First Search
- A* Search
- Bidirectional Search
- Tabu Search
- Beam Search
- Simulated Annealing
- Hill Climbing
- Constraint Satisfaction Problems

Search Algorithms in Artificial Intelligence

Search algorithms are one of the most important areas of Artificial Intelligence. This topic will explain all about the search algorithms in AI.

Problem-solving agents

In Artificial Intelligence, Search techniques are universal problem-solving methods. **Rational agents** or **Problem-solving agents** in AI mostly used these search strategies or algorithms to solve a specific problem and provide the bestresult. Problem-solving agents are the goal-based agents and use atomic representation. In this topic, we will learn various problem-solving searchalgorithms.

Search Algorithm Terminologies

- **Search:** Searching is a step-by-step procedure to solve a search-problem in a given search space. A search problem can have three main factors:

    a. **Search Space:** Search space represents a set of possible solutions, which asystem may have.

    b. **Start State:** It is a state from where agent begins **the search**.

- **Goal test:** It is a function which observe the current state and returns whether the goal state is achieved or not.
- **Search tree:** A tree representation of search problem is called Search tree. The root of the search tree is the root node which is corresponding to the initial state.
- **Actions:** It gives the description of all the available actions to the agent.
- **Transition model:** A description of what each action do, can be represented as atransition model.
- **Path Cost:** It is a function which assigns a numeric cost to each path.
- **Solution:** It is an action sequence which leads from the start node to the goalnode.
- **Optimal Solution:** If a solution has the lowest cost among all solutions.

Properties of Search Algorithms

Following are the four essential properties of search algorithms to compare theefficiency of these algorithms:

Completeness: A search algorithm is said to be complete if it guarantees to returna solution if at least any solution exists for any random input.

Optimality: If a solution found for an algorithm is guaranteed to be the best solution (lowest path cost) among all other solutions, then such a solution for issaid to be an optimal solution.

Time Complexity: Time complexity is a measure of time for an algorithm tocomplete its task.

Space Complexity: It is the maximum storage space required at any point duringthe search, as the complexity of the problem.

Types of search algorithms

Based on the search problems we can classify the search algorithms intouninformed (Blind search) search and informed search (Heuristic search)algorithms.

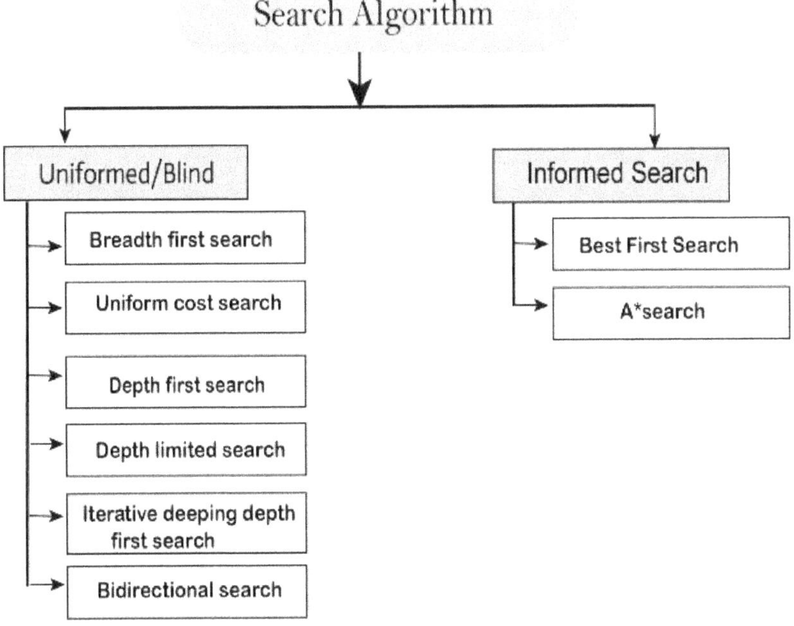

Uninformed/Blind Search

The uninformed search does not contain any domain knowledge such as closeness, the location of the goal. It operates in a brute-force way as it only includes information about how to traverse the tree and how to identify leaf andgoal nodes.

Uninformed search applies a way in which search tree is searched without any information about the search space like initial state operators and test for the goal, so it is also called blind search. It examines each node of the treeuntil it achieves the goal node.

It can be divided into five main types:
- Breadth-first search
- Uniform cost search
- Depth-first search
- Iterative deepening depth-first search
- Bidirectional Search

Informed Search

Informed search algorithms use domain knowledge. In an informed search, problem information is available which can guide the search. Informed search strategies can find a solution more efficiently than an uninformed search strategy.Informed search is also called a Heuristic search.

A heuristic is a way which might not always be guaranteed for best solutions but guaranteed to find a good solution in reasonable time. Informed search can solve much complex problem which could not be solved inanother way.

An example of informed search algorithms is a traveling salesman problem.

1) Greedy Search
2) A* Search

Heuristics of Software Testability
- **Controllability** - Software and hardware states can be controlled by test engineers and the Software modules can be tested independently
- **Observability** - Check for the object or System states and all other factorsaffecting the output.
- **Availability** - Check if Source code is accessible as product evolves in stages.
- **Simplicity** - Check if the design is consistent. Check for functional simplicity,structural simplicity, and code simplicity.
- **Stability** - Check if the Changes to the software are infrequent and changesare controlled and communicated.

Heuristics Interface for User Interface Design (UID)
- Visibility of system status
- Match between system and the real world
- Consistency and standards
- Error prevention
- Flexibility and efficiency of use
- Aesthetic and minimalist design
- Help and documentation

Game Playing

Game Playing is an important domain of artificial intelligence. Games don't require much knowledge; the only knowledge we need to provide is the rules,legal moves, and the conditions of winning or losing the game.

Both players try to win the game. So, both of them try to make the best move possible at each turn. Searching techniques like BFS (Breadth First Search) are no accurate for this as the branching factor is very high, so searching will take a lot oftime.

So, we need another search procedures that improve:

- **Generate procedure** so that only good moves are generated.
- **Test procedure** so that the best move can be explored first.

The most common search technique in game playing is **Minimax search procedure**. It is depth-first depth-limited search procedure. It is used for gameslike chess and tic-tac-toe.

Minimax algorithm uses two functions

MOVEGEN: It generates all the possible moves that can be generated from thecurrent position.

STATICEVALUATION: It returns a value depending upon the goodness from theviewpoint two-player.

This algorithm is a two-player game, so we call the first player as PLAYER1 and second player as PLAYER2. The value of each node is backed-up from its children.For PLAYER1 the backed-up value is the maximum value of its children and for PLAYER2 the backed-up value is the minimum value of its children.

It provides most promising move to PLAYER1, assuming that the PLAYER2 has make the best move. It is a recursive algorithm, as same procedure occurs at each level.

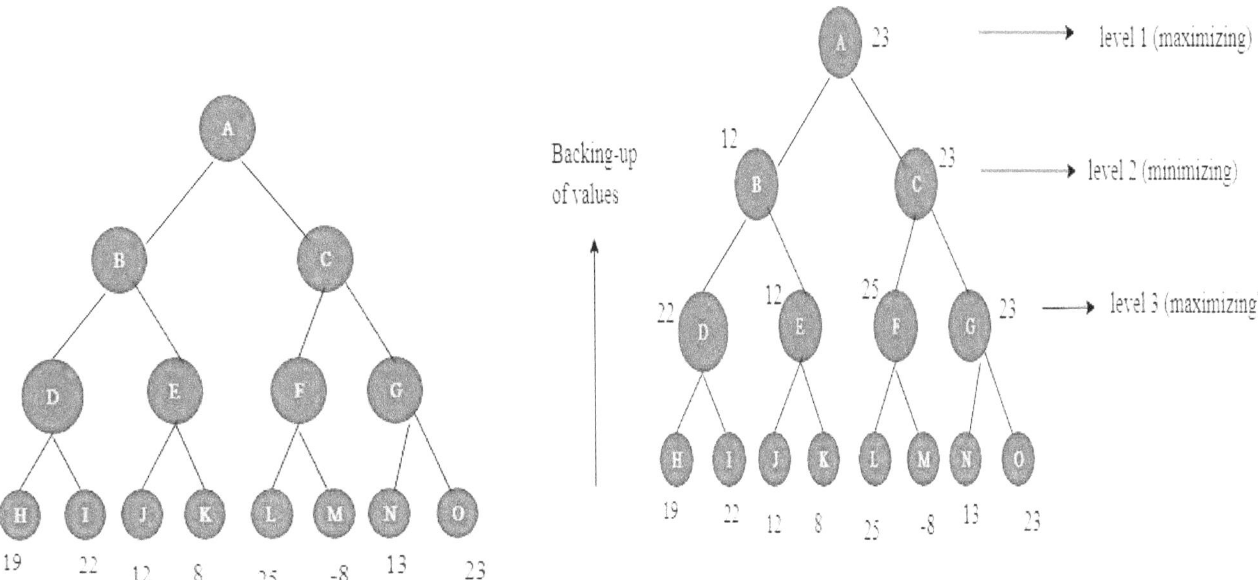

Figure 2: After backing-up of values

We assume that PLAYER1 will start the game. 4 levels are generated. The value tonodes H, I, J, K, L, M, N, O is provided by STATICEVALUATION function. Level 3 is maximizing level, so all nodes of level 3 will take maximum values of their children.

Level 2 is minimizing level, so all its nodes will take minimum values of their children. This process continues. The value of A is 23. That means A should choose C move to win.

Mini-Max Algorithm in Artificial Intelligence

- Mini-max algorithm is a recursive or backtracking algorithm which is used indecision-making and game theory. It provides an optimal move for the player assuming that opponent is also playing optimally.
- Mini-Max algorithm uses recursion to search through the game-tree.
- Min-Max algorithm is mostly used for game playing in AI. Such as Chess,Checkers, tic-tac-toe, go, and various tow-players game. This Algorithm computes the minimax decision for the current state.
- In this algorithm two players play the game; one is called MAX and other iscalled MIN.
- Both the players fight it as the opponent player gets the minimum benefitwhile they get the maximum benefit.
- Both Players of the game are opponent of each other, where MAX willselect the maximized value and MIN will select the minimized value.
- The minimax algorithm performs a depth-first search algorithm for theexploration of the complete game tree.
- The minimax algorithm proceeds all the way down to the terminal node ofthe tree, then backtrack the tree as the recursion.

Pseudo-code for Minimax Algorithm:

function minimax (node, depth, maximizing Player) is
if depth ==0 or node is a terminal node then
return static evaluation of node
if Maximizing Player then   // for Maximizer Player
maxEva= -infinity
for each child of node **do**
 eva= minimax(child, depth-1, **false**)
maxEva= max(maxEva,eva)
//gives Maximum of the values
return maxEva
else   // for Minimizer player
minEva= +infinity
for each child of node **do**
eva= minimax(child, depth-1, **true**)
minEva= min(minEva, eva)   //gives minimum of the values
return minEva

Initial call:

Minimax (node, 3, true) Working of Min-Max Algorithm:

- The working of the minimax algorithm can be easily described using anexample. Below we have taken an example of game-tree which is representing the two-player game.
- In this example, there are two players one is called Maximizer and other iscalled Minimizer.
- Maximizer will try to get the Maximum possible score, and Minimizer willtry to get the minimum possible score.
- This algorithm applies DFS, so in this game-tree, we have to go all the waythrough the leaves to reach the terminal nodes.
- At the terminal node, the terminal values are given so we will compare those value and backtrack the tree until the initial state occurs.

Followingare the main steps involved in solving the two-player game tree:
Step-1: In the first step, the algorithm generates the entire game-tree and apply the utility function to get the utility values for the terminal states. In the below tree diagram, let's take A is the initial state of the tree. Suppose maximizer takes first turn which has worst-case initial value =- infinity, and minimizer will take nextturn which has worst-case initial value = + infinity.

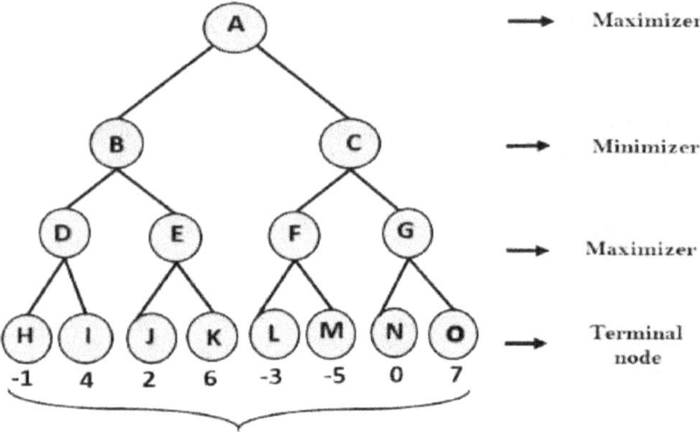

Step 2: Now, first we find the utilities value for the Maximizer, its initial value is -∞, so we will compare each value in terminal state with initial value of Maximizerand determines the higher nodes values. It will find the maximum among all.

- For node D max(-1,- -∞) => max(-1,4)= 4
- For Node E max(2, -∞) => max(2, 6)= 6
- For Node F max (-3, -∞) => max (-3,-5) = -3

- For node G max (0, -∞) = max (0, 7) = 7

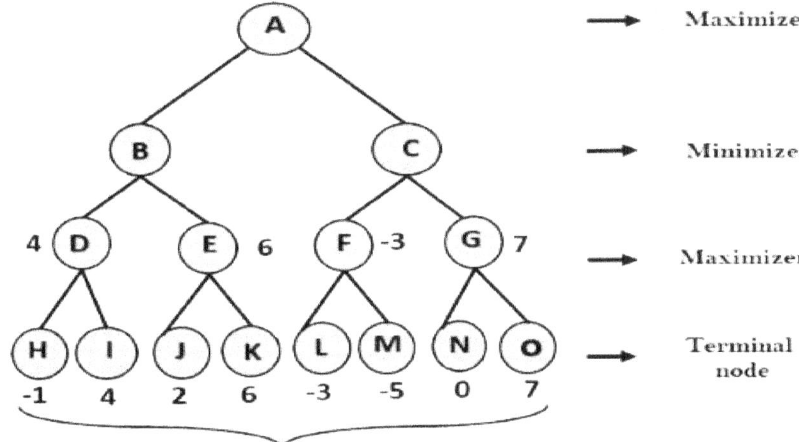

Step 3: In the next step, it's a turn for minimizer, so it will compare all nodes value with +∞, and will find the 3rd layer node values.
- For node B= min (4,6) = 4
- For node C= min (-3, 7) = -3

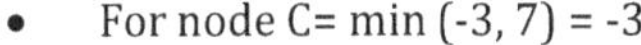

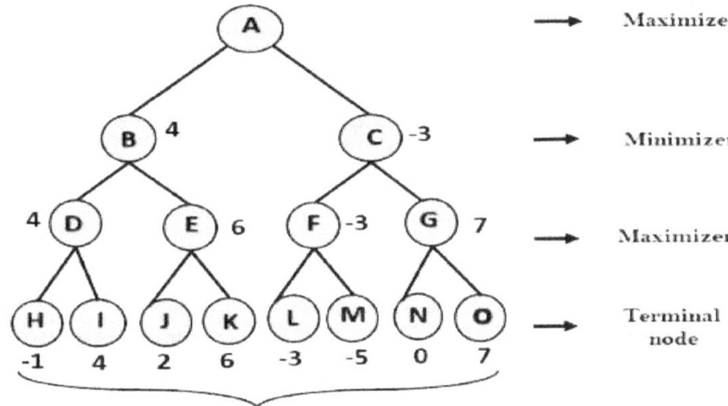

Step 3: Now it's a turn for Maximizer, and it will again choose the maximum of all nodes value and find the maximum value for the root node. In this game tree, there are only 4 layers, hence we reach immediately to the root node, but in real games, there will be more than 4 layers.
- For node A max(4, -3)= 4

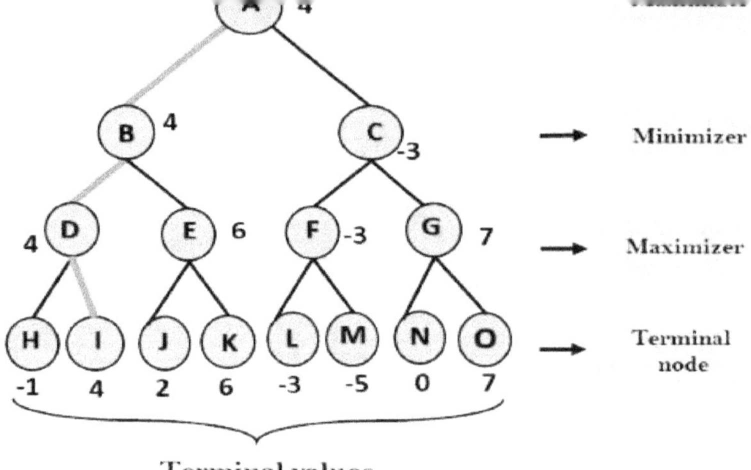

That was the complete workflow of the minimax two player game.

Properties of Mini-Max algorithm

- **Complete-** Min-Max algorithm is Complete. It will definitely find a solution(if exist), in the finite search tree.
- **Optimal-** Min-Max algorithm is optimal if both opponents are playingoptimally.
- **Time complexity-** As it performs DFS for the game-tree, so the time complexity of Min-Max algorithm is $O(b^m)$, where b is branching factor ofthe game-tree, and m is the maximum depth of the tree.
- **Space Complexity-** Space complexity of Mini-max algorithm is also similarto DFS which is $O(bm)$.

Limitation of the minimax Algorithm:

The main drawback of the minimax algorithm is that it gets really slow for complex games such as Chess, go, etc. This type of games has a huge branching factor, and the player has lots of choices to decide. This limitation of the minimaxalgorithm can be improved from **alpha-beta pruning** which we have discussed in the next topic.

Alpha-Beta Pruning

- Alpha-beta pruning is a modified version of the minimax algorithm. It is an optimization technique for the minimax algorithm.
- As we have seen in the minimax search algorithm that the number of game states it has to examine are exponential in depth of the tree. Since we cannot eliminate the exponent, but we can cut it to half.
  Hence there is a technique by which without checking each node of the game tree we can compute the correct minimax decision, and this technique is called **pruning**.

  This involves two threshold parameter Alpha and beta for future expansion,so it is called **alpha-beta pruning**. It is also called as **Alpha-Beta Algorithm**.
- Alpha-beta pruning can be applied at any depth of a tree, and sometimes itnot only prune the tree leaves but also entire sub-tree.
- The two-parameter can be defined as:
  a.   **Alpha:** The best (highest-value) choice we have found so far at any pointalong the path of Maximizer. The initial value of alpha is **-∞**.
  b.   **Beta:** The best (lowest-value) choice we have found so far at any pointalong the path of Minimizer. The initial value of beta is **+∞**.

The Alpha-beta pruning to a standard minimax algorithm returns the same moveas the standard algorithm does, but it removes all the nodes which are not really affecting the final decision but making algorithm slow. Hence by pruning thesenodes, it makes the algorithm fast.

Note: To better understand this topic, kindly study the minimax algorithm.

Condition for Alpha-beta pruning:

The main condition which required for alpha-beta pruning is:

1) $\alpha >= \beta$

Key points about alpha-beta pruning:

- The Max player will only update the value of alpha.
- The Min player will only update the value of beta.

- While backtracking the tree, the node values will be passed to upper nodesinstead of values of alpha and beta.
- We will only pass the alpha, beta values to the child nodes.

Pseudo-code for Alpha-beta Pruning:

```
function minimax(node, depth, alpha, beta, maximizingPlayer) is
if depth ==0 or node is a terminal node then
return static evaluation of node

if MaximizingPlayer then     // for Maximizer Player maxEva= -infinity
for each child of node do

eva= minimax(child, depth-1, alpha, beta, False) maxEva= max(maxEva, eva)
 alpha= max(alpha, maxEva)


 if beta<=alpha

break
return maxEva
else  // for Minimizer player
minEva= +infinity
for each child of node do
eva= minimax(child, depth-1, alpha, beta, true) minEva= min(minEva, eva)
beta= min(beta, eva)
if beta<=alpha
break
return minEva
```

Working of Alpha-Beta Pruning:

Let's take an example of two-player search tree to understand the working ofAlpha-beta pruning

Step 1: At the first step the, Max player will start first move from node A whereα= -∞ and β= +∞, these value of alpha and beta passed down to node B whereagain α= -∞ and β= +∞, and Node B passes the same value to its child D.

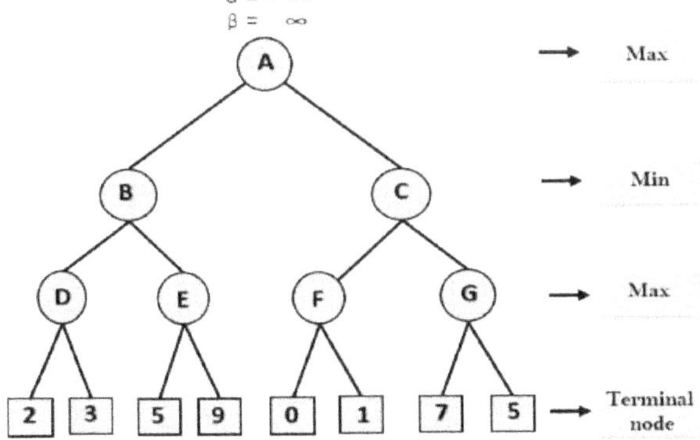

Step 2: At Node D, the value of α will be calculated as its turn for Max. The valueof α is compared with firstly 2 and then 3, and the max (2, 3) = 3 will be the valueof α at node D and node value will also 3.

Step 3: Now algorithm backtrack to node B, where the value of β will change asthis is a turn of Min, Now β= +∞, will compare with the available subsequent nodes value, i.e. min (∞, 3) = 3, hence at node B now α= -∞, and β= 3.

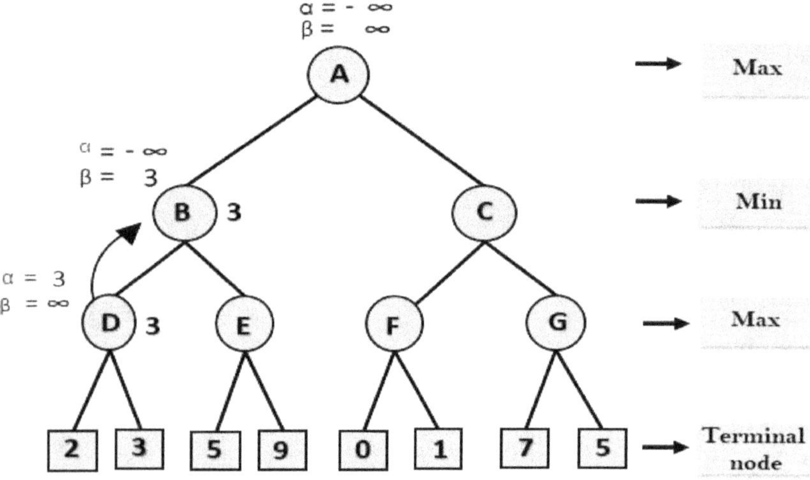

In the next step, algorithm traverse the next successor of Node B which is node E,and the values of α= -∞, and β= 3 will also be passed.

Step 4: At node E, Max will take its turn, and the value of alpha will change. The current value of alpha will be compared with 5, so max (-∞, 5) = 5, hence at nodeE α= 5 and β= 3, where α>=β, so the right successor of E will be pruned, and algorithm will not traverse it, and the value at node E will be

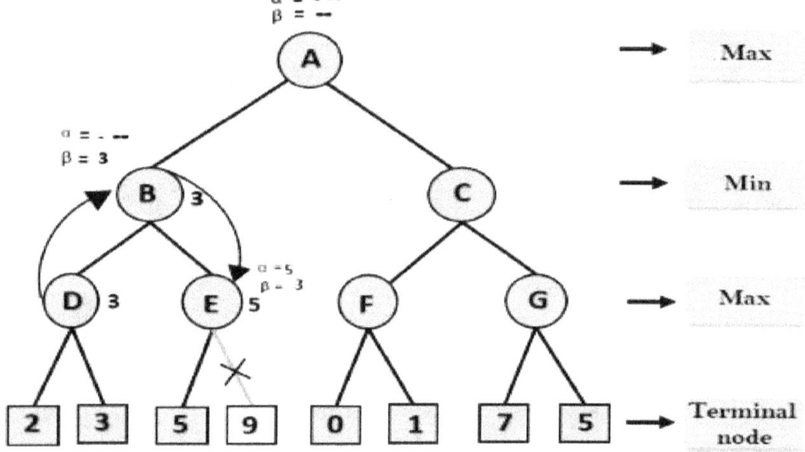

Step 5: At next step, algorithm again backtrack the tree, from node B to node A. At node A, the value of alpha will be changed the maximum available value is 3 asmax (-∞, 3)= 3, and β= +∞, these two values now passes to right successor of A which is Node C. At node C, α=3 and β= +∞, and the same values will be passed on to node F.

Step 6: At node F, again the value of α will be compared with left child which is 0,and max(3,0)= 3, and then compared with right child which is 1, and max(3,1)= 3 still α remains 3, but the node value of F will become 1.

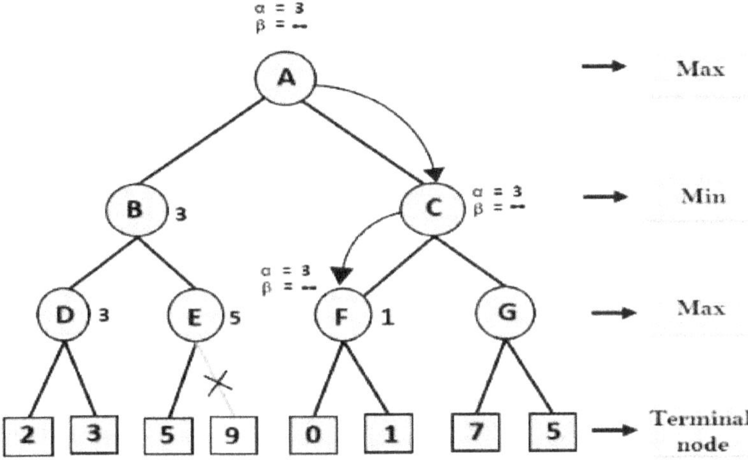

Step 7: Node F returns the node value 1 to node C, at C α= 3 and β= +∞, here the value of beta will be changed, it will compare with 1 so min (∞, 1) = 1. Now at C, α=3 and β= 1, and again it satisfies the condition α>=β, so the next child of C which is G will be pruned, and the algorithm will not compute the entire sub-treeG.

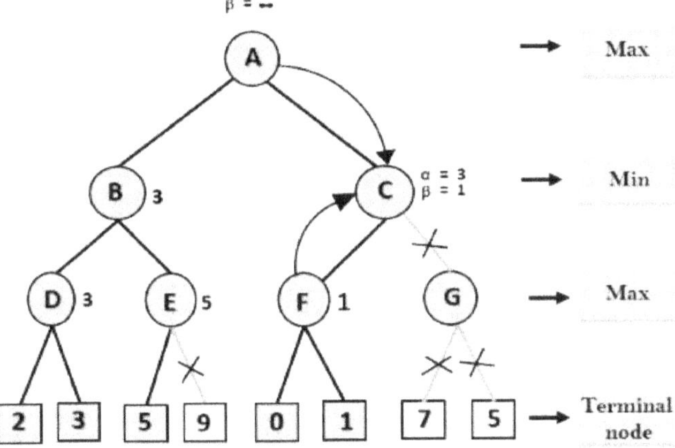

Step 8: C now returns the value of 1 to A here the best value for A is max (3, 1) =3

Following is the final game tree which is the showing the nodes which are computed and nodes which has never computed. Hence the optimal value for themaximizer is 3 for this example.

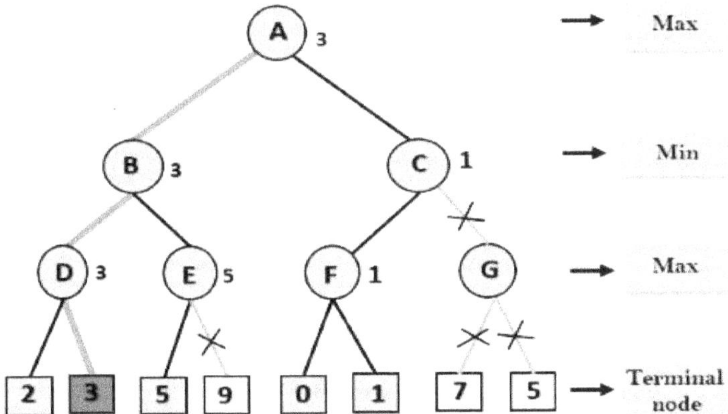

Move Ordering in Alpha-Beta pruning:

The effectiveness of alpha-beta pruning is highly dependent on the order in which each node is examined. Move order is an important aspect of alpha-beta pruning.

It can be of two types:
- **Worst ordering:** In some cases, alpha-beta pruning algorithm does not prune any of the leaves of the tree, and works

exactly as minimax algorithm. In this case, it also consumes more time because of alpha-beta factors, such a move of pruning is called worst ordering.

In this case, the best move occurs on the right side of the tree. The time complexity for suchan order is O(b^m).
- **Ideal ordering:** The ideal ordering for alpha-beta pruning occurs when lots of pruning happens in the tree, and best moves occur at the left side of thetree.

We apply DFS hence it first search left of the tree and go deep twice as minimax algorithm in the same amount of time. Complexity in ideal ordering is $O(b^{m/2})$.

Rules to find good ordering:

Following are some rules to find good ordering in alpha-beta pruning:
- Occur the best move from the shallowest node.
- Order the nodes in the tree such that the best nodes are checked first.
- Use domain knowledge while finding the best move. Ex: for Chess, try order: captures first, then threats, then forward moves, backward moves.
- We can bookkeep the states, as there is a possibility that states may repeat.

Knowledge Representation

- **Artificial intelligence** is a system that is concerned with the study of understanding, designing and implementing the ways, associated withknowledge representation to computers.
- In any intelligent system, representing the knowledge is supposed to be animportant technique to encode the knowledge.
- The main objective of AI system is to design the programs that provide information to the computer, which can be helpful to interact with humansand solve problems in various fields which require human intelligence.

What is Knowledge?

- Knowledge is an useful term to judge the understanding of an individual ona given subject.
- In intelligent systems, domain is the main focused subject area. So, thesystem specifically focuses on acquiring the domain knowledge.

Types of knowledge in AI
Depending on the type of functionality, the knowledge in AI is categorized as:
1) **Declarative knowledge**
    - The knowledge which is based on concepts, facts and objects, is termed as'Declarative Knowledge'.
    - It provides all the necessary information about the problem in termsof simple statements, either true or false.
2) **Procedural knowledge**
    - Procedural knowledge derives the information on the basis of rules,strategies, agendas and procedure.
    - It describes how a problem can be solved.
    - Procedural knowledge directs the steps on how to perform something.
    - **For example:** Computer program.
3) **Heuristic knowledge**
    - Heuristic knowledge is based on thumb rule.
    - It provides the information based on a thumb rule, which is useful inguiding the reasoning process.
    - In this type, the knowledge representation is based on the strategies to solve the problems through the experience of past problems, compiled byan expert. Hence, it is also known as **Shallow knowledge.**
4) **Meta-knowledge**
    - This type gives an idea about the other types of knowledge that are suitablefor solving problem.
    - Meta-knowledge is helpful in enhancing the efficiency of problem solvingthrough proper reasoning process.
5) **Structural knowledge**
    - Structural knowledge is associated with the information based on rules,sets, concepts and relationships.
    - It provides the information necessary for developing the knowledge structures and overall **mental model** of the problem.

Issues in knowledge representation

The main objective of knowledge representation is to draw the conclusions from the knowledge, but there are many issues associated with the use of knowledgerepresentation techniques.

Some of them are listed below:

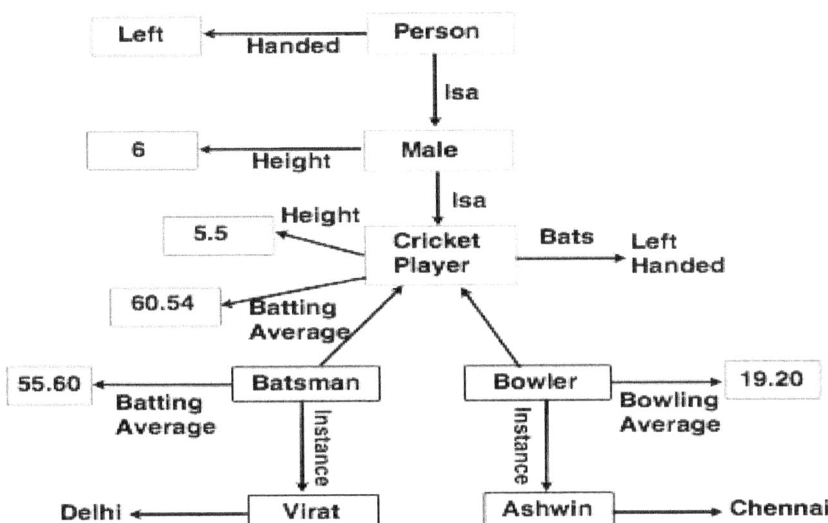

Fig: Inheratable Knowledge Representation

Refer to the above diagram to refer to the following issues.

1) **Important attributes**

    There are two attributes shown in the diagram, **instance** and **isa.** Since these attributes support property of inheritance, they are of prime importance.

2) **Relationships among attributes**

    Basically, the attributes used to describe objects are nothing but the entities. However, the attributes of an object do not depend on the encoded specificknowledge.

3) **Choosing the granularity of representation**

    While deciding the granularity of representation, it is necessary to know thefollowing:

    I.   What are the primitives and at what level should the knowledge berepresented?

    II.   What should be the number (small or large) of low-level primitives or high-levelfacts?

    High-level facts may be insufficient to draw the conclusion while Low-levelprimitives may require a lot of storage.

    For example: Suppose that we are interested in following facts:John spotted Alex.
    Now, this could be represented as "Spotted (agent(John), object (Alex))"
    Such a representation can make it easy to answer questions such as: Who spottedAlex?

    Suppose we want to know : "Did John see Sue?"
    Given only one fact, user cannot discover that answer.
    Hence, the user can add other facts, such as "Spotted (x, y) → saw (x, y)"

4) **Representing sets of objects.**

    There are some properties of objects which satisfy the condition of a set togetherbut not as individual;

    Example: Consider the assertion made in the sentences:

    "There are more sheep than people in Australia", and "English speakers can befound all over the world."
    These facts can be described by including an assertion to the sets representingpeople, sheep, and English.

5) Finding the right structure as needed

To describe a particular situation, it is always important to find the access of rightstructure. This can be done by selecting an initial structure and then revising the choice.

While selecting and reversing the right structure, it is necessary to solve followingproblem statements. **They include the process on how to:**

- Select an initial appropriate structure.
- Fill the necessary details from the current situations.
- Determine a better structure if the initially selected structure is notappropriate to fulfill other conditions.
- Find the solution if none of the available structures is appropriate.
- Create and remember a new structure for the given condition.
- There is no specific way to solve these problems, but some of the effectiveknowledge representation techniques have the potential to solve them.

Techniques of knowledge representation

There are mainly four ways of knowledge representation which are given asfollows:
1) Logical Representation
2) Semantic Network Representation
3) Frame Representation
4) Production Rules

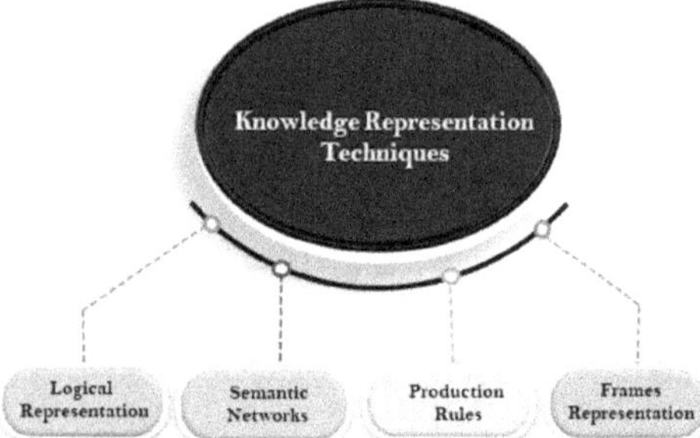

1) Logical Representation

Logical representation is a language with some concrete rules which deals with propositions and has no ambiguity in representation. Logical representation means drawing a conclusion based on various conditions. This representation laysdown some important communication rules.

It consists of precisely defined syntaxand semantics which supports the sound inference. Each sentence can be translated into logics using syntax and semantics. Facts are the general statements that may be either True or False. Thus, logic canbe used to represent such simple facts.

To build a Logic-based representation:

- User has to define a set of primitive symbols along with the requiredsemantics.
- The symbols are assigned together to define legal sentences in thelanguage for representing TRUE facts.

New logical statements are formed from the existing ones. The statements whichcan be either TRUE or false but not both , are called propositions. A declarative sentence expresses a statement with a proposition as content;

Example: The declarative "Cotton is white" expresses that Cotton is white. So, thesentence "Cotton is white" is a true statement.

Propositional logic in Artificial intelligence

Propositional logic (PL) is the simplest form of logic where all the statements are made by propositions. A proposition is a declarative statement which is either true or false. It is a technique of knowledge representation in logical and mathematical form.

Example:

a) It is Sunday.
b) The Sun rises from West (False proposition)
c) 3+3= 7(False proposition)

d) 5 is a prime number.

Following are some basic facts about propositional logic:

- Propositional logic is also called Boolean logic as it works on 0 and 1.
- In propositional logic, we use symbolic variables to represent the logic, and we can use any symbol for a representing a proposition, such A, B, C, P, Q, R, etc.
- Propositions can be either true or false, but it cannot be both.
- Propositional logic consists of an object, relations or function, and **logicalconnectives**.
- These connectives are also called logical operators.
- The propositions and connectives are the basic elements of thepropositional logic.
- Connectives can be said as a logical operator which connects twosentences.
- A proposition formula which is always true is called **tautology**, and it is alsocalled a valid sentence.
- A proposition formula which is always false is called **Contradiction**.
- A proposition formula which has both true and false values is called
- Statements which are questions, commands, or opinions are not propositions such as "**Where is Rohini**", "**How are you**", "**What is yourname**", are not propositions.

Syntax of propositional logic:

The syntax of propositional logic defines the allowable sentences for the knowledge representation. There are two types of Propositions:

a. **Atomic Propositions**
b. **Compound propositions**

- **Atomic Proposition:** Atomic propositions are the simple propositions. Itconsists of a single proposition symbol. These are the sentences which must be either true or false.

    Example:
    1) 2+2 is 4, it is an atomic proposition as it is a **true** fact.
    2) "The Sun is cold" is also a proposition as it is a **false** fact.

- **Compound proposition:** Compound propositions are constructed by combining simpler or atomic propositions, using parenthesis and logicalconnectives.

    Example:
    1) "It is raining today, and street is wet."
    2) "Ankit is a doctor, and his clinic is in Mumbai."

Logical Connectives:

Logical connectives are used to connect two simpler propositions or representinga sentence logically. We can create compound propositions with the help of logical connectives. There are mainly five connectives, which are given as follows:

1) **Negation:** A sentence such as ¬ P is called negation of P. A literal can beeither Positive literal or negative literal.
2) **Conjunction:** A sentence which has ⏑ connective such as, **P ⏑ Q** is called aconjunction.
Example: Rohan is intelligent and hardworking. It can be written as,
P= Rohan is intelligent,
Q= Rohan is hardworking. → P⏑ Q.
3) **Disjunction:** A sentence which has ∨ connective, such as **P ∨ Q**. is calleddisjunction, where P and Q are the propositions.
    Example: "Ritika is a doctor or Engineer",
    Here P= Ritika is Doctor. Q= Ritika is Doctor, so we can write it as **P ∨ Q**.
4) **Implication:** A sentence such as P → Q, is called an implication. Implications are also known as if-then rules. It can be represented as
    If it is raining, then the street is wet.
    Let P= It is raining, and Q= Street is wet, so it is represented as P → Q
5) **Biconditional:** A sentence such as P⇔ Q is a Biconditional sentence,example If I am breathing, then I am alive
    P= I am breathing, Q= I am alive, it can be represented as P ⇔ Q.

Following is the summarized table for Propositional Logic Connectives:

Connective symbols	Word	Technical term	Example
∧	AND	Conjunction	A ∧ B
∨	OR	Disjunction	A ∨ B
→	Implies	Implication	A → B
⇔	If and only if	Biconditional	A ⇔ B
¬ or ~	Not	Negation	¬ A or ¬ B

Truth Table:

propositional logic, we need to know the truth values of propositions in all possible scenarios. We can combine all the possible combination with logical connectives, and the representation of these combinations in a tabular format is called **Truth table**. Following is the truth table for all logical connectives:

For Negation:

P	¬ P
True	False
False	True

For Conjunction:

P	Q	P∧ Q
True	True	True
True	False	False
False	True	False
False	False	False

For disjunction:

P	Q	P ∨ Q.
True	True	True
False	True	True
True	False	True
False	False	False

For Implication:

P	Q	P→ Q
True	True	True
True	False	False
False	True	True
False	False	True

In

Truth table with three propositions:

We can build a proposition composing three propositions P, Q, and R. This truth table is made-up of 8n Tuples as we have taken

P	Q	R	¬R	Pv Q	PvQ→¬R
True	True	True	False	True	False
True	True	False	True	True	True
True	False	True	False	True	False
True	False	False	True	True	True
False	True	True	False	True	False
False	True	False	True	True	True
False	False	True	False	False	True
False	False	False	True	False	True

three proposition symbols.

Precedence of connectives:

Just like arithmetic operators, there is a precedence order for propositional connectors or logical operators. This order should be followed while evaluating a propositional problem. Following is the list of the precedence order for operators:

Precedence	Operators
First Precedence	Parenthesis
Second Precedence	Negation
Third Precedence	Conjunction (AND)
Fourth Precedence	Disjunction (OR)
Fifth Precedence	Implication

For Biconditional:

P	Q	P⟺Q
True	True	True
True	False	False
False	True	False
False	False	True

Six Precedence	Biconditional

Note: For better understanding use parenthesis to make sure of the correct interpretations. Such as ¬RV Q, It can be interpreted as (¬R) ∨ Q.

Logical equivalence:

Logical equivalence is one of the features of propositional logic. Two propositions are said to be logically equivalent if and only if the columns in the truth table are identical to each other.

Let's take two propositions A and B, so for logical equivalence, we can write it as A⟺B. In below truth table we can see that column for ¬AV B and A→B, are identical hence A is Equivalent to B

A	B	¬A	¬AV B	A→B
T	T	F	T	T
T	F	F	F	F
F	T	T	T	T
F	F	T	T	T

Properties of Operators:

- **Commutativity:**
  - PA Q= Q A P, or
  - P ∨ Q = Q ∨ P.
- **Associativity:**
  - (P A Q) A R= P A (Q A R),
  - (P ∨ Q) ∨ R= P ∨ (Q ∨ R)
- **Identity element:**
  - P A True = P,
  - P ∨ True= True.

- **Distributive:**
  - PA (Q ∨ R) = (P A Q) ∨ (P A R).
  - P ∨ (Q A R) = (P ∨ Q) A (P ∨ R).
- **DE Morgan's Law:**
  - ¬ (P A Q) = (¬P) ∨ (¬Q)
  - ¬ (P ∨ Q) = (¬ P) A (¬Q).
- **Double-negation elimination:**
  - ¬ (¬P) = P.

Limitations of Propositional logic:

- We cannot represent relations like ALL, some, or none with propositionallogic. Example:
a. **All the girls are intelligent.**
b. **Some apples are sweet.**

Propositional logic has limited expressive power.

In propositional logic, we cannot describe statements in terms of their propertiesor logical relationships.

Syntax:

- Syntaxes are the rules which decide how we can construct legal sentencesin the logic.
- It determines which symbol we can use in knowledge representation.
- How to write those symbols.

Semantics:

- Semantics are the rules by which we can interpret the sentence in the logic.
- Semantic also involves assigning a meaning to each sentence.

Logical representation can be categorized into mainly two logics:

a) Propositional Logics
b) Predicate logics

Note: We will discuss Prepositional Logics and Predicate logics in later chapters.

Advantages of logical representation:

1) Logical representation enables us to do logical reasoning.
2) Logical representation is the basis for the programming languages.

Disadvantages of logical Representation:

1) Logical representations have some restrictions and are challenging to workwith.
2) Logical representation technique may not be very natural, and inferencemay not be so efficient.

Note: Do not be confused with logical representation and logical reasoning as logical representation is a representation language and reasoning is a process ofthinking logically.

2) Semantic Network Representation

Semantic networks are alternative of predicate logic for knowledge representation. In Semantic networks, we can represent our knowledge in the form of graphical networks. This network consists of nodes representing objects and arcs which describe the relationship between those objects. Semantic networks can categorize the object in different forms and can also link those objects. Semantic networks are easy to understand and can be easily extended.

A semantic network or net is a graph structure for representing knowledge in patterns of interconnected nodes and arcs. Computer implementations of semantic networks were first developed for artificial intelligence and machine translation, but earlier versions have long been used in philosophy, psychology,and linguistics. The Giant Global Graph of the Semantic Web is a large semanticnetwork.

What is common to all semantic networks is a declarative graphic representation that can be used to represent knowledge and support automated systems for reasoning about the knowledge. Some versions are highly informal, but others are formally defined systems of logic.

Following are six of the most common kinds of semantic networks:

1) Definitional networks emphasize the subtype or is-a relation between aconcept type and a newly defined subtype. The resulting network, also called a generalization or subsumption hierarchy, supports the rule of inheritance for copying properties defined for a supertype to all of its subtypes. Since definitions are true by definition, the information in these networks is often assumed to be necessarily true.

2) Assertional networks are designed to assert propositions. Unlike definitional networks, the information in an assertional network is assumedto be contingently true, unless it is explicitly marked with a modal operator.

3) Some assertional networks have been proposed as models of the conceptual structures underlying natural language semantics.

4) Implicational networks use implication as the primary relation for connecting nodes. They may be used to represent patterns of beliefs,causality, or inferences.

5) Executable networks include some mechanism, such as marker passing or attached procedures, which can perform inferences, pass messages, or search for patterns and associations.
   Learning networks build or extend their representations by acquiring knowledge from examples. The new knowledge may change the old network by adding and deleting nodes and arcs or by modifying numerical values, called weights, associated with the nodes and arcs.

6) Hybrid networks combine two or more of the previous techniques, either ina single network or in separate, but closely interacting networks. Some networks were explicitly designed to implement hypotheses about human cognitive mechanisms, while others have been designed primarily for computer efficiency. Sometimes, computational issues may lead to the same conclusions aspsychological evidence.

Network notations and linear notations are capable of expressing equivalent information. But certain kinds of information are easier to express or process in one form or the other. Since the boundary lines are vague, it is impossible to state necessary and sufficient conditions that include all semantic networks while excluding other systems that are not usually called semantic networks.

This representation consists of mainly two types of relations:

a.   IS-A relation (Inheritance)

b.   Kind-of-relation

Example: Following are some statements which we need to represent in the formof nodes and arcs.
Statements:
a. Jerry is a cat.
b. Jerry is a mammal
c. Jerry is owned by Priya.
d. Jerry is brown colored.
e. All Mammals are animal.

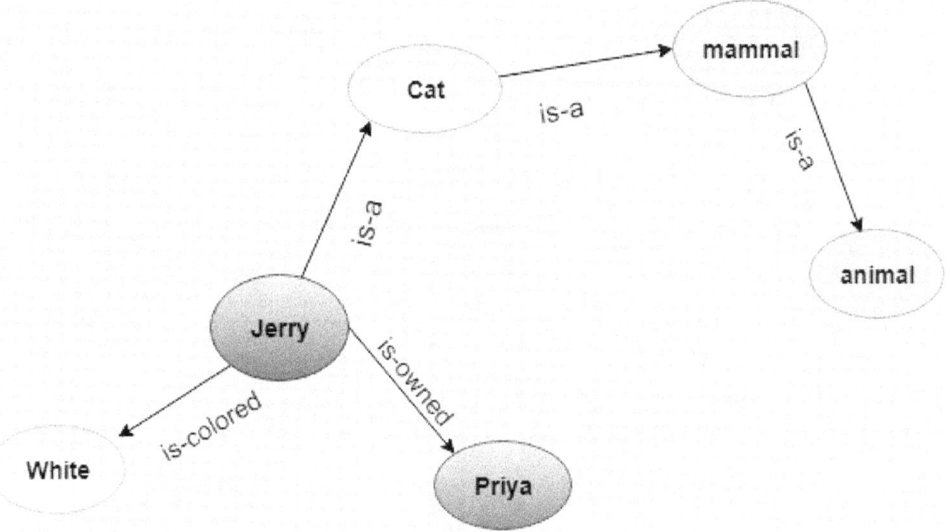

In the above diagram, we have represented the different type of knowledge in the form of nodes and arcs. Each object is connected with another object by some relation.

Drawbacks in Semantic representation:

1) Semantic networks take more computational time at runtime as we need to traverse the complete network tree to answer some questions. It might be possible in the worst-case scenario that after traversing the entire tree, we find that the solution does not exist in this network.

2) Semantic networks try to model human-like memory (Which has 1015 neurons and links) to store the information, but in practice, it is not possible to build such a vast semantic network.

3) These types of representations are inadequate as they do not have any equivalent quantifier, e.g., for all, for some, none, etc.

4) Semantic networks do not have any standard definition for the link names.

5) These networks are not intelligent and depend on the creator of the system.

Advantages of Semantic network:

1) Semantic networks are a natural representation of knowledge.

2) Semantic networks convey meaning in a transparent manner.

3) These networks are simple and easily understandable.

3) Frame Representation

A frame is a record like structure which consists of a collection of attributes and its values to describe an entity in the world. Frames are the AI data structure which divides knowledge into substructures by representing stereotypes situations. It consists of a collection of slots and slot values. These slots may be of any type and sizes. Slots have names and values which are called facets.

Facets: The various aspects of a slot is known as **Facets**. Facets are features of frames which enable us to put constraints on the frames. Example: IF-NEEDED facts are called when data of any particular slot is needed. A frame may consist of any number of slots, and a slot may include any number of facets and facets may have any number of values. A frame is also known as **slot-filter knowledge representation** in artificial intelligence.

Frames are derived from semantic networks and later evolved into our modern- day classes and objects. A single frame is not much useful. Frames system consist of a collection of frames which are connected. In the frame, knowledge about an object or event can be stored together in the knowledge base. The frame is a type of technology which is widely used in various applications including Natural language processing and machine visions.

Example: 1

An example of a frame for a book

Slots	Filters
Title	Artificial Intelligence
Genre	Computer Science
Author	Peter Norvig
Edition	Third Edition
Year	1996
Page	1152

Example 2:

suppose we are taking an entity, Peter. Peter is an engineer as a profession, and his age is 25, he lives in city London, and the country is England. So following is the frame representation for this:

Slots	Filter

Name	Peter
Profession	Doctor
Age	25
Marital status	Single
Weight	78

Advantages of frame representation:

1) The frame knowledge representation makes the programming easier bygrouping the related data.
2) The frame representation is comparably flexible and used by manyapplications in AI.
3) It is very easy to add slots for new attribute and relations.
4) It is easy to include default data and to search for missing values.
5) Frame representation is easy to understand and visualize.

Disadvantages of frame representation:

1) In frame system inference mechanism is not be easily processed.
2) Inference mechanism cannot be smoothly proceeded by framerepresentation.
3) Frame representation has a much-generalized approach.

4) Production Rules

Production rules system consist of (**condition, action**) pairs which mean, "Ifcondition then action". It has mainly three parts:

- The set of production rules
- Working Memory
- The recognize-act-cycle

In production rules agent checks for the condition and if the condition exists thenproduction rule fires and corresponding action is carried out. The condition part of the rule determines which rule may be applied to a problem. And the action part carries out the associated problem-solving steps. This complete process is called a recognize-act cycle.

The working memory contains the description of the current state of problems-solving and rule can write knowledge to the working memory. This knowledge match and may fire other rules.

If there is a new situation (state) generates, then multiple production rules will befired together, this is called conflict set. In this situation, the agent needs to selecta rule from these sets, and it is called a conflict resolution.

Example:

- IF (at bus stop AND bus arrives) THEN action (get into the bus)
- IF (on the bus AND paid AND empty seat) THEN action (sit down).

- IF (on bus AND unpaid) THEN action (pay charges).
- IF (bus arrives at destination) THEN action (get down from the bus).

Advantages of Production rule:

1) The production rules are expressed in natural language.
2) The production rules are highly modular, so we can easily remove, add ormodify an individual rule.

Disadvantages of Production rule:

1) Production rule system does not exhibit any learning capabilities, as it doesnot store the result of the problem for the future uses.
2) During the execution of the program, many rules may be active hence rule-based production systems are inefficient.

Rules for Knowledge Representation

One way to represent knowledge is by using rules that express what must happenor what does happen when certain conditions are met.

Rules are usually expressed in the form of IF . . . THEN . . . statements, such as: IF A THEN B This can be considered to have a similar logical meaning as the following: A→B

A is called the antecedent and B is the consequent in this statement. In expressing rules, the consequent usually takes the form of an action or a conclusion.

In other words, the purpose of a rule is usually to tell a system (such as an expert system) what to do in certain circumstances, or what conclusions to draw from a set of inputs about the current situation.

In general, a rule can have more than one antecedent, usually combined either by AND or by OR (logically the same as the operators ∧ and ∨).
Similarly, a rule may have more than one consequent, which usually suggests that there are multiple actions to be taken.

In general, the antecedent of a rule compares an object with a possible value, using an operator.
For example, suitable antecedents in a rule might be IF x > 3
IF name is "Bob" IF weather is cold
Here, the objects being considered are x, name, and weather; the operators are ">" and "is", and the values are 3, "Bob," and cold.

Note that an object is not necessarily an object in the real-world sense—the weather is not a real-world object, but rather a state or condition of the world.

An object in this sense is simply a variable that represents some physical object or state in the real world.

An example of a rule might be IF name is "Bob"
AND weather is cold
THEN tell Bob 'Wear a coat'

This is an example of a recommendation rule, which takes a set of inputs and gives advice as a result. The conclusion of the rule is actually an action, and the action takes the form of a recommendation to Bob that he should wear a coat.

In some cases, the rules provide more definite actions such as "move left" or "close door," in which case the rules are being used to represent directives.
Rules can also be used to represent relations such as:

IF temperature is below 0 THEN weather is cold **Scripts**
A script is a knowledge representation scheme similar to a frame, but instead of describing an object, the script describes a sequence of events. Like the frame, the script portrays a stereotyped situation. Unlike the frame, it is usually presented in a particular context. To describe a sequence of events, the script uses a series of slots containing information about the people, objects, and actions that are involved in the events.

Some of the elements of a typical script include entry conditions, props, roles, tracks, and scenes. The entry conditions describe situations that must be satisfied before events in this script can occur or be valid. Props refer to objects that are used in the sequence of events that occur. Roles refer to the people involved in the script. The result is conditions that exist after the events in the script have

occurred. Track refers to variations that might occur in a particular script. And finally, scenes describe the actual sequence of events that occur.

A typical script is shown in Figure. It is a variation of the well-known restaurant example that has been used in AI to show how knowledge is represented in script format. Going to a restaurant is a stereotyped situation with predictable entry conditions, props, roles, and scenes.

As we can see, such a script accurately describes what occurs in almost every fast-food restaurant situation. The scenes are miniscripts within the main script that describes the various subdivisions of the entire process. Note the optional scene that describes a take-out situation rather than an eat-in situation. Another option may be a drive-through scene.

Finally, note the results.

A script is useful in predicting what will happen in a specific situation. Even though certain events have not been observed, the script permits the computer to predict what will happen to whom and when. If the computer triggers a script, questions can be asked and accurate answers derived with little or no original input knowledge. Like frames, scripts are a particularly useful form of knowledge representation because there are so many stereotypical situations and events that people use every day.

Knowledge like this is generally taken for granted, but in computer problem-solving situations, such knowledge must often be simulated to solve a particular problem using artificial intelligence. To use the script, we store knowledge in the computer in symbolic form. This is best done using LISP or another symbolic language. We can then ask questions about various persons and conditions.

A search and pattern-matching process examines the script for the answers. For example, what does the customer do first? Well, he parks the car, then goes into the restaurant. Whom does he pay? The server, of course. The whole thing is totally predictable.

```
Restaurant Script
Track: Fast-food restaurant
Roles: Customer (C)
       Server (S)
Props: Counter
       Tray
       Food
       Money
       Napkins
       Salt/Pepper/Catsup/Straws
Entry Conditions: Customer in hungry.
                  Customer has money.

Scene 1: Entry
• Customer parks car.
• Customer enters restaurant.
• Customer waits in line at the counter.
• Customer reads the menu on the wall and makes a
  decision about what to order.

Scene 2: Order
• Customer gives order to server.
• Server fills order by putting food on tray.
• Customer pays server.

Scene 3: Eating
• Customer gets napkins, straws, salt, etc.
• Customer takes tray to an unoccupied table.
• Customer eats food quickly.

Scene 3A (option): Take-out
• Customer takes food and exits.

Scene 4: Exit
• Customer cleans up table.
• Customer discards trash.
• Customer leaves restaurant.
• Customer drives away.

Results:
• Customer is no longer hungry.
• Customer has less money.
• Customer is happy.*
• Customer is unhappy.*
• Customer is too full.*
• Customer has upset stomach.*

* Options
```

Typical Script

Script representation is interrelated with case-based reasoning.

Conceptual Dependency (CD)

This representation is used in natural language processing in order to represent the meaning of the sentences in such a way that inference we can be made from the sentences. It is independent of the language in which the sentences were originally stated. CD representations of a sentence is built out of primitives, which are not words belonging to the language but are conceptual, these

primitives are combined to form the meaning s of the words. As an example consider the event represented by the sentence. Conceptual Dependency originally developed to represent knowledge acquiredfrom natural language input.

The goals of this theory are:
- To help in the drawing of inference from sentences.
- To be independent of the words used in the original input.
- That is to say: For any 2 (or more) sentences that are identical in meaningthere should be only one representation of that meaning.

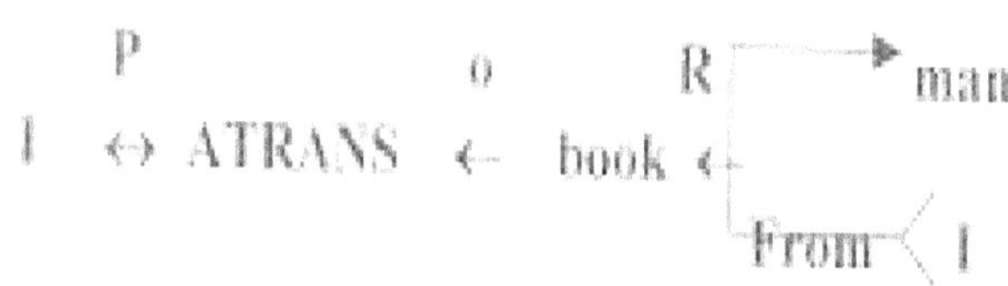

In the above representation the symbols have the following meaning:
Arrows indicate direction of dependency
Double arrow indicates two may link between actor and the actionP indicates past tense
ATRANS is one of the primitive acts used by the theory . it indicates transfer ofpossession
0 indicates the object case relation
R indicates the recipient case relation

Conceptual dependency provides a structure in which knowledge can be represented and also a set of building blocks from which representations can bebuilt. A typical set of primitive actions are
ATRANS - Transfer of an abstract relationship (Eg: give) PTRANS - Transfer of the physical location of an object(Eg: go)PROPEL - Application of physical force to an object (Eg: push) MOVE - Movement of a body part by its owner (eg : kick) GRASP - Grasping of an object by an actor(Eg: throw)

INGEST - Ingesting of an object by an animal (Eg: eat)
EXPEL - Expulsion of something from the body of an animal (cry)MTRANS - Transfer of mental information(Eg: tell)

MBUILD - Building new information out of old(Eg: decide)SPEAK - Production of sounds(Eg: say)
ATTEND - Focusing of sense organ toward a stimulus (Eg: listen)
A second set of building block is the set of allowable dependencies among theconceptualization describe in a sentence.

Conceptual Ontologies
ontology is the study of what exists. In AI, an **ontology** is a specification of the meanings of the symbols in an information system. That is, it is a specification of aconceptualization. It is a specification of what individuals and relationships are assumed to exist and what terminology is used for them. Typically, it specifies what types of individuals will be modeled, specifies what properties will be used, and gives some axioms that restrict the use of that vocabulary.

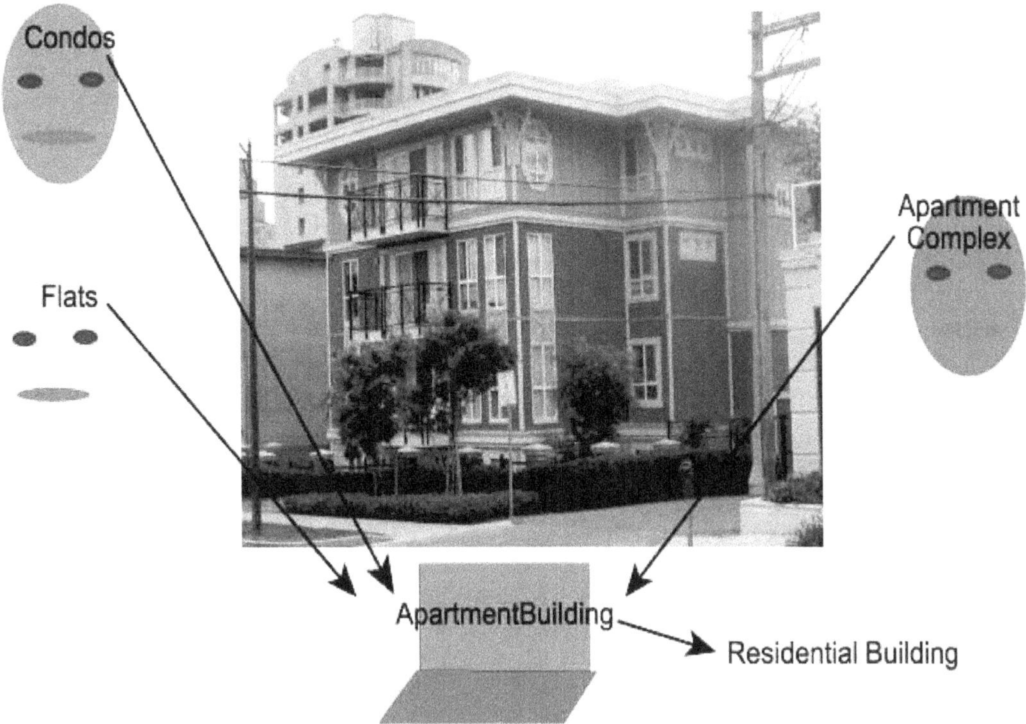

Figure 13.4: Mapping from a conceptualization to a symbol

Example 13.13: An ontology of individuals that could appear on a map could specify that the symbol "Apartment Building" will represent apartment buildings. The ontology will not define an apartment building, but it will describe it well enough so that others can understand the definition. We want other people, whomay be inclined to use different symbols, to be able to use the ontology to find the appropriate symbol to use.

Multiple people are able to use the symbol consistently. An ontology should also enable a person to verify what a symbol means. That is, given a concept, they want to be able to find the symbol, and, given the symbol, they want to be able to determine what it means.

An ontology may give axioms to restrict the use of some symbol. For example, it may specify that apartment buildings are buildings, which are human-constructedartifacts. It may give some restriction on the size of buildings so that shoeboxes cannot be buildings or that cities cannot be buildings.
It may state that a building cannot be at two geographically dispersed locations at the same time (so if you take off some part of the building and move it to a different location, it is nolonger a single building). Because apartment buildings are buildings, these restrictions also apply to apartment buildings.

Ontologies are usually written independently of a particular application and often involve a community to agree on the meanings of symbols. An ontology consists of

- A vocabulary of the categories of the things (both classes and properties)that a knowledge base may want to represent;
- An organization of the categories, for example into an inheritance hierarchyusing sub Class Of or sub Property Of, or using Aristotelian definitions; and
- A set of axioms restricting the meanings of some of the symbols to better reflect their meaning - for example, that some property is transitive, or thatthe domain and range are restricted, or that there are some restriction on the number of values a property can take for each individual. Sometimes relationships are defined in terms of more primitive relationships but, ultimately, the relationships are grounded out into **primitive** relationships that are not actually defined.

Aristotelian Definitions

Categorizing objects, the basis for modern ontologies, has a long history. Aristotle (350 B.C.) suggested the definition of a class C in terms of

- **Genus**: a superclass of C. The plural of genus is genera.
- **Differentia**: the properties that make members of the class C different fromother members of the superclass of C.

He anticipated many of the issues that arise in definitions:

If genera are different and co-ordinate, their differentiae are themselves different in kind. Take as an instance the genus "animal" and the genus "knowledge". "With feet", "two-footed", "winged", "aquatic", are differentiae of "animal", the species of knowledge are not distinguished by the same differentiae. One species of knowledge does not differ from another in being "two-footed".

Note that "co-ordinate" here means neither is subordinate to the other. In the style of modern ontologies, we would say that "animal" is a class, and "knowledge" is a class. The property "two-footed" has domain "animal". If something is an instance of knowledge, it does not have a value for the property "two-footed".

To build an ontology based on **Aristotelian definitions**:

- For each class you may want to define, determine a relevant superclass, and then select those attributes that distinguish the class from other subclasses. Each attribute gives a property and a value.
- For each property, define the most general class for which it makes sense, and define the domain of the property to be this class. Make the range another class that makes sense (perhaps requiring this range class to be defined, either by enumerating its values or by defining it using an Aristotelian definition).

This can get quite complicated. For example, defining "luxury furniture", perhaps the superclass you want is "furniture" and the distinguishing characteristics are cost is high and luxury furniture is soft. The softness of furniture is different than the softness of rocks. we also probably want to distinguish the squishiness from the texture (both of which may be regarded as soft).

This methodology does not, in general, give a tree hierarchy of classes. Objects can be in many classes. Each class does not have a single most-specific superclass. However, it is still straightforward to check whether one class is a subclass of another, to check the meaning of a class, and to determine the class that corresponds to a concept in your head.

In rare cases, this results in a tree structure, most famously in the **Linnaean taxonomy** of living things. It seems that the reason this is a tree is because of evolution. Trying to force a tree structure in other domains has been much less successful.

An ontology does not specify the individuals not known at design time. For example, an ontology of buildings would typically not include actual buildings. An ontology would specify those individuals that are fixed and should be shared, such as the days of the week, or colors.

Example 13.14: Consider a trading agent that is designed to find accommodations. Users could use such an agent to describe what accommodation they want. The trading agent could search multiple knowledge bases to find suitable accommodations or to notify users when some appropriate accommodation becomes available. An ontology is required to specify the meaning of the symbols for the user and to allow the knowledge bases to interoperate. It provides the semantic glue to tie together the users' needs with the knowledge bases.

In such a domain, houses and apartment buildings may both be residential buildings. Although it may be sensible to suggest renting a house or an apartment in an apartment building, it may not be sensible to suggest renting an apartment building to someone who does not actually specify that they want to rent the whole building. A "living unit" could be defined to be the collection of rooms that some people, who are living together, live in.

A living unit may be what a rental agency offers to rent. At some stage, the designer may have to decide whether a room for rent in a house is a living unit, or even whether part of a shared room that is rented separately is a living unit. Often the boundary cases - cases that may not be initially anticipated - are not clearly delineated but become better defined as the ontology evolves.

The ontology would not contain descriptions of actual houses or apartments because the actual available accommodation would change over time and would not change the meaning of the vocabulary.

The primary purpose of an ontology is to document what the symbols mean - the mapping between symbols (in a computer) and concepts (in someone's head).

Given a symbol, a person is able to use the ontology to determine what it means. When someone has a concept to be represented, the ontology is used to find the appropriate symbol or to determine that the concept does not exist in the ontology. The secondary purpose, achieved by the use of axioms, is to allow inference or to determine that some combination of values is inconsistent. The main challenge in building an ontology is the organization of the concepts to allow a human to map concepts into symbols in the computer, and for the computer to infer useful new knowledge from stated facts.

Expert System

An expert system is a computer program that is designed to solve complex problems and to provide decision-making ability like a human expert. It performs this by extracting knowledge from its knowledge base using the reasoning and inference rules according to the user queries.

The expert system is a part of AI, and the first ES was developed in the year 1970, which was the first successful approach of artificial intelligence. It solves the mostcomplex issue as an expert by extracting the knowledge stored in its knowledge base.

The system helps in decision making for complex problems using **both factsand heuristics like a human expert**. It is called so because it contains the expert knowledge of a specific domain and can solve any complex problem of that particular domain. These systems are designed for a specific domain, such as **medicine, science,** etc.

The performance of an expert system is based on the expert's knowledge stored in its knowledge base. The more knowledge stored in the KB, the more that system improves its performance. One of the common examples of an ES is a suggestion of spelling errors while typing in the Google search box.

Below is the block diagram that represents the working of an expert system:

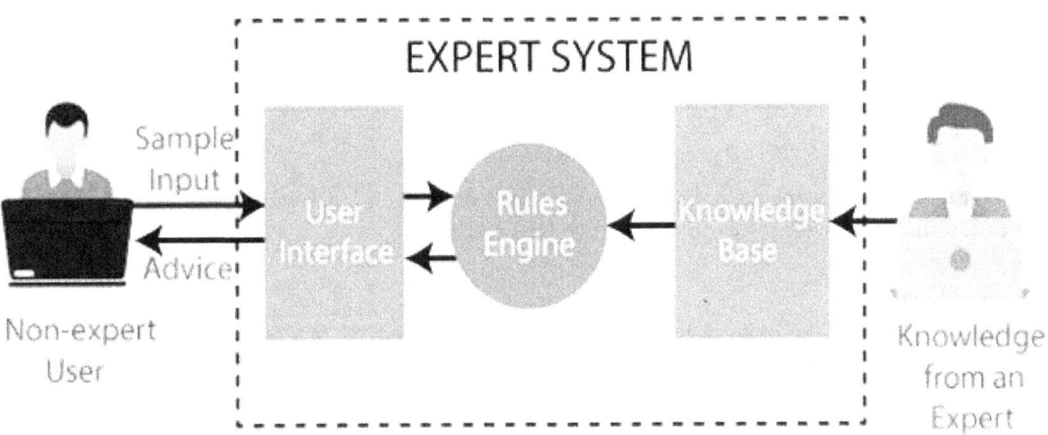

Note: It is important to remember that an expert system is not used to replace the human experts; instead, it is used to assist the human in making a complex decision. These systems do not have human capabilities of thinking and work onthe basis of the knowledge base of the particular domain.

Below are some popular examples of the Expert System:

- **DENDRAL:** It was an artificial intelligence project that was made as a chemical analysis expert system. It was used in organic chemistry to detect unknown organic molecules with the help of their mass spectra and knowledge base of chemistry.
- **MYCIN:** It was one of the earliest backward chaining expert systems that was designed to find the bacteria causing infections like bacteraemia and meningitis. It was also used for the recommendation of antibiotics and the diagnosis of blood clotting diseases.
- **PXDES:** It is an expert system that is used to determine the type and level oflung cancer. To determine the disease, it takes a picture from the upper body, which looks like the shadow. This shadow identifies the type and degree of harm.
- **CaDeT:** The CaDet expert system is a diagnostic support system that candetect cancer at early stages.

Characteristics of Expert System

- **High Performance:** The expert system provides high performance forsolving any type of complex problem of a specific domain with high efficiency and accuracy.
- **Understandable:** It responds in a way that can be easily understandable bythe user. It can take input in human language and provides the output in the same way.
- **Reliable:** It is much reliable for generating an efficient and accurate output.
- **Highly responsive:** ES provides the result for any complex query within avery short period of time.

Components of Expert System

An expert system mainly consists of three components:

- **User Interface**
- **Inference Engine**
- **Knowledge Base**

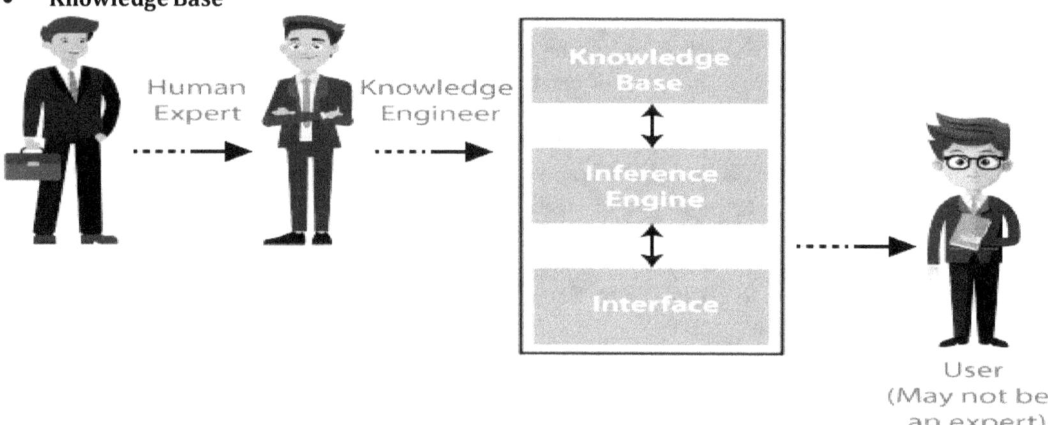

1) User Interface

With the help of a user interface, the expert system interacts with the user, takes queries as an input in a readable format, and passes it to the inference engine.

After getting the response from the inference engine, it displays the output to the user. In other words, **it is an interface that helps a non-expert user to communicate with the expert system to find a solution**.

2) Inference Engine (Rules of Engine)

- The inference engine is known as the brain of the expert system as it is the main processing unit of the system. It applies inference rules to the knowledge base to derive a conclusion or deduce new information. It helps in deriving an error-free solution of queries asked by the user.
- With the help of an inference engine, the system extracts the knowledge from the knowledge base.
- There are two types of inference engine:
- **Deterministic Inference engine:** The conclusions drawn from this type of inference engine are assumed to be true. It is based on **facts** and **rules**.
- **Probabilistic Inference engine:** This type of inference engine contains uncertainty in conclusions and based on the probability.

Inference engine uses the below modes to derive the solutions:

- **Forward Chaining:** It starts from the known facts and rules, and applies the inference rules to add their conclusion to the known facts.
- **Backward Chaining:** It is a backward reasoning method that starts from the goal and works backward to prove the known facts.

3) Knowledge Base

- The knowledge base is a type of storage that stores knowledge acquired from the different experts of the particular domain. It is considered as big storage of knowledge. The more the knowledge base, the more precise will be the Expert System.
- It is similar to a database that contains information and rules of a particular domain or subject.
- One can also view the knowledge base as collections of objects and their attributes. Such as a Lion is an object and its attributes are it is a mammal, it is not a domestic animal, etc.

Components of Knowledge Base

- **Factual Knowledge:** The knowledge which is based on facts and accepted by knowledge engineers comes under factual knowledge.

- **Heuristic Knowledge:** This knowledge is based on practice, the ability to guess, evaluation, and experiences.
- **Knowledge Representation:** It is used to formalize the knowledge stored in the knowledge base using the If-else rules.
- **Knowledge Acquisitions:** It is the process of extracting, organizing, and structuring the domain knowledge, specifying the rules to acquire the knowledge from various experts, and store that knowledge into the knowledge base.

Development of Expert System

Here, we will explain the working of an expert system by taking an example of MYCIN ES. Below are some steps to build an MYCIN:

- Firstly, ES should be fed with expert knowledge. In the case of MYCIN, human experts specialized in the medical field of bacterial infection, provide information about the causes, symptoms, and other knowledge in that domain.
- The KB of the MYCIN is updated successfully. In order to test it, the doctor provides a new problem to it. The problem is to identify the presence of the bacteria by inputting the details of a patient, including the symptoms, current condition, and medical history.
- The ES will need a questionnaire to be filled by the patient to know the general information about the patient, such as gender, age, etc.
- Now the system has collected all the information, so it will find the solution for the problem by applying if-then rules using the inference engine and using the facts stored within the KB.
- In the end, it will provide a response to the patient by using the user interface.

Participants in the development of Expert System

There are three primary participants in the building of Expert System:

1) **Expert:** The success of an ES much depends on the knowledge provided by human experts. These experts are those persons who are specialized in that specific domain.
2) **Knowledge Engineer:** Knowledge engineer is the person who gathers the knowledge from the domain experts and then codifies that knowledge to the system according to the formalism.
3) **End-User:** This is a particular person or a group of people who may not be experts, and working on the expert system needs the solution or advice for his queries, which are complex.

Why Expert System?

Before using any technology, we must have an idea about why to use that technology and hence the same for the ES. Although we have human experts in every field, then what is the need to develop a computer-based system. So below are the points that are describing the need of the ES:

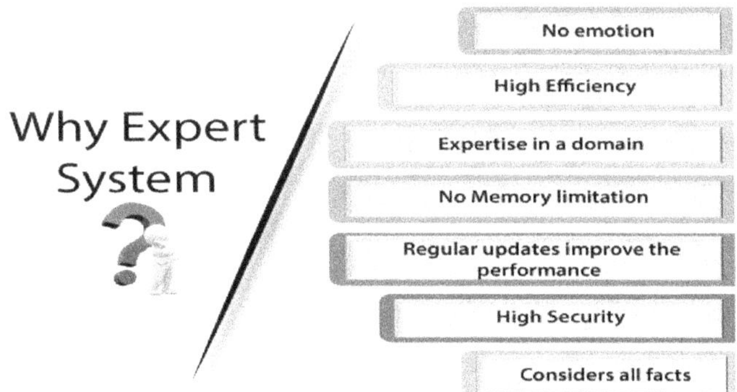

1) **No memory Limitations:** It can store as much data as required and can memorize it at the time of its application. But for human experts, there are some limitations to memorize all things at every time.
2) **High Efficiency:** If the knowledge base is updated with the correct knowledge, then it provides a highly efficient output, which may not be possible for a human.
3) **Expertise in a domain:** There are lots of human experts in each domain, and they all have different skills, different experiences, and different skills, so it is not easy to get a final output for the query. But if we put the knowledge gained from human experts into the expert system, then it provides an efficient output by mixing all the facts and knowledge.
4) **Not affected by emotions:** These systems are not affected by human emotions such as fatigue, anger, depression, anxiety,

etc.. Hence theperformance remains constant.

5) **High security:** These systems provide high security to resolve any query.

6) **Considers all the facts:** To respond to any query, it checks and considers all the available facts and provides the result accordingly. But it is possible thata human expert may not consider some facts due to any reason.

7) **Regular updates improve the performance:** If there is an issue in the result provided by the expert systems, we can improve the performance of the system by updating the knowledge base.

Capabilities of the Expert System

Below are some capabilities of an Expert System:

- **Advising:** It is capable of advising the human being for the query of anydomain from the particular ES.
- **Provide decision-making capabilities:** It provides the capability of decision making in any domain, such as for making any financial decision, decisionsin medical science, etc.
- **Demonstrate a device:** It is capable of demonstrating any new productssuch as its features, specifications, how to use that product, etc.
- **Problem-solving:** It has problem-solving capabilities.
- **Explaining a problem:** It is also capable of providing a detailed descriptionof an input problem.
- **Interpreting the input:** It is capable of interpreting the input given by theuser.
- **Predicting results:** It can be used for the prediction of a result.
- **Diagnosis:** An ES designed for the medical field is capable of diagnosing adisease without using multiple components as it already contains variousinbuilt medical tools.

Advantages of Expert System

- These systems are highly reproducible.
- They can be used for risky places where the human presence is not safe.
- Error possibilities are less if the KB contains correct knowledge.
- The performance of these systems remains steady as it is not affected byemotions, tension, or fatigue.
- They provide a very high speed to respond to a particular query.

Limitations of Expert System

- The response of the expert system may get wrong if the knowledge basecontains the wrong information.
- Like a human being, it cannot produce a creative output for differentscenarios.
- Its maintenance and development costs are very high.
- Knowledge acquisition for designing is much difficult.
- For each domain, we require a specific ES, which is one of the biglimitations.
- It cannot learn from itself and hence requires manual updates.

Applications of Expert System

- **In designing and manufacturing domain**

  It can be broadly used for designing and manufacturing physical devicessuch as camera lenses and automobiles.
- **In the knowledge domain**

  These systems are primarily used for publishing the relevant knowledge to the users. The two popular ES used for this domain is an advisor and a tax advisor.
- **In the finance domain**

  In the finance industries, it is used to detect any type of possible fraud, suspicious activity, and advise bankers that if they should provide loans forbusiness or not.
- **In the diagnosis and troubleshooting of devices**

  In medical diagnosis, the ES system is used, and it was the first area wherethese systems were used.
- **Planning and Scheduling**

  The expert systems can also be used for planning and scheduling someparticular tasks for achieving the goal of that task.

Causes of uncertainty:

Following are some leading causes of uncertainty to occur in the real world.

1) Information occurred from unreliable sources.

2) Experimental Errors
3) Equipment fault
4) Temperature variation
5) Climate change.

Probabilistic reasoning:

Probabilistic reasoning is a way of knowledge representation where we apply the concept of probability to indicate the uncertainty in knowledge. In probabilistic reasoning, we combine probability theory with logic to handle the uncertainty.

We use probability in probabilistic reasoning because it provides a way to handlethe uncertainty that is the result of someone's laziness and ignorance.

In the real world, there are lots of scenarios, where the certainty of something is not confirmed, such as "It will rain today," "behavior of someone for some situations," "A match between two teams or two players." These are probable sentences for which we can assume that it will happen but not sure about it, so here we use probabilistic reasoning.

Need of probabilistic reasoning in AI:

- When there are unpredictable outcomes.
- When specifications or possibilities of predicates becomes too large tohandle.
- When an unknown error occurs during an experiment.

In probabilistic reasoning, there are two ways to solve problems with uncertainknowledge:

- **Bayes' rule**
- **Bayesian Statistics**

Note: We will learn the above two rules in later chapters.

As probabilistic reasoning uses probability and related terms, so before understanding probabilistic reasoning, let's understand some common terms:

Probability: Probability can be defined as a chance that an uncertain event will occur. It is the numerical measure of the likelihood that an event will occur. Thevalue of probability always remains between 0 and 1 that represent ideal uncertainties.

1) $0 \le P(A) \le 1$,   where $P(A)$ is the probability of an event A.
2) $P(A) = 0$, indicates total uncertainty in an event A.
3) $P(A) = 1$, indicates total certainty in an event A.

We can find the probability of an uncertain event by using the below formula.

$$\textbf{Probability of occurrence} = \frac{\text{Number of desired outcomes}}{\text{Total number of outcomes}}$$

- $P(\neg A)$ = probability of a not happening event.
- $P(\neg A) + P(A) = 1$.

Event: Each possible outcome of a variable is called an event.
Sample space: The collection of all possible events is called sample space.
Random variables: Random variables are used to represent the events andobjects in the real world.
Prior probability: The prior probability of an event is probability computed beforeobserving new information.

Posterior Probability: The probability that is calculated after all evidence or information has taken into account. It is a combination of prior probability andnew information.

Conditional probability:
Conditional probability is a probability of occurring an event when another eventhas already happened.

Let's suppose, we want to calculate the event A when event B has already occurred, "the probability of A under the conditions of

B", it can be written as:

$$P(A\,|\,B) = \frac{P(A \wedge B)}{P(B)}$$

Where P(A∧B) = Joint probability of a and BP(B) = Marginal probability of B.
If the probability of A is given and we need to find the probability of B, then it willbe given as:

$$P(B\,|\,A) = \frac{P(A \wedge B)}{P(A)}$$

It can be explained by using the below Venn diagram, where B is occurred event,so sample space will be reduced to set B, and now we can only calculate event Awhen event B is already occurred by dividing the probability of **P(A∧B) by P(B)**.

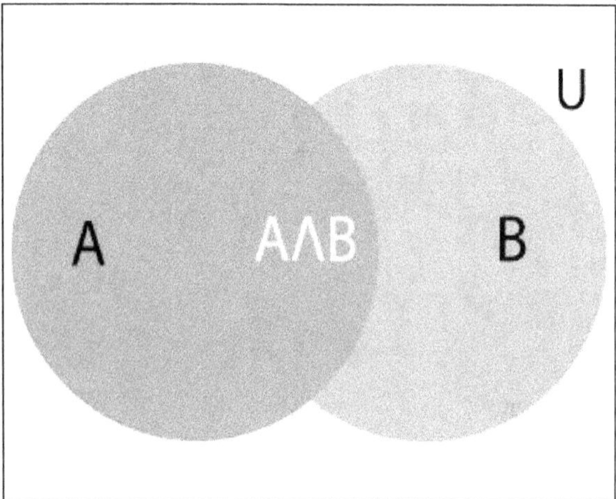

Example:
In a class, there are 70% of the students who like English and 40% of the studentswho likes English and mathematics, and then what is the percent of students those who like English also like mathematics?

Solution:
Let, A is an event that a student likes MathematicsB is an event that a student likes English.
Hence, 57% are the students who like English also like Mathematics.

$$P(A\,|\,B) = \frac{P(A \wedge B)}{P(B)} = \frac{0.4}{0.7} = 57\%$$

planning in AI?

- The planning in Artificial Intelligence is about the decision making tasks performed by the robots or computer programs to achieve a specific goal.
- The execution of planning is about choosing a sequence of actions with ahigh likelihood to complete the specific task.

Blocks-World planning problem

- The blocks-world problem is known as **Sussman Anomaly.**
- Noninterleaved planners of the early 1970s were unable to solve thisproblem, hence it is considered as anomalous.
- When two subgoals G1 and G2 are given, a noninterleaved planner produces either a plan for G1 concatenated with a plan for G2, or vice-versa.
- In blocks-world problem, three blocks labeled as 'A', 'B', 'C' are allowed torest on the flat surface. The given condition is that only one block can be moved at a time to achieve the goal.
- The start state and goal state are shown in the following diagram.

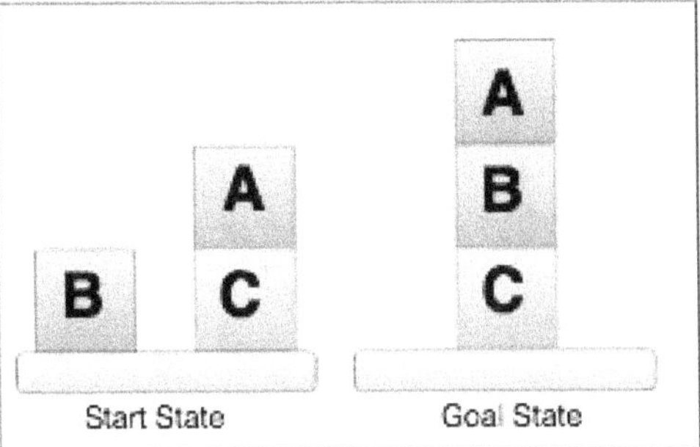

Fig: Blocks-World Planning Problem

Components of Planning System
The planning consists of following important steps:

- Choose the best rule for applying the next rule based on the best availableheuristics.
- Apply the chosen rule for computing the new problem state.
- Detect when a solution has been found.
- Detect dead ends so that they can be abandoned and the system's effort isdirected in more fruitful directions.
- Detect when an almost correct solution has been found.

Goal stack planning
This is one of the most important planning algorithms, which is specifically usedby **STRIPS.**

- The stack is used in an algorithm to hold the action and satisfy the goal. Aknowledge base is used to hold the current state, actions.
- Goal stack is similar to a node in a search tree, where the branches arecreated if there is a choice of an action.

The important steps of the algorithm are as stated below:

(a) Start by pushing the original goal on the stack. Repeat this until the stackbecomes empty. If stack top is a compound goal, then push its unsatisfied subgoals on the stack.

(b) If stack top is a single unsatisfied goal then, replace it by an action and push theaction's precondition on the stack to satisfy the condition.

(c) If stack top is an action, pop it from the stack, execute it and change theknowledge base by the effects of the action.

(d) If stack top is a satisfied goal, pop it from the stack.

Non-linear planning
This planning is used to set a goal stack and is included in the search space of allpossible subgoal orderings. It handles the goal interactions by interleaving method.

Advantage of non-Linear planning
Non-linear planning may be an optimal solution with respect to plan length(depending on search strategy used).

Disadvantages of Nonlinear planning
- It takes larger search space, since all possible goal orderings are taken intoconsideration.
- Complex algorithm to understand.

Algorithm

1) Choose a goal 'g' from the goalset
2) If 'g' does not match the state, then
    - Choose an operator 'o' whose add-list matches goal g
    - Push 'o' on the opstack
    - Add the preconditions of 'o' to the goalset
3) While all preconditions of operator on top of opstack are met in state
    - Pop operator o from top of opstack
    - state = apply(o, state)

- plan = [plan; o]

Hierarchical Task Network Planning

Hierarchies are the most common structure used to understand the world better. In galaxies, for instance, multiple-star systems are organised in a hierarchical system. Then, governmental and company organisations are structured using a hierarchy, while the Internet, which is used on a daily basis, has a space of domainnames arranged hierarchically.

Since Artificial Intelligence (AI) planning portrays information about the world and reasons to solve some of world's problems, Hierarchical Task Network (HTN) planning has been introduced almost 40 years ago to represent and deal with hierarchies. Its requirement for rich domain knowledge to characterise the world enables HTN planning to be very useful, but also to perform well.

However, the history of almost 40 years obfuscates the current understanding of HTN planning in terms of accomplishments, planning models, similarities and differences among hierarchical planners, and its current and objective image. On top of these issues, attention attracts the ability of hierarchical planning to truly cope with the requirements of applications from the real world. We propose a framework-based approach to remedy this situation.

First, we provide a basis for defining different formal models of hierarchical planning, and define two models that comprise a large portion of HTN planners.Second, we provide a set of concepts that helps to interpret HTN planners fromthe aspect of their search space. Then, we analyse and compare the planners based on a variety of properties organised in five segments, namely domain authoring, expressiveness, competence, performance and applicability.

Furthermore, we select Web service composition as a real-world and current application, and classify and compare the approaches that employ HTN planningto solve the problem of service composition. Finally, we conclude with our findings and present directions for future work.

Hierarchical Task Network (HTN) planning is an Artificial Intelligence (AI) planningtechnique that breaks with the tradition of classical planning. The basic idea behind this technique includes an initial state description, a task network as an objective to be achieved, and domain knowledge consisting of networks of primitive and compound tasks.

A task network represents a hierarchy of tasks each of which can be executed, if the task is primitive, or decomposed into refined subtasks. The planning process starts by decomposing the initial task network and continues until all compound tasks are decomposed, that is, a solution is found. The solution is a plan which equates to a set of primitive tasks applicable to the initial world state.

Beside being a tradition breaker, HTN planning appears to be controversial as well. The controversy lies in its requirement for well-conceived and well- structured domain knowledge. Such knowledge is likely to contain rich information and guidance on how to solve a planning problem, thus encoding more of the solution than was envisioned for classical planning techniques.

Thisstructured and rich knowledge gives a primary advantage to HTN planners in terms of speed and scalability when applied to real-world problems and compared to their counterparts in classical world.

The biggest contribution towards this kind of "popular" image of HTN planning has emerged after the proposal of the Simple Hierarchical Ordered Planner (SHOP) and its successors. SHOP is an HTN-based planner that shows efficient performance even on complex problems, but at the expense of providing well- written and possibly algorithmic-like domain knowledge.

Several situations may confirm our observation, but the most well-known is the disqualification of SHOPfrom the International Planning Competition (IPC) in 2000 with the reason that the domain knowledge was not well-written so that the planner produced plans that were not solutions to the competition problems. Furthermore, the disqualification was followed by a dispute on whether providing such knowledgeto a planner should be considered as "cheating" in the world of AI planning.

SHOP's style of HTN planning was introduced by the end of 1990s, but HTN planning existed long before that. The initial idea of hierarchical planning was presented by the Nets of Action Hierarchies (NOAH) planner in 1975. It was followed by a series of studies on practical implementations and theoretical contributions on HTN planning up until today.

We believe that the fruitful ideas and scientific contribution of nearly 40 years must not be easily reduced to controversy and antagonism towards HTN planning. On the other hand, we are faced with a situation full of fuzziness in terms of difficulty to understand what kind of planning style other HTN planners perform, how it is achieved and implemented, what are the similarities and differences among these planners, and finally, what is their actual contribution to the creation of the overall and possibly objective image of HTN planning.

The situation cannot be effortlessly clarified because the current literature on HTN planning, despite being very rich, reports little or nothing at all on any of these issues, especially in a consolidated form. In addition to these issues, we observe the applicability of AI planning techniques as an ultimate goal of their development. We are especially interested in novel and real-world domains which may require reconsidering established techniques.

The growing trend on other than classical and synthetic domains leads to the need for algorithms and systems that reflect planning better and more closely to the real world. This perspective gives another view to the abilities of HTN

planners (and HTN planning in general) to cope with various properties of an application in the real world. We aim to consolidate and synthesise a number of existing studies on HTN planning in a manner that will clarify, categorise and analyse HTN planners, and allow us to make statements that are not merely based on contributions of a single HTN planner.

We also hope to rectify the perception of HTN planning as being controversial and antagonistic in the AI planning community. Finally, we choose a non-traditional, dynamic and uncertain application domain to ascertain HTN planning with respect to various domain characteristics.

Partial-Order Planning

The forward and regression planners enforce a total ordering on actions at all stages of the planning process. The CSP planner commits to the particular time that the action will be carried out. This means that those planners have to commit to an ordering of actions that cannot occur concurrently when adding them to a partial plan, even if there is no particular reason to put one action before another.

The idea of a **partial-order planner** is to have a partial ordering between actions and only commit to an ordering between actions when forced. This is sometimes also called a **non-linear planner**, which is a misnomer because such planners often produce a linear plan.

A partial ordering is a less-than relation that is transitive and asymmetric. A **partial-order plan** is a set of actions together with a partial ordering, representing a "before" relation on actions, such that any total ordering of the actions, consistent with the partial ordering, will solve the goal from the initial state. Write $act_0 < act_1$ if action act_0 is before action act_1 in the partial order. This means that action act_0 must occur before action act_1.

For uniformity, treat start as an action that achieves the relations that are true in the initial state, and treat finish as an action whose precondition is the goal to be solved. The pseudoaction start is before every other action, and finish is after every other action. The use of these as actions means that the algorithm does not require special cases for the initial situation and for the goals. When the preconditions of finish hold, the goal is solved.

An action, other than start or finish, will be in a partial-order plan to achieve a precondition of an action in the plan. Each precondition of an action in the plan is either true in the initial state, and so achieved by start, or there will be an action in the plan that achieves it.

We must ensure that the actions achieve the conditions they were assigned to achieve. Each precondition P of an action act_1 in a plan will have an action act_0 associated with it such that act_0 achieves precondition P for act_1. The triple $\langle act_0, P, act_1 \rangle$ is a **causal link**. The partial order specifies that action act_0 occurs before action act_1, which is written as $act_0 < act_1$. Any other action A that makes P false must either be before act_0 or after act_1.

Informally, a partial-order planner works as follows: Begin with the actions start and finish and the partial order start < finish. The planner maintains an agenda that is a set of $\langle P, A \rangle$ pairs, where A is an action in the plan and P is an atom that is a precondition of A that must be achieved. Initially the agenda contains pairs $\langle G, finish \rangle$, where G is an atom that must be true in the goal state.

At each stage in the planning process, a pair $\langle G, act_1 \rangle$ is selected from the agenda, where P is a precondition for action act_1. Then an action, act_0, is chosen to achieve P. That action is either already in the plan - it could be the start action, for example - or it is a new action that is added to the plan. Action act_0 must happen before act_1 in the partial order. It adds a causal link that records that act_0 achieves P for action act_1.

Any action in the plan that deletes P must happen either before act_0 or after act_1. If act_0 is a new action, its preconditions are added to the agenda, and the process continues until the agenda is empty.

This is a non-deterministic procedure. The "choose" and the "either ...or ..." form choices that must be searched over. There are two choices that require search:

- which action is selected to achieve G and
- whether an action that deletes G happens before act_0 or after act_1.

non-deterministic procedure PartialOrderPlanner (Gs)2: **Inputs**
3: Gs: set of atomic propositions to achieve4: **Output**
5: linear plan to achieve Gs6: **Local**
7: Agenda: set of $\langle P,A \rangle$ pairs where P is atom and A an action8: Actions: set of actions in the current plan
9: Constraints: set of temporal constraints on actions10: CausalLinks: set of $\langle act_0,P,act_1 \rangle$ triples
11: Agenda $\leftarrow \{\langle G,finish \rangle : G \in Gs\}$12: Actions $\leftarrow \{start,finish\}$
13: Constraints $\leftarrow \{start<finish\}$
14: CausalLinks $\leftarrow \{\}$
15: **repeat**
16: select and remove $\langle G,act_1 \rangle$ from Agenda
17: **either**
18: choose $act_0 \in$ Actions such that act_0 achieves G19: **or**
20: choose $act_0 \notin$ Actions such that act_0 achieves G
21: Actions $\leftarrow$ Actions $\cup \{act_0\}$
22: Constraints $\leftarrow$ add_const(start<act_0,Constraints)
23: **for each** CL$\in$CausalLinks **do**
24: Constraints $\leftarrow$ protect(CL,act_0,Constraints)
25: Agenda $\leftarrow$ Agenda $\cup \{\langle P,act_0 \rangle$: P is a precondition of act_0 $\}$
27: Constraints $\leftarrow$ add_const(act_0<act_1,Constraints)
29: CausalLinks $\cup \{\langle act_0,G,act_1 \rangle\}$
30: **for each** A$\in$Actions **do**
31: Constraints $\leftarrow$ protect($\langle act_0,G,act_1 \rangle$,A,Constraints)
32: **until** Agenda=$\{\}$
34: **return** total ordering of Actions consistent with Constraints
Partial-order planner

The algorithm PartialOrderPlanner is given
The function add_const(act_0<act_1,Constraints) returns the constraints formed by adding the constraint act_0<act_1 to Constraints, and it fails if act_0<act_1 is incompatible with Constraints. There are many ways this function can be implemented.

The function protect($\langle act_0,G,act_1 \rangle$,A,Constraints) checks whether A$\neq act_0$ and A$\neq act_1$ and A deletes G. If so, it returns either { A<act_0 } $\cup$ Constraints or { act_1<A } $\cup$ Constraints. This is a non-deterministic choice that is searched over. Otherwise it returns Constraints.

The preceding algorithm has glossed over one important detail. It is sometimes necessary to perform some action more than once in a plan. The preceding algorithm will not work in this case, because it will try to find a partial ordering with both instances of the action occurring at the same time. To fix this problem, the ordering should be between action instances, and not actions themselves.

To implement this, assign an index to each instance of an action in the plan, and the ordering is on the action instance indexes and not the actions themselves. This is left as an exercise.

Natural Language Processing (NLP)

Natural Language Processing (NLP) refers to AI method of communicating with an intelligent system using a natural language such as English. Processing of Natural Language is required when we want an intelligent system like robot to perform as per our instructions, when we want to hear decision from a dialogue based clinical expert system, etc.

The field of NLP involves making computers to perform useful tasks with the natural language's humans use. The input and output of an NLP system can be –

- Speech
- Written Text

Components of NLP

There are two components of NLP as given –**Natural Language Understanding (NLU)** Understanding involves the following tasks –

- Mapping the given input in natural language into useful representations.
- Analyzing different aspects of the language.

Natural Language Generation (NLG)

It is the process of producing meaningful phrases and sentences in the form of natural language from some internal representation.

It involves –

- **Text planning** – It includes retrieving the relevant content from knowledgebase.
- **Sentence planning** – It includes choosing required words, formingmeaningful phrases, setting tone of the sentence.
- **Text Realization** – It is mapping sentence plan into sentence structure.The NLU is harder than NLG.

Difficulties in NLU

NL has an extremely rich form and structure.

It is very ambiguous. There can be different levels of ambiguity –

- **Lexical ambiguity** – It is at very primitive level such as word-level. For example, treating the word "board" as noun or verb?
- **Syntax Level ambiguity** – A sentence can be parsed in different ways.
  For example, "He lifted the beetle with red cap." – Did he use cap to lift thebeetle or he lifted a beetle that had red cap?
- **Referential ambiguity** – Referring to something using pronouns. For example, Rima went to Gauri. She said, "I am tired." – Exactly who is tired?
- One input can mean different meanings.
- Many inputs can mean the same thing.

NLP Terminology

- **Phonology** – It is study of organizing sound systematically.
- **Morphology** – It is a study of construction of words from primitivemeaningful units.
- **Morpheme** – It is primitive unit of meaning in a language.
- **Syntax** – It refers to arranging words to make a sentence. It also involvesdetermining the structural role of words in the sentence and in phrases.
- **Semantics** – It is concerned with the meaning of words and how tocombine words into meaningful phrases and sentences.
- **Pragmatics** – It deals with using and understanding sentences in differentsituations and how the interpretation of the sentence is affected.
- **Discourse** – It deals with how the immediately preceding sentence canaffect the interpretation of the next sentence.
- **World Knowledge** – It includes the general knowledge about the world.

Steps in NLP

There are general five steps –

- **Lexical Analysis** – It involves identifying and analyzing the structure of words. Lexicon of a language means the collection of words and phrases ina language. Lexical analysis is dividing the whole chunk of txt into paragraphs, sentences, and words.
- **Syntactic Analysis (Parsing)** – It involves analysis of words in the sentencefor grammar and arranging words in a manner that shows the relationshipamong the words. The sentence such as "The school goes to boy" is rejected by English syntactic analyzer.

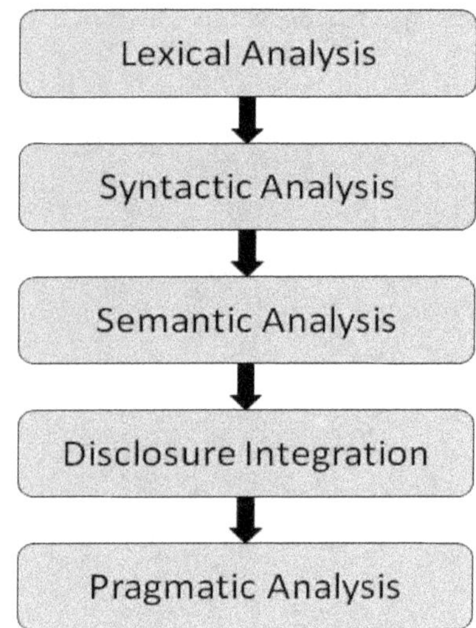

- **Semantic Analysis** – It draws the exact meaning or the dictionary meaning from the text. The text is checked for meaningfulness. It is done by mapping syntactic structures and objects in the task domain. The semantic analyzer disregards sentence such as "hot ice-cream".
- **Discourse Integration** – The meaning of any sentence depends upon the meaning of the sentence just before it. In addition, it also brings about themeaning of immediately succeeding sentence.
- **Pragmatic Analysis** – During this, what was said is re-interpreted on what itactually meant. It involves deriving those aspects of language which requirereal world knowledge.
- **Implementation Aspects of Syntactic Analysis**
- There are a number of algorithms researchers have developed for syntactic analysis, but we consider only the following simple methods –
    - Context-Free Grammar
    - Top-Down Parser

Context-Free Grammar

It is the grammar that consists rules with a single symbol on the left-hand side ofthe rewrite rules. Let us create grammar to parse a sentence –

"The bird pecks the grains"

Articles (DET) – a | an | the

Nouns – bird | birds | grain | grains

Noun Phrase (NP) – Article + Noun | Article + Adjective + Noun = DET N | DET ADJ N

Verbs – pecks | pecking | pecked

Verb Phrase (VP) – NP V | V NP

Adjectives (ADJ) – beautiful | small | chirping

The parse tree breaks down the sentence into structured parts so that the computer can easily understand and process it. In order for the parsing algorithmto construct this parse tree, a set of rewrite rules, which describe what tree structures are legal, need to be constructed.

These rules say that a certain symbol may be expanded in the tree by a sequence of other symbols. According to first order logic rule, if there are two strings Noun Phrase (NP) and Verb Phrase (VP), then the string combined by NP followed by VP is a sentence. The rewrite rules for the sentence are as follows –

S → NP VP

NP → DET N | DET ADJ NVP → V NP

Lexocon –

DET → a | the

ADJ → beautiful | perching

N → bird | birds | grain | grainsV → peck | pecks | pecking

The parse tree can be created as shown –

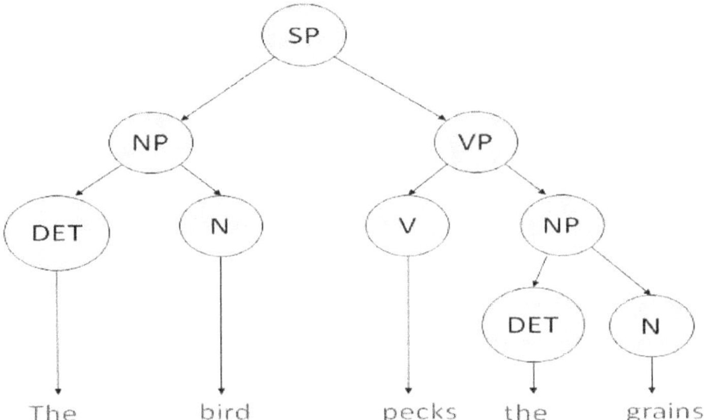

Now consider the above rewrite rules. Since V can be replaced by both, "peck" or "pecks", sentences such as "The bird peck the grains" can be wrongly permitted. i.e. the subject-verb agreement error is approved as correct.

Merit – The simplest style of grammar, therefore widely used one.
Demerits –
- They are not highly precise. For example, "The grains peck the bird", is asyntactically correct according to parser, but even if it makes no sense, parser takes it as a correct sentence.
- To bring out high precision, multiple sets of grammar need to be prepared. It may require a completely different sets of rules for parsing singular and plural variations, passive sentences, etc., which can lead to creation of hugeset of rules that are unmanageable.

Top-Down Parser
Here, the parser starts with the S symbol and attempts to rewrite it into a sequence of terminal symbols that matches the classes of the words in the inputsentence until it consists entirely of terminal symbols.

These are then checked with the input sentence to see if it matched. If not, the process is started over again with a different set of rules. This is repeated until aspecific rule is found which describes the structure of the sentence.

Merit – It is simple to implement.
Demerits –
- It is inefficient, as the search process has to be repeated if an error occurs.
- Slow speed of working.

Grammars and Languages
The types of grammars that exist are Noam Chomsky invented a hierarchy ofgrammars.
The hierarchy consists of four main types of grammars.
The simplest grammars are used to define regular languages.

A regular language is one that can be described or understood by a finite state automaton. Such languages are very simplistic and allow sentences such as "aaaaabbbbbb." Recall that a finite state automaton consists of a finite number ofstates, and rules that define how the automaton can transition from one state to another.

A finite state automaton could be designed that defined the language thatconsisted of a string of one or more occurrences of the letter a. Hence, thefollowing strings would be valid strings in this

Language:
Regular languages are of interest to computer scientists, but are not of great interest to the field of natural language processing because they are not powerfulenough to represent even simple formal languages, let alone the more complex natural languages.

Sentences defined by a regular grammar are often known as regular expressions. The grammar that we defined above using rewrite rules is a context-free grammar.

It is context free because it defines the grammar simply in terms of which word types can go together—it does not specify the way that words should agree witheach. A stale dog climbs Mount Rushmore.

It also, allows the following sentence, which is not grammatically correct:Chickens eats.
A context-free grammar can have only at most one terminal symbol on the right-hand side of its rewrite rules.
Rewrite rules for a context-sensitive grammar, in contrast, can have more than one terminal symbol on the right-hand side. This enables the grammar to specifynumber, case, tense, and gender agreement.

Each context-sensitive rewrite rule must have at least as many symbols on theright-hand side as it does on the left-hand side. Rewrite rules for context-sensitive grammars have the following form:

A X B→A Y B
which means that in the context of A and B, X can be rewritten as Y.

Each of A, B, X, and Y can be either a terminal or a nonterminal symbol.

Context-sensitive grammars are most usually used for natural language processing because they are powerful enough to define the kinds of grammarsthat natural languages use. Unfortunately, they tend to involve a much larger number of rules and are a much less natural way to describe language, makingthem harder for human developers to design than context free grammars.

The final class of grammars in Chomsky's hierarchy consists of recursivelyenumerable grammars (also known as unrestricted grammars). A recursively enumerable grammar can define any language and has no restrictions on the structure of its rewrite rules. Such grammars are of interest tocomputer scientists but are not of great use in the study of natural language processing.

Parsing: Syntactic Analysis
As we have seen, morphologic analysis can be used to determine to which part ofspeech each word in a sentence belongs. We will now examine how this information is used to determine the syntactic structure of a sentence.

This process, in which we convert a sentence into a tree that represents thesentence's syntactic structure, is known as parsing.

Parsing a sentence tells us whether it is a valid sentence, as defined by ourgrammar
If a sentence is not a valid sentence, then it cannot be parsed. Parsing a sentenceinvolves producing a tree, such as that shown in Fig 10.1, which shows the parse tree for the following sentence:

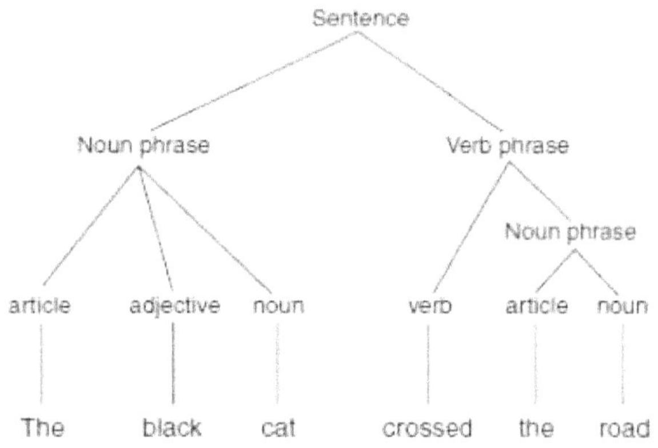

Fig 10.1

The black cat crossed the road.
This tree shows how the sentence is made up of a noun phrase and a verb phrase. The noun phrase consists of an article, an adjective, and a noun. The verb phraseconsists of a verb and a further noun phrase, which in turn consists of an article and a noun. Parse trees can be built in a bottom-up fashion or in a top-down fashion.

Building a parse tree from the top down involves starting from a sentence and determining which of the possible rewrites for Sentence can be applied to the sentence that is being parsed. Hence, in this case, Sentence would be rewritten using the following rule:

Sentence→NounPhrase VerbPhrase

Then the verb phrase and noun phrase would be broken down recursively in the same way, until only terminal symbols were left. When a parse tree is built from the top down, it is known as a derivation tree.

To build a parse tree from the bottom up, the terminal symbols of the sentence are first replaced by their corresponding nonterminals (e.g., cat is replaced by noun), and then these nonterminals are combined to match the right-hand sides of rewrite rules.

Parsing Techniques

Transition Networks

A transition network is a finite state automaton that is used to represent a part of a grammar. A transition network parser uses a number of these transition networks to represent its entire grammar. Each network represents one nonterminal symbol in the grammar. Hence, in the grammar for the English language, we would have one transition network for Sentence, one for Noun Phrase, one for Verb Phrase, one for Verb, and so on.

Fig shows the transition network equivalents for three production rules.

In each transition network, S1 is the start state, and the accepting state, or final state, is denoted by a heavy border. When a phrase is applied to a transition network, the first word is compared against one of the arcs leading from the first state.

If this word matches one of those arcs, the network moves into the state to which that arc points. Hence, the first network shown in Fig 10.2, when presented with a Noun Phrase, will move from state S1 to state S2.

If a phrase is presented to a transition network and no match is found from the current state, then that network cannot be used and another network must be tried. Hence, when starting with the phrase the cat sat on the mat, none of the networks shown in Fig 10.2 will be used because they all have only nonterminal symbols, whereas all the symbols in the cat sat on the mat are terminal.

Hence, we need further networks, such as the ones shown in Figure 10.2, which deal with terminal symbols.

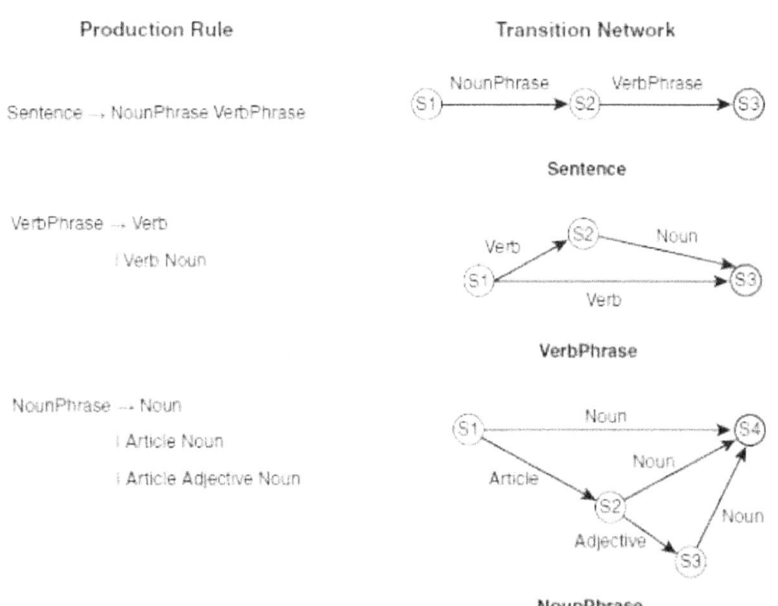

<table>
<tr><th>Production Rule</th><th>Transition Network</th></tr>
</table>

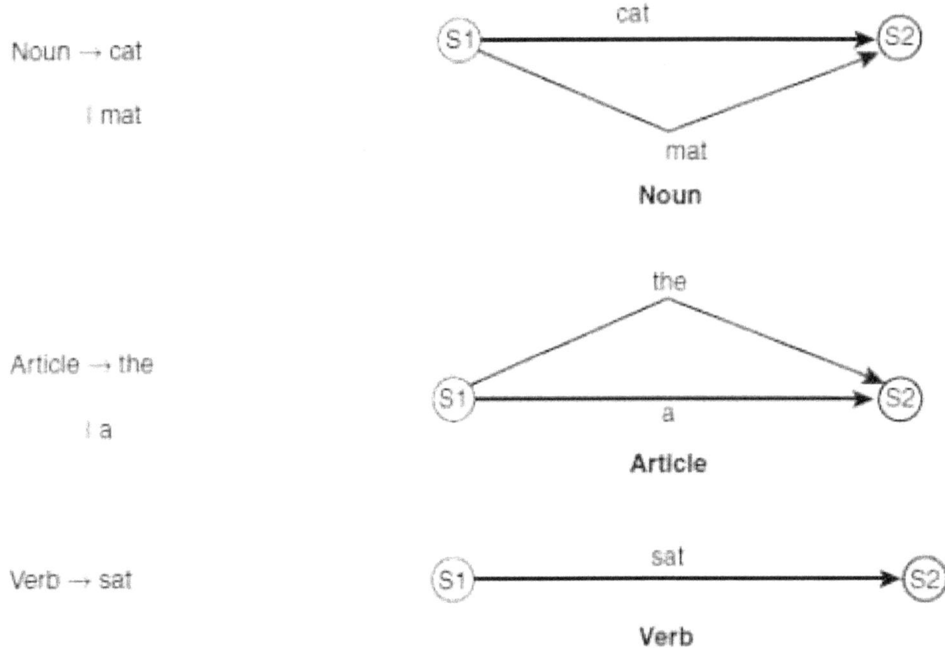

Fig 10.2

Transition networks can be used to determine whether a sentence is grammatically correct, at least according to the rules of the grammar the networks represent. Parsing using transition networks involves exploring a search space of possible parses in a depth-first fashion. the parse of the following simple sentence:

A cat sat.
We begin in state S1 in the Sentence transition network. To proceed, we mustfollow the arc that is labeled NounPhrase. We thus move out of the Sentence network and into the NounPhrase network.

The first arc of the NounPhrase network is labeled Noun. We thus move into the Noun network. We now follow each of the arcs in the Noun network and discoverthat our first word, A, does not match any of them. Hence, we backtrack to the next arc in the NounPhrase network.

This arc is labeled Article, so we move on to the Article transition network. Here,on examining the second label, we find that the first word is matched by the terminal symbol on this arc.

We therefore consume the word, A, and move on to state S2 in the Article network. Because this is a success node, we are able to return to the NounPhrasenetwork and move on to state S2 in this network. We now have an arc labeled Noun.

As before, we move into the Noun network and find that our next word, cat, matches. We thus move to state S4 in the NounPhrase network. This is a success node, and so we move back to the Sentence network and repeat the process for the VerbPhrase arc.

It is possible for a system to use transition networks to generate a derivation treefor a sentence, so that as well as determining whether the sentence is grammatically valid, it parses it fully to obtain further information by semantic analysis from the sentence.

This can be done by simply having the system build up the tree by noting whicharcs it successfully followed. When, for example, it successfully follows the NounPhrase arc in the Sentence network, the system generates a root node labeled Sentence and an arc leading from that node to a new node labeled NounPhrase.

When the system follows the NounPhrase network and identifies an article and a noun, these are similarly added to the tree. In this way, the full parse tree for the sentence can be generated using transitionnetworks.

Parsing using transition networks is simple to understand but is not necessarily as efficient or as effective as we might hope for. In particular, it does not pay any attention to potential ambiguities or the need for words to agree with each other in case, gender, or number.

Parsing

Parsing can be defined as top-down or bottom-up based on how the parse-tree isconstructed.

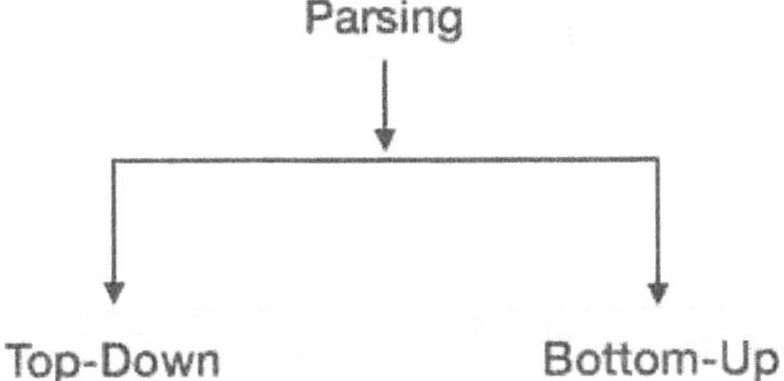

Top-Down Parsing

We have learnt in the last chapter that the top-down parsing technique parsesthe input, and starts constructing a parse tree from the root node gradually moving down to the leaf nodes. The types of top-down parsing are depicted below:

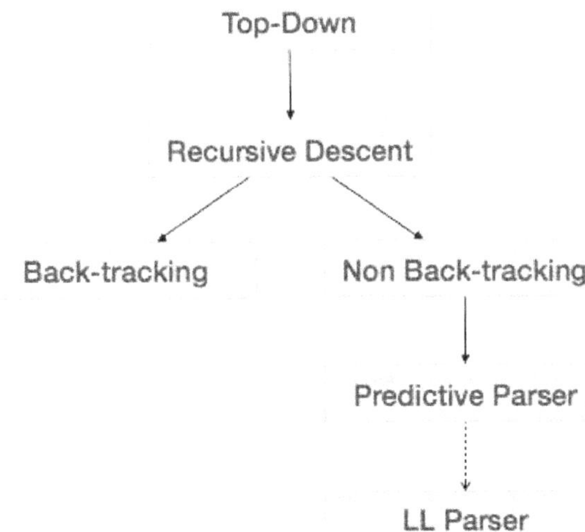

Recursive Descent Parsing

Recursive descent is a top-down parsing technique that constructs the parse treefrom the top and the input is read from left to right. It uses procedures for every terminal and non-terminal entity. This parsing technique recursively parses the input to make a parse tree, which may or may not require back-tracking. But the grammar associated with it (if not left factored) cannot avoid back-tracking. A form of recursive-descent parsing that does not require any back-tracking is known as **predictive parsing**.

This parsing technique is regarded recursive as it uses context-free grammarwhich is recursive in nature.

Back-tracking

Top- down parsers start from the root node (start symbol) and match the inputstring against the production rules to replace them (if matched). To understandthis, take the following example of CFG:

S → rXd | rZdX → oa | eaZ → ai

For an input string: read, a top-down parser, will behave like this: It will start with S from the production rules and will match its yield to the left- most letter of the input, i.e. 'r'. The very production of S (S → rXd) matches with it. So the top-down parser advances to the next input letter (i.e. 'e').

The parser tries to expand non-terminal 'X' and checks its production from the left (X → oa). It does not match with the next input symbol. So the top-down parser backtracksto obtain the next production rule of X, (X → ea). Now the parser matches all the input letters in an ordered manner. The string isaccepted.

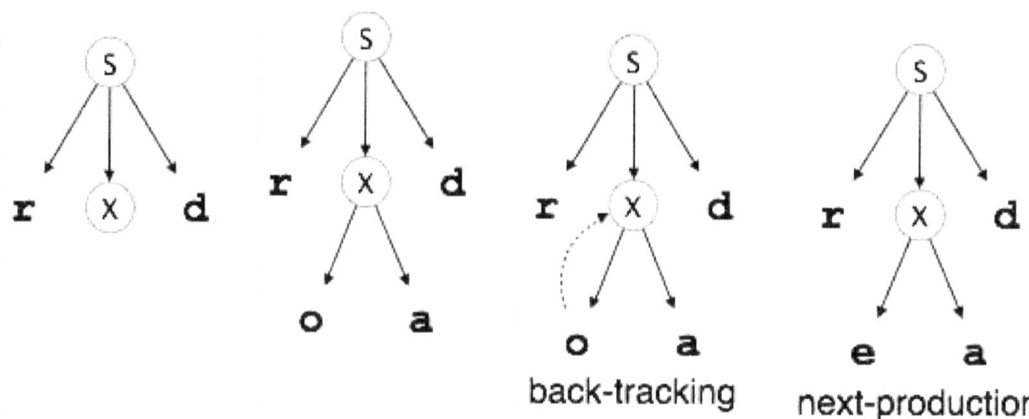

Predictive Parser

Predictive parser is a recursive descent parser, which has the capability to predictwhich production is to be used to replace the input string. The predictive parser does not suffer from backtracking. To accomplish its tasks, the predictive parser uses a look-ahead pointer, which points to the next input symbols.

To make the parser back-tracking free, the predictive parser puts some constraints on the grammar and accepts only a classof grammar known as LL(k) grammar.

Predictive parsing uses a stack and a parsing table to parse the input and generatea parse tree. Both the stack and the input contains an end symbol $ to denote that the stack is empty and the input is consumed. The parser refers to the parsing table to take any decision on the input and stack element combination.

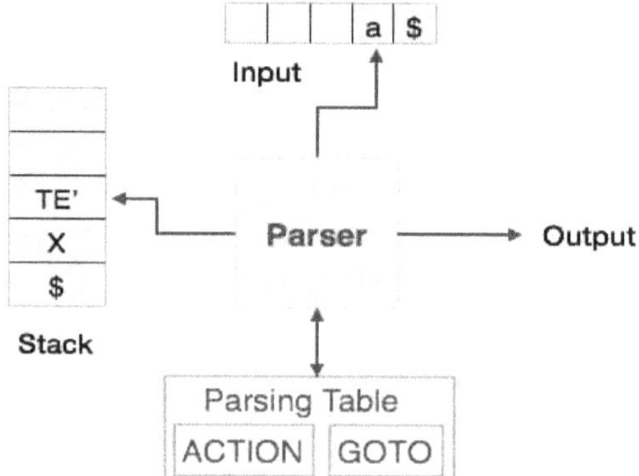

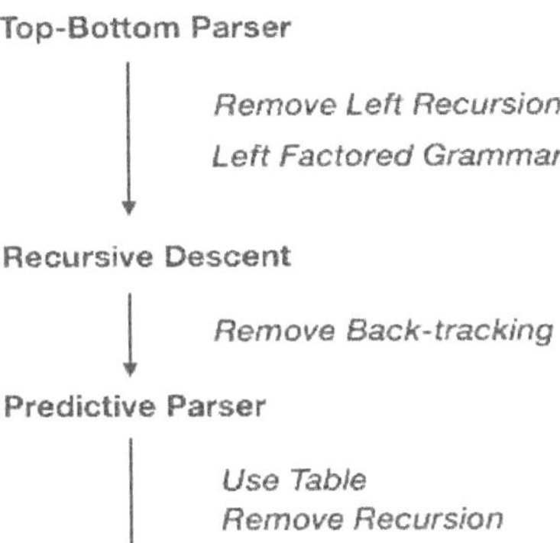

In recursive descent parsing, the parser may have more than one production to choose from for a single instance of input, whereas in predictive parser, each step has at most one production to choose. There might be instances where there is no production matching the input string, making the parsing procedure to fail.

LL Parser

An LL Parser accepts LL grammar. LL grammar is a subset of context-free grammar but with some restrictions to get the simplified version, in order to achieve easy implementation. LL grammar can be implemented by means of both algorithms namely, recursive-descent or table-driven.

LL parser is denoted as LL(k). The first L in LL(k) is parsing the input from left to right, the second L in LL(k) stands for left-most derivation and k itself represents the number of look aheads. Generally k = 1, so LL(k) may also be written as LL(1).

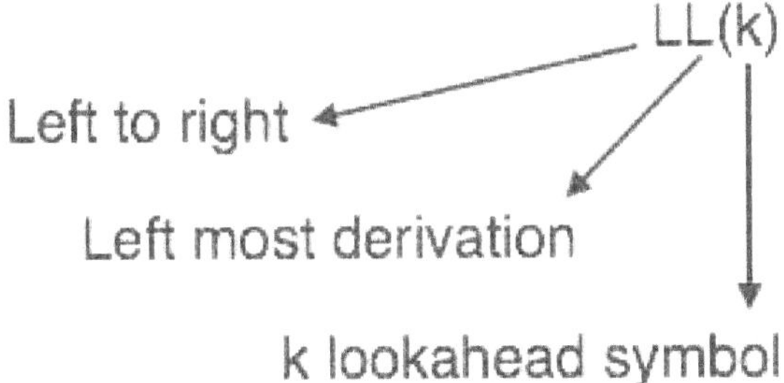

LL Parsing Algorithm

We may stick to deterministic LL(1) for parser explanation, as the size of table grows exponentially with the value of k. Secondly, if a given grammar is not LL(1), then usually, it is not LL(k), for any given k. Given below is an algorithm for LL(1) Parsing:Input:
string ω

parsing table M for grammar GOutput:
If ω is in L(G) then left-most derivation of ω,error otherwise.
Initial State : $S on stack (with S being start symbol)$\omega$$ in the input buffer
SET ip to point the first symbol of $\omega$$.repeat
let X be the top stack symbol and a the symbol pointed by ip.if X$\in$ V_t or $
if X = a

POP X and advance ip.else
error()endif
else   /* X is non-terminal */ if M[X,a] = X $\rightarrow$ Y1, Y2,... Yk
POP X

PUSH Yk, Yk-1,... Y1 /* Y1 on top */ Output the production X $\rightarrow$ Y1, Y2,... Yk
else

error()endif

endif
until X = $ /* empty stack */

A grammar G is LL(1) if A → α | β are two distinct productions of G:
- for no terminal, both α and β derive strings beginning with a.
- at most one of α and β can derive empty string.
- if β → t, then α does not derive any string beginning with a terminal in FOLLOW (A).

Bottom-up Parsing

Bottom-up parsing starts from the leaf nodes of a tree and works in upward direction till it reaches the root node. Here, we start from a sentence and then apply production rules in reverse manner in order to reach the start symbol. The image given below depicts the bottom-up parsers available.

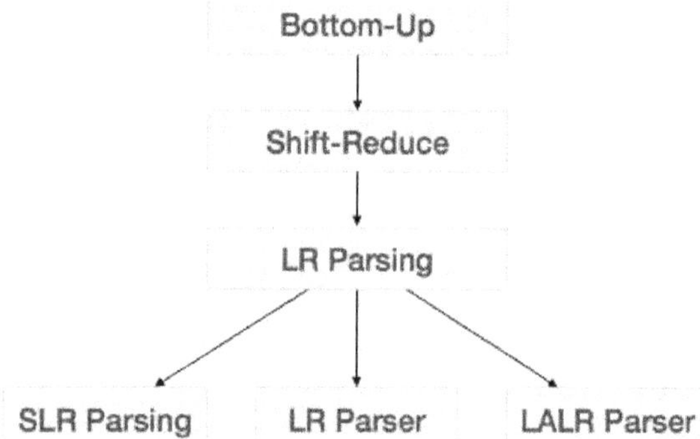

Shift-Reduce Parsing

Shift-reduce parsing uses two unique steps for bottom-up parsing. These steps are known as shift-step and reduce-step.
- **Shift step**: The shift step refers to the advancement of the input pointer to the next input symbol, which is called the shifted symbol. This symbol is pushed onto the stack. The shifted symbol is treated as a single node of the parse tree.
- **Reduce step** : When the parser finds a complete grammar rule (RHS) and replaces it to (LHS), it is known as reduce-step. This occurs when the top of the stack contains a handle. To reduce, a POP function is performed on the stack which pops off the handle and replaces it with LHS non-terminal symbol.

LR Parser

The LR parser is a non-recursive, shift-reduce, bottom-up parser. It uses a wide class of context-free grammar which makes it the most efficient syntax analysis technique. LR parsers are also known as LR(k) parsers, where L stands for left-to-right scanning of the input stream; R stands for the construction of right-most derivation in reverse, and k denotes the number of lookahead symbols to make decisions.

There are three widely used algorithms available for constructing an LR parser:
- SLR(1) – Simple LR Parser:
  - Works on smallest class of grammar
  - Few number of states, hence very small table
  - Simple and fast construction

- LR(1) – LR Parser:
  - Works on complete set of LR(1) Grammar
  - Generates large table and large number of states
  - Slow construction

- LALR(1) – Look-Ahead LR Parser:
  - Works on intermediate size of grammar
  - Number of states are same as in SLR(1)LR Parsing Algorithm

Here we describe a skeleton algorithm of an LR parser:token = next_token()
repeat forever
s = top of stack

if action[s, token] = "shift si" thenPUSH token
PUSH si
token = next_token()

else if action[s, tpken] = "reduce A::= β" thenPOP 2 * |β| symbols
s = top of stackPUSH A
PUSH goto[s,A]

else if action[s, token] = "accept" thenreturn
else
error()LL vs. LR

LL	LR
Does a leftmost derivation.	Does a rightmost derivation in reverse.
Starts with the root nonterminal on the stack.	Ends with the root nonterminal on the stack.
Ends when the stack is empty.	Starts with an empty stack.
Uses the stack for designating what is still to be expected.	Uses the stack for designating what is already seen.
Builds the parse tree top-down.	Builds the parse tree bottom-up.
Continuously pops a nonterminal off the stack, and pushes the corresponding right hand side.	Tries to recognize a right hand side on the stack, pops it, and pushes the corresponding nonterminal.
Expands the non-terminals.	Reduces the non-terminals.
Reads the terminals when it pops one off the stack.	Reads the terminals while it pushes them on the stack.
Pre-order traversal of the parse tree.	Post-order traversal of the parse tree.

Semantic Analysis

The purpose of semantic analysis is to draw exact meaning, or you can say dictionary meaning from the text. The work of semantic analyzer is to check the text for meaningfulness. Semantic analysis is concerned with the meaning representation. It mainlyfocuses on the literal meaning of words, phrases, and sentences.

We already know that lexical analysis also deals with the meaning of the words, then how is semantic analysis different from lexical analysis? Lexical analysis is based on smaller token but on the other side semantic analysis focuses on larger chunks. That is why semantic analysis can be divided into the following two parts–

Studying meaning of individual word It is the first part of the semantic analysis in which the study of the meaning ofindividual words is performed. This part is called lexical semantics. Studying the combination of individual words

In the second part, the individual words will be combined to provide meaning insentences. The most important task of semantic analysis is to get the proper meaning of the sentence. For example, analyze the sentence **"Ram is great."** In this sentence, the speaker is talking either about Lord Ram or about a person whose name is Ram.

That is why the job, to get the proper meaning of the sentence, of semanticanalyzer is important.

Elements of Semantic Analysis

Followings are some important elements of semantic analysis –

Hyponymy

It may be defined as the relationship between a generic term and instances of that generic term. Here the generic term is called hypernym and its instances are called hyponyms. For example, the word color is hypernym and the color blue,yellow etc. are hyponyms.

Homonymy

It may be defined as the words having same spelling or same form but having different and unrelated meaning. For example, the word "Bat" is a homonymyword because bat can be an implement to hit a ball or bat is a nocturnal flyingmammal also.

Polysemy

Polysemy is a Greek word, which means "many signs". It is a word or phrase withdifferent but related sense. In other words, we can say that polysemy has the same spelling but different and related meaning. For example, the word "bank" isa polysemy word having the following meanings –

- A financial institution.
- The building in which such an institution is located.
- A synonym for "to rely on".

Difference between Polysemy and Homonymy

Both polysemy and homonymy words have the same syntax or spelling. The maindifference between them is that in polysemy, the meanings of the words are related but in homonymy, the meanings of the words are not related.

For example, if we talk about the same word "Bank", we can write the meaning 'afinancial institution' or 'a riverbank'. In that case it would be the example of homonym because the meanings are unrelated to each other.

Synonymy

It is the relation between two lexical items having different forms but expressingthe same or a close meaning. Examples are 'author/writer', 'fate/destiny'.

Antonymy

It is the relation between two lexical items having symmetry between their
semantic components relative to an axis. The scope of antonymy is as follows –

- **Application of property or not** – Example is 'life/death','certitude/incertitude'
- **Application of scalable property** – Example is 'rich/poor', 'hot/cold'
- **Application of a usage** – Example is 'father/son', 'moon/sun'.

Meaning Representation

Semantic analysis creates a representation of the meaning of a sentence. But before getting into the concept and approaches related to meaning representation, we need to understand the building blocks of semantic system.

Building Blocks of Semantic System

In word representation or representation of the meaning of the words, thefollowing building blocks play an important role –

- **Entities** – It represents the individual such as a particular person, locationetc. For example, Haryana. India, Ram all are entities.
- **Concepts** – It represents the general category of the individuals such as aperson, city, etc.
- **Relations** – It represents the relationship between entities and concept. Forexample, Ram is a person.
- **Predicates** – It represents the verb structures. For example, semantic roles and case grammar are the examples of predicates.

Now, we can understand that meaning representation shows how to put togetherthe building blocks of semantic systems. In other words, it shows how to put together entities, concepts, relation and predicates to describe a situation. It also enables the reasoning about the semantic world.

Approaches to Meaning Representations

Semantic analysis uses the following approaches for the representation ofmeaning –

- First order predicate logic (FOPL)
- Semantic Nets
- Frames
- Conceptual dependency (CD)
- Rule-based architecture
- Case Grammar
- Conceptual Graphs

Need of Meaning Representations

A question that arises here is why do we need meaning representation? Followings are the reasons for the same –Linking of linguistic elements to non-linguistic elements The very first reason is that with the help of meaning representation the linking of linguistic elements to the non-linguistic elements can be done.

Representing variety at lexical level

With the help of meaning representation, unambiguous, canonical forms can berepresented at the lexical level. Can be used for reasoning Meaning representation can be used to reason for verifying what is true in theworld as well as to infer the knowledge from the semantic representation.

Lexical Semantics

The first part of semantic analysis, studying the meaning of individual words iscalled lexical semantics. It includes words, sub-words, affixes (sub-units), compound words and phrases also. All the words, sub-words, etc. are collectivelycalled lexical items. In other words, we can say that lexical semantics is the relationship between lexical items, meaning of sentences and syntax of sentence.

Following are the steps involved in lexical semantics –

- Classification of lexical items like words, sub-words, affixes, etc. isperformed in lexical semantics.
- Decomposition of lexical items like words, sub-words, affixes, etc. isperformed in lexical semantics.
- Differences as well as similarities between various lexical semanticstructures is also analyzed.

Pragmatic Analysis

It is the fourth phase of NLP. Pragmatic analysis simply fits the actual objects/events, which exist in a given context with object references obtainedduring the last phase (semantic analysis). For example, the sentence "Put the banana in the basket on the shelf" can have two semantic interpretations andpragmatic analyzer will choose between these two possibilities.

The pragmatic analysis means handling the situation in a much more practical or realistic manner than using a theoretical approach. As we know that a sentence can have different meanings in various situations. For example, The average is 18.

The average is 18. (average may be of sequence)The average is 18. (average may be of a vehicle)
The average is 18. (average may be of a mathematical term) We can see that for the same input there can be different perceptions. To interpret the meaning of the sentence we need to understand the situation. To tackle such problems we use pragmatic analysis. The pragmatic analysis tends to make the understanding of the language much more clear and easy to interpret.

Implementation:

Language processing are required to follow an order. Each phase takes its input from the previous phase's output and sends it along to the next phase for processing. While this process input can get rejected half-way if it does not followthe rules defining it for the next phase.

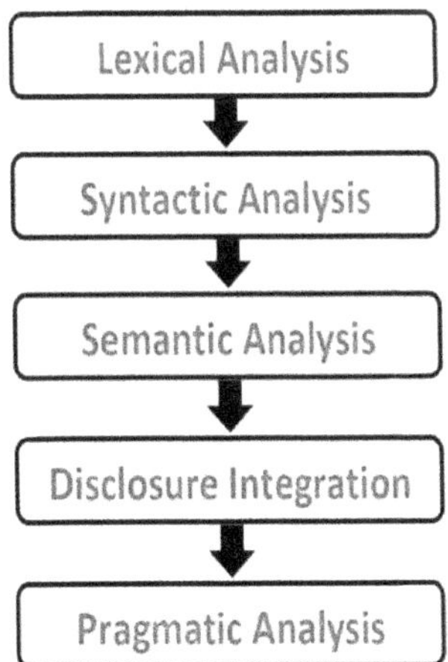

Agents in Artificial Intelligence

An AI system can be defined as the study of the rational agent and its environment. The agents sense the environment through sensors and act on their environment through actuators. An AI agent can have mental properties such as knowledge, belief, intention, etc.

Agent

An agent can be anything that perceive its environment through sensors and act upon that environment through actuators. An Agent runs in the cycle of **perceiving**, **thinking**, and **acting**. An agent can be:

- **Human-Agent:** A human agent has eyes, ears, and other organs which work for sensors and hand, legs, vocal tract work for actuators.
- **Robotic Agent:** A robotic agent can have cameras, infrared range finder, NLP for sensors and various motors for actuators.
- **Software Agent:** Software agent can have keystrokes, file contents as sensory input and act on those inputs and display output on the screen.

Hence the world around us is full of agents such as thermostat, cellphone, camera, and even we are also agents. Before moving forward, we should first know about sensors, effectors, and actuators.

Sensor: Sensor is a device which detects the change in the environment and sends the information to other electronic devices. An agent observes its environment through sensors.

Actuators: Actuators are the component of machines that converts energy into motion. The actuators are only responsible for moving and controlling a system. An actuator can be an electric motor, gears, rails, etc.

Effectors: Effectors are the devices which affect the environment. Effectors can be legs, wheels, arms, fingers, wings, fins, and display screen.

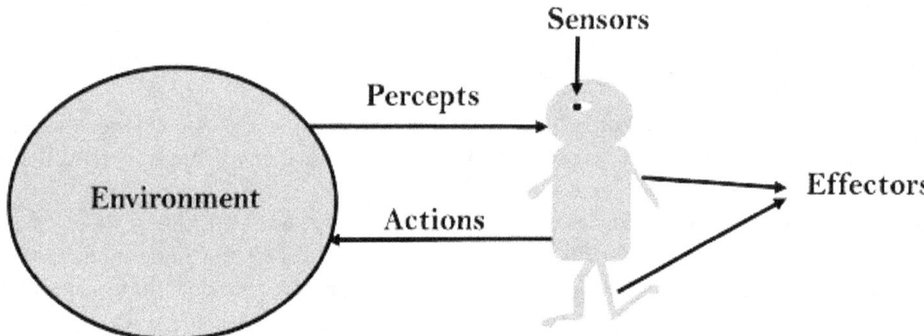

Intelligent Agents:

An intelligent agent is an autonomous entity which act upon an environment using sensors and actuators for achieving goals. An intelligent agent may learn from the environment to achieve their goals. A thermostat is an example of an intelligent agent.

Following are the main four rules for an AI agent:

- **Rule 1:** An AI agent must have the ability to perceive the environment.
- **Rule 2:** The observation must be used to make decisions.
- **Rule 3:** Decision should result in an action.
- **Rule 4:** The action taken by an AI agent must be a rational action.

Rational Agent:

A rational agent is an agent which has clear preference, models uncertainty, and acts in a way to maximize its performance measure with all possible actions. A rational agent is said to perform the right things. AI is about creating rational agents to use for game theory and decision theory for various real-world scenarios.

For an AI agent, the rational action is most important because in AI reinforcement learning algorithm, for each best possible action, agent gets the positive reward and for each wrong action, an agent gets a negative reward.

Note: Rational agents in AI are very similar to intelligent agents.

Rationality:

The rationality of an agent is measured by its performance measure. Rationality can be judged on the basis of following points:

- Performance measure which defines the success criterion.

- Agent prior knowledge of its environment.
- Best possible actions that an agent can perform.
- The sequence of percepts.

Note: Rationality differs from Omniscience because an Omniscient agent knows the actual outcome of its action and act accordingly, which is not possible in reality.

Structure of an AI Agent

The task of AI is to design an agent program which implements the agent function. The structure of an intelligent agent is a combination of architecture andagent program.
It can be viewed as: Agent = Architecture + Agent program

Following are the main three terms involved in the structure of an AI agent:
Architecture: Architecture is machinery that an AI agent executes on.
Agent Function: Agent function is used to map a percept to an action.
f:P* → A

Agent program: Agent program is an implementation of agent function. An agentprogram executes on the physical architecture to produce function f.

PEAS Representation

PEAS is a type of model on which an AI agent works upon. When we define an AIagent or rational agent, then we can group its properties under PEAS representation model. It is made up of four words:
- **P:** Performance measure
- **E:** Environment
- **A:** Actuators
- **S:** Sensors

Here performance measure is the objective for the success of an agent's behavior.

PEAS for self-driving cars:
suppose a self-driving car then PEAS representation will be:
Performance: Safety, time, legal drive, comfort
Environment: Roads, other vehicles, road signs, pedestrian
Actuators: Steering, accelerator, brake, signal, horn

Sensors: Camera, GPS, speedometer, odometer, accelerometer, sonar.

Types of AI Agents

Agents can be grouped into five classes based on their degree of perceived intelligence and capability. All these agents can improve their performance andgenerate better action over the time. These are given below:
- Simple Reflex Agent
- Model-based reflex agent
- Goal-based agents
- Utility-based agent
- Learning agent

1) Simple Reflex agent:

- The Simple reflex agents are the simplest agents. These agents take decisions on the basis of the current percepts and ignore the rest of thepercept history.
- These agents only succeed in the fully observable environment.
- The Simple reflex agent does not consider any part of percepts historyduring their decision and action process.
- The Simple reflex agent works on Condition-action rule, which means it maps the current state to action. Such as a Room Cleaner agent, it worksonly if there is dirt in the room.
- Problems for the simple reflex agent design approach:
- They have very limited intelligence
- They do not have knowledge of non-perceptual parts of the currentstate
- Mostly too big to generate and to store.
- Not adaptive to changes in the environment.

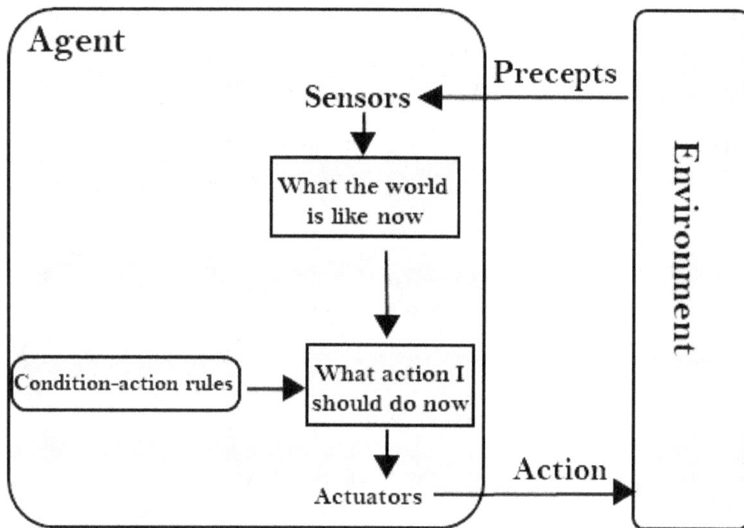

2) Model-based reflex agent

- The Model-based agent can work in a partially observable environment, and track the situation.
- A model-based agent has two important factors:
- **Model:** It is knowledge about "how things happen in the world," so itis called a Model-   based agent.
- **Internal State:** It is a representation of the current state based onpercept history.
  - These agents have the model, "which is knowledge of the world" and basedon the model they perform actions.
  - Updating the agent state requires information about:
    a. How the world evolves
    b. How the agent's action affects the world.

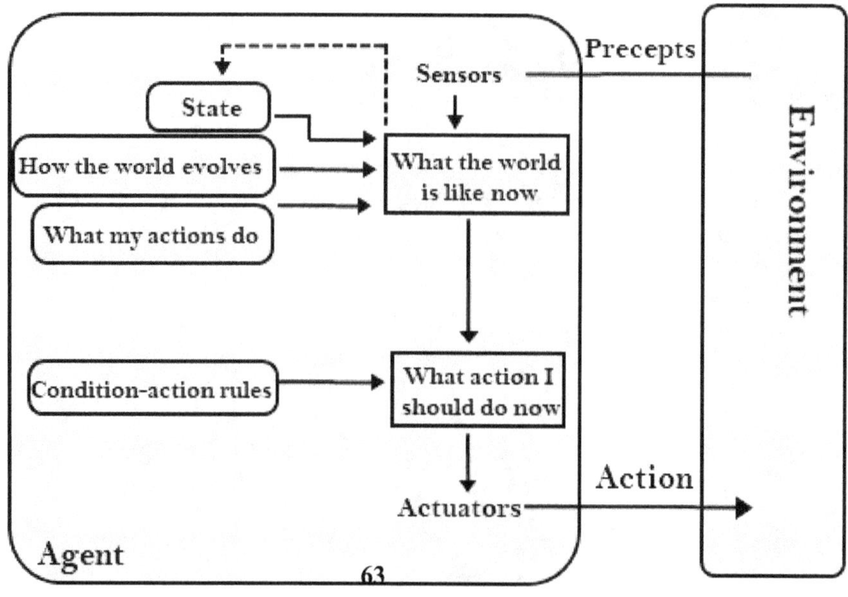

3) Goal-based agents

- The knowledge of the current state environment is not always sufficient todecide for an agent to what to do.
- The agent needs to know its goal which describes desirable situations.
- Goal-based agents expand the capabilities of the model-based agent byhaving the "goal" information.
- They choose an action, so that they can achieve the goal.
- These agents may have to consider a long sequence of possible actions before deciding whether the goal is achieved or not. Such considerations ofdifferent scenario are called searching and planning, which makes an agentproactive.

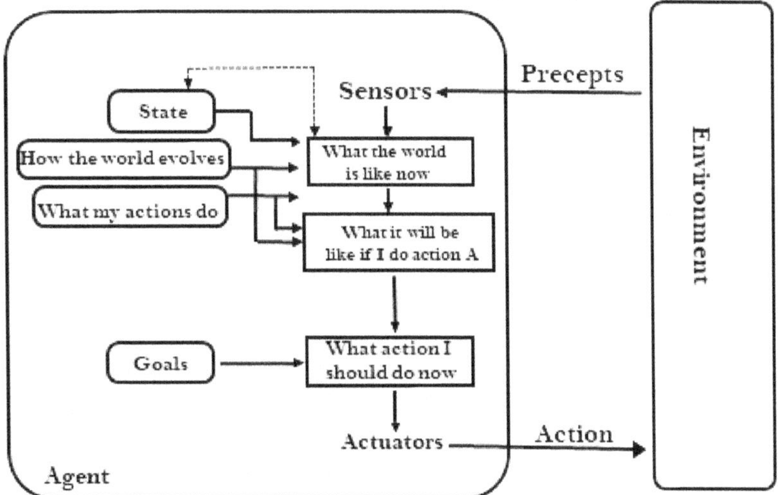

4) Utility-based agents

- These agents are similar to the goal-based agent but provide an extracomponent of utility measurement which makes them different by providing a measure of success at a given state.
- Utility-based agent act based not only goals but also the best way toachieve the goal.
- The Utility-based agent is useful when there are multiple possible alternatives, and an agent has to choose in order to perform the bestaction.
- The utility function maps each state to a real number to check howefficiently each action achieves the goals.

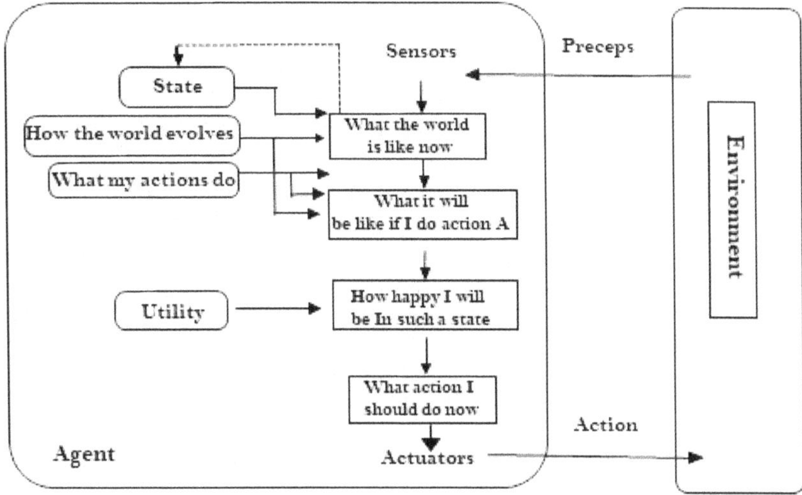

5) Learning Agents

- A learning agent in AI is the type of agent which can learn from its pastexperiences, or it has learning capabilities.
- It starts to act with basic knowledge and then able to act and adaptautomatically through learning.
- A learning agent has mainly four conceptual components, which are:
    a. **Learning element:** It is responsible for making improvements by learningfrom environment
    b. **Critic:** Learning element takes feedback from critic which describes thathow well the agent is doing with respect to a fixed performance standard.
    c. **Performance element:** It is responsible for selecting external action.

d. **Problem generator:** This component is responsible for suggesting actions that will lead to new and informative experiences.

Hence, learning agents are able to learn, analyze performance, and look for new ways to improve the performance.

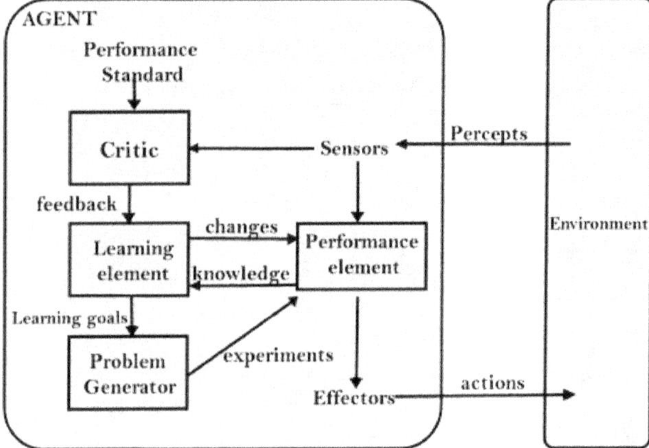

Semantic Web

Current World Wide Web (WWW) is a huge library of interlinked documents that are transferred by computers and presented to people. It has grown from hypertext systems, but the difference is that anyone can contribute to it. This also means that the quality of information or even the persistence of documents cannot be generally guaranteed.

Current WWW contains a lot of information and knowledge, but machines usually serve only to deliver and present the content of documents describing the knowledge. People have to connect all the sources of relevant information and interpret them themselves.

Semantic Web Architecture

Semantic web is an effort to enhance current web so that computers can process the information presented on WWW, interpret and connect it, to help humans to find required knowledge. In the same way as WWW is a huge distributed hypertext system, semantic web is intended to form a huge distributed knowledge based system. The focus of semantic web is to share data instead of documents.

In other words, it is a project that should provide a common framework that allows data to be shared and reused across application, enterprise, and community boundaries. It is a collaborative effort led by World Wide Web Consortium (W3C).

The architecture of semantic web is illustrated in the figure below. The first layer, URI and Unicode, follows the important features of the existing WWW. Unicode is a standard of encoding international character sets and it allows that all human languages can be used (written and read) on the web using one standardized form.

Uniform Resource Identifier (URI) is a string of a standardized form that allows to uniquely identify resources (e.g., documents). A subset of URI is Uniform Resource Locator (URL), which contains access mechanism and a (network) location of a document - such as http://www.example.org/. Another subset of URI is URN that allows to identify a resource without implying its location and means of dereferencing it - an example is urn:isbn: 0-123-45678-9.

The usage of URI is important for a distributed internet system as it provides understandable identification of all resources. An international variant to URI is Internationalized Resource Identifier (IRI) that allows usage of Unicode characters in identifier and for which a mapping to URI is defined. In the rest of this text, whenever URI is used, IRI can be used as well as a more general concept.

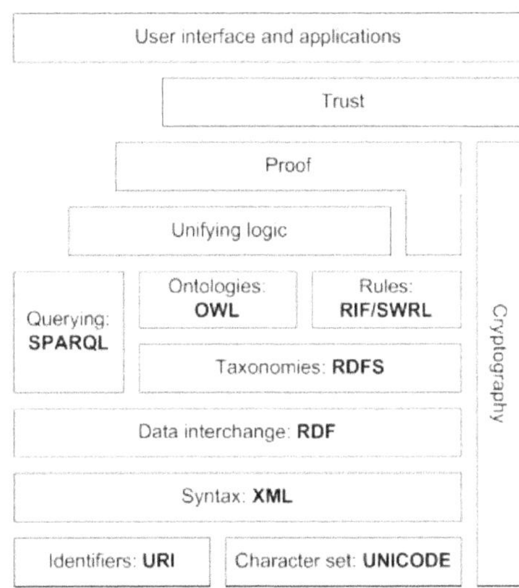

Extensible Markup Language (XML) layer with XML namespace and XML schema definitions makes sure that there is a common syntax used in the semantic web. XML is a general purpose markup language for documents containing structured information. A XML document contains elements that canbe nested and that may have attributes and content. XML namespaces allow to
specify different markup vocabularies in one XML document. XML schema servesfor expressing schema of a particular set of XML documents.

A core data representation format for semantic web is Resource Description Framework (RDF). RDF is a framework for representing information about resources in a graph form. It was primarily intended for representing metadata about WWW resources, such as the title, author, and modification date of a Webpage, but it can be used for storing any other data.

It is based on triples subject- predicate-object that form graph of data. All data in the semantic web use RDF as the primary representation language. The normative syntax for serializing RDF isXML in the RDF/XML form. Formal semantics of RDF is defined as well.

RDF itself serves as a description of a graph formed by triples. Anyone can definevocabulary of terms used for more detailed description. To allow standardized description of taxonomies and other ontological constructs, a RDF Schema (RDFS) was created together with its formal semantics within RDF. RDFS can be used to describe taxonomies of classes and properties and use them to create lightweight ontologies.

More detailed ontologies can be created with Web Ontology Language OWL. The OWL is a language derived from description logics, and offers more constructs over RDFS. It is syntactically embedded into RDF, so like RDFS, it provides additional standardized vocabulary. OWL comes in three species - OWL Lite for taxonomies and simple constrains, OWL DL for full description logic support, and OWL Full for maximum expressiveness and syntactic freedom of RDF.

Since OWL is based on description logic, it is not surprising that a formal semantics is definedfor this language. RDFS and OWL have semantics defined and this semantics can be used for reasoning within ontologies and knowledge bases described using these languages. To provide rules beyond the constructs available from these languages, rule languages are being standardized for the semantic web as well.Two standards are emerging - RIF and SWRL.

For querying RDF data as well as RDFS and OWL ontologies with knowledge bases,a Simple Protocol and RDF Query Language (SPARQL) is available. SPARQL is SQL- like language, but uses RDF triples and resources for both matching part of the query and for returning results of the query. Since both RDFS and OWL are built on RDF, SPARQL can be used for querying ontologies and knowledge bases directly as well. Note that SPARQL is not only query language, it is also a protocol for accessing RDF data.

It is expected that all the semantics and rules will be executed at the layers belowProof and the result will be used to prove deductions. Formal proof together with trusted inputs for the proof will mean that the results can be trusted, which is shown in the top layer of the figure. For reliable inputs, cryptography means areto be used, such as digital signatures for verification of the origin of the sources.On top of these layers, application with user interface can be built.

Agent communication

Agent communication is based on message passing, where **agents communicate** by formulating and sending individual messages to each other. The FIPA ACL specifies a standard message language by setting out the encoding, semantics and pragmatics of the messages.

Components of communicating agents Speaker

1) **Intention:** Before speaking anything, we know the intention of what we want to convey to the other person. The same thing is implemented in the communicating systems. This makes communication valid and relevant from the side of the communicating system.

2) **Generation:** After knowing the intention of what is to be conveyed, the system must gather words so that the information can be reached to the user in his very own communicating language. So, the generation of relevant words is done by the system after the intention process.

3) **Synthesis:** Once the agent has all the relevant words, yet they have to be uttered in away that they have some meaning. So, after the generation of words, the formation of meaningful sentences takes places and finally, the agent speaks them out to the user.

Hearer

1) **Perception:** In the perception phase, the communicating system perceives what the user has spoken to it. This is a sort of an audio input signal which the agent receives from the user and then this signal is sent for the further processing by the system.

2) **Analysis:** After getting the audio input from the user which is a sequence of sentences and phrases, the system tries to analyze them by extracting the meaningful terms out of the sentences by removing the articles, connectors and other words which are there only for the sake of sentence formation.

3) **Disambiguation:** This is the most important thing that a communicating system carries out. After the analyzing process, the agent must understand the meaning of the sentences that the user have spoken. So, this understanding phase in which the system tries to derive the meaning of the sentences by removing various ambiguities and errors is known as disambiguation. This is done by understanding the Syntax, Semantics, and Pragmatics of the sentences.

4) **Incorporation:** In incorporation, the system figures out whether the understanding that it has derived out of the audio signal is correct or not. Whether it is meaningful, whether the system should consider it or ask the user for further input for resolving any sort of ambiguity.

Fuzzy sets

Fuzzy sets can be considered as an extension and gross oversimplification of classical sets. It can be best understood in the context of set membership. Basically it allows partial membership which means that it contain elements that have varying degrees of membership in the set.

From this, we can understand the difference between classical set and fuzzy set. Classical set contains elements that satisfy precise properties of membership while fuzzy set contains elements that satisfy imprecise properties of membership.

Mathematical Concept

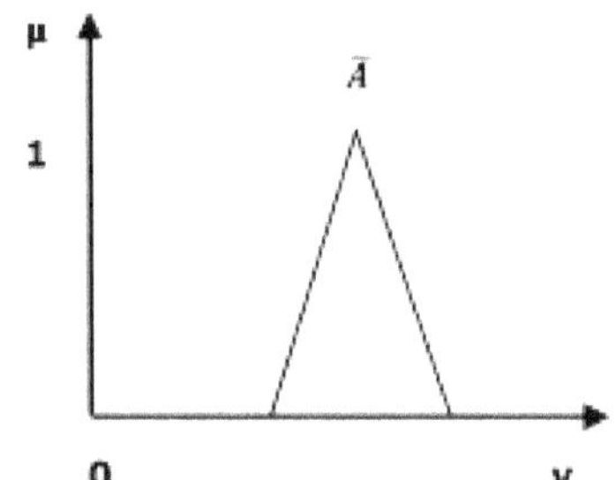
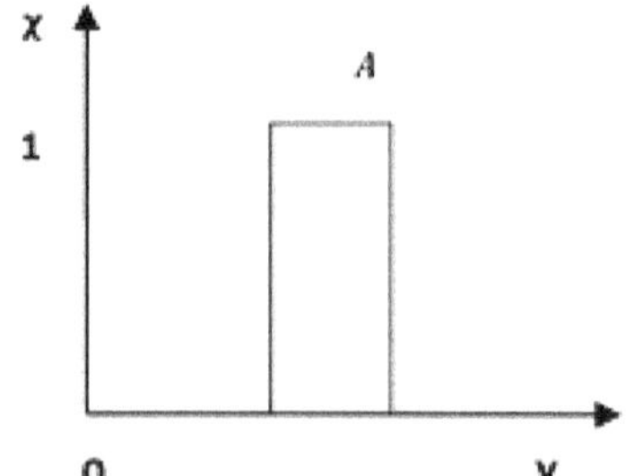

Membership Function of Fuzzy set $\tilde{A}$ Membership Function of classical set A

A fuzzy set $A\tilde{A}\sim$ in the universe of information UU can be defined as a set of ordered pairs and it can be represented mathematically as –

$\tilde{A} = \{(y, \mu\tilde{A}(y)) | y \in U\}$

Here $\mu\tilde{A}(y)$ = degree of membership of yy in $\widetilde{A}$, assumes values in the range from 0 to 1, i.e., $\mu\tilde{A}(y) \in [0,1]$.

Representation of fuzzy set

Let us now consider two cases of universe of information and understand how afuzzy set can be represented.

Case 1

$$\tilde{A} = \left\{ \frac{\mu_{\tilde{A}}(y_1)}{y_1} + \frac{\mu_{\tilde{A}}(y_2)}{y_2} + \frac{\mu_{\tilde{A}}(y_3)}{y_3} + \dots \right\}$$

$$= \left\{ \sum_{i=1}^{n} \frac{\mu_{\tilde{A}}(y_i)}{y_i} \right\}$$

When universe of information UU is discrete and finite –

Case 2

When universe of information UU is continuous and infinite –

$$\tilde{A} = \left\{ \int \frac{\mu_{\tilde{A}}(y)}{y} \right\}$$

In the above representation, the summation symbol represents the collection ofeach element.

Operations on Fuzzy Sets

Having two fuzzy sets A~A~ and B~B~, the universe of information UU and an element y of the universe, the following relations express the union, intersectionand complement operation on fuzzy sets.

Union/Fuzzy 'OR'

Let us consider the following representation to understand how the **Union/Fuzzy 'OR'** relation works – μA~UB~(y)=μA~VμB~∀y∈UHere V represents the 'max' operation.

Semantic   web   architecture   in   layers

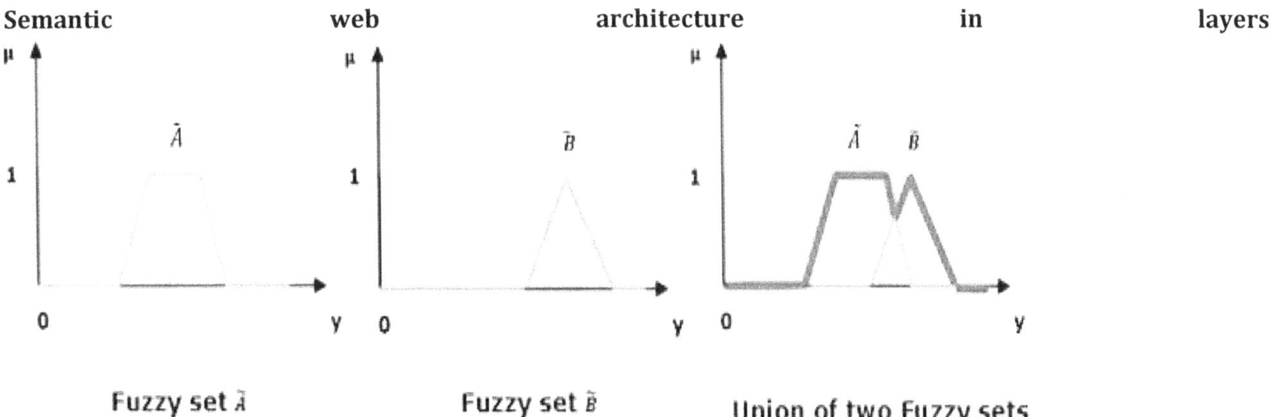

Intersection/Fuzzy 'AND'

Let us consider the following representation to understand how the **Intersection/Fuzzy 'AND'** relation works – μA~∩B~(y)=μA~AμB~∀y∈U Here A represents the 'min' operation.

Complement/Fuzzy 'NOT'

Let us consider the following representation to understand how the **Complement/Fuzzy 'NOT'** relation woks – μA~=1−μA~(y)y∈U

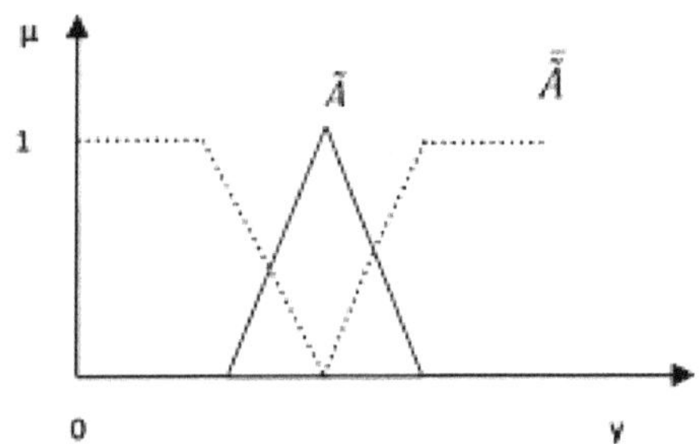

Complement of a fuzzy set

Properties of Fuzzy Sets

the different properties of fuzzy sets.

Commutative Property

Having two fuzzy sets A~A~ and B~B~, this property states –

A~UB~=B~UA~A~∩B~=B~∩A~

Associative Property

Having three fuzzy sets A~A~, B~B~ and C~C~, this property states –

(\widetilde{A}\cup \left \widetilde{B}) \cup \widetilde{C} \right = \left \widetilde{
A} \cup (\widetilde{B}\right)\cup \widetilde{C})
(\widetilde{A}\cap \left \widetilde{B}) \cap \widetilde{C} \right = \left \widetilde{
A} \cup (\widetilde{B}\right \cap \widetilde{C})

Distributive Property

Having three fuzzy sets A~, B~ and C~, this property states –A~U(B~∩C~)=(A~UB~)∩(A~UC~)
A~∩(B~UC~)=(A~∩B~)U(A~∩C~)

Idempotency Property

For any fuzzy set A~A~, this property states –A~UA~=A~A~UA~=A~
A~∩A~=A~A~∩A~=A~

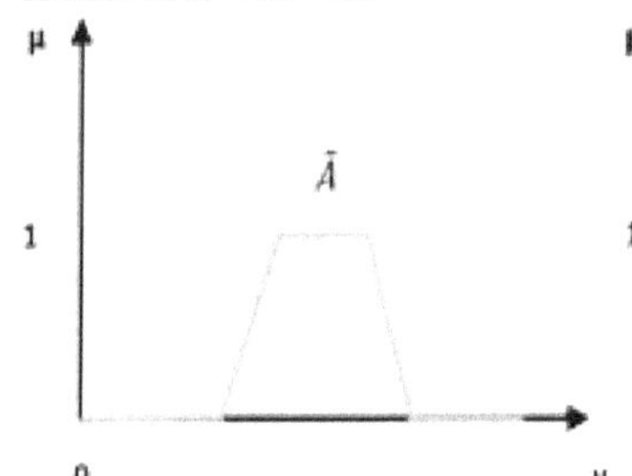

Fuzzy set $\tilde{A}$

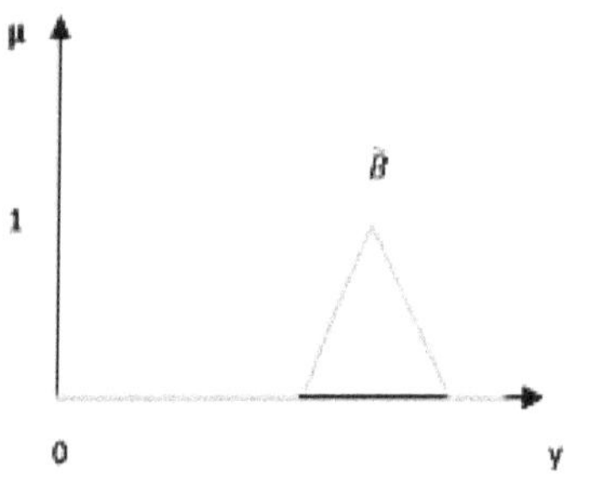

Fuzzy set $\tilde{B}$

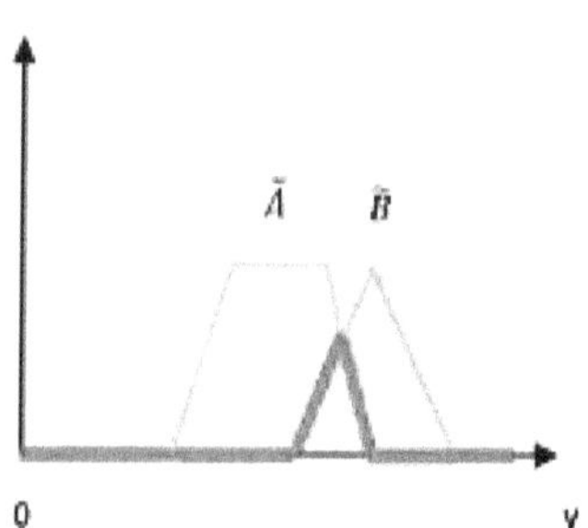

Intersection of two Fuzzy sets

Identity Property

For fuzzy set A~A~ and universal set UU, this property states –A~Uφ=A~
A~∩U=A~A~∩φ=φ
A~UU=U

Transitive Property

Having three fuzzy sets A~, B~ and C~, this property states –

$$If\ \tilde{\tilde{A}} \subseteq \tilde{B} \subseteq \tilde{C},\ then\ \tilde{A} \subseteq \tilde{C}$$

Involution Property

For any fuzzy set A~, this property states –

$$\overline{\overline{\tilde{A}}} = \tilde{A}$$

De Morgan's Law

This law plays a crucial role in proving tautologies and contradiction. This law states –

$$\overline{\tilde{A} \cap \tilde{B}} = \overline{\tilde{A}} \cup \overline{\tilde{B}}$$

$$\overline{\tilde{A} \cup \tilde{B}} = \overline{\tilde{A}} \cap \overline{\tilde{B}}$$

Membership Function

We already know that fuzzy logic is not logic that is fuzzy but logic that is used to describe fuzziness. This fuzziness is best characterized by its membership function. In other words, we can say that membership function represents the degree of truth in fuzzy logic.

Following are a few important points relating to the membership function –

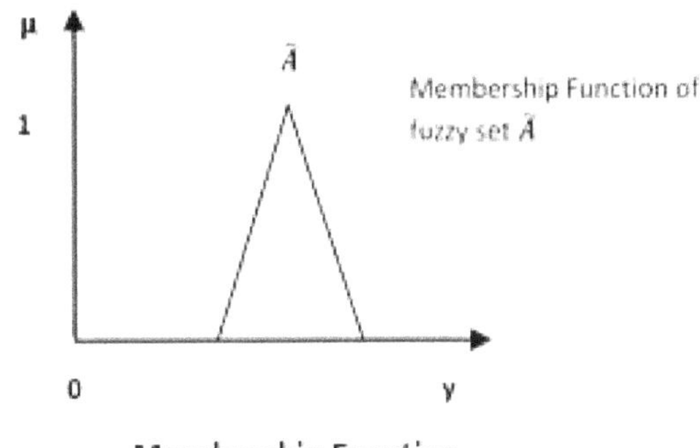

Membership Function

- Membership functions were first introduced in 1965 by Lofti A. Zadeh in his first research paper "fuzzy sets".
- Membership functions characterize fuzziness (i.e., all the information in fuzzy set), whether the elements in fuzzy sets are discrete or continuous.
- Membership functions can be defined as a technique to solve practical problems by experience rather than knowledge.
- Membership functions are represented by graphical forms.
- Rules for defining fuzziness are fuzzy too.

Mathematical Notation

We have already studied that a fuzzy set Ã in the universe of information U can be defined as a set of ordered pairs and it can be represented mathematically as –

A~={(y,μA~(y))|y∈U}

Here μA~(·) = membership function of A~; this assumes values in the range from 0 to 1, i.e., μA~(·)∈[0,1]. The membership function μA~(·) maps UU to the membership space MM. The dot (·) in the membership function described above, represents the element in a fuzzy set; whether it is discrete or continuous.

Features of Membership Functions

We will now discuss the different features of Membership Functions.

Core

For any fuzzy set A~, the core of a membership function is that region of universe that is characterize by full membership in the set. Hence, core consists of all those elements yy of the universe of information such that,

μA~(y)=1μA~(y)=1

Support

For any fuzzy set A~A~, the support of a membership function is the region of universe that is characterize by a nonzero membership in the set. Hence coreconsists of all those elements yy of the universe of information such that,

μA~(y)>0

Boundary

For any fuzzy set A~A~, the boundary of a membership function is the region ofuniverse that is characterized by a nonzero but incomplete membership in the set. Hence, core consists of all those elements yy of the universe of informationsuch that,

1>μA~(y)>0

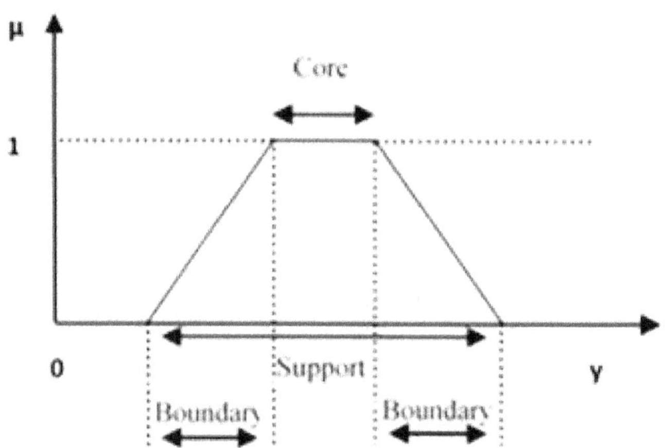

Features of Membership Function

Fuzzification

It may be defined as the process of transforming a crisp set to a fuzzy set or a fuzzy set to fuzzier set. Basically, this operation translates accurate crisp input values into linguistic variables. Following are the two important methods of fuzzification –
Support Fuzzification(s-fuzzification) Method
In this method, the fuzzified set can be expressed with the help of the followingrelation –
A~=μ1Q(x1)+μ2Q(x2)+...+μnQ(xn)
Here the fuzzy set Q(xi)Q(xi) is called as kernel of fuzzification. This method isimplemented by keeping μiμi constant and xi being transformed to a fuzzy set Q(xi).

Grade Fuzzification (g-fuzzification) Method

It is quite similar to the above method but the main difference is that itkept xixi constant and μiμi is expressed as a fuzzy set.

Defuzzification

It may be defined as the process of reducing a fuzzy set into a crisp set or toconvert a fuzzy member into a crisp member. We have already studied that the fuzzification process involves conversion fromcrisp quantities to fuzzy quantities. In a number of engineering applications, it is necessary to defuzzify the result or rather "fuzzy result" so that it must be converted to crisp result. Mathematically, the process of Defuzzification is also called "rounding it off".

The different methods of Defuzzification are described below –

Max-Membership Method

This method is limited to peak output functions and also known as height method. Mathematically it can be represented as follows –
μA~(x∗)>μA~(x)forallx∈XμA~(x∗)>μA~(x)forallx∈X Here, x∗is the defuzzified output.

Centroid Method

This method is also known as the center of area or the center of gravity method.Mathematically, the defuzzified output x∗x∗ will be represented as –

$$x^* = \frac{\int \mu_{\tilde{A}}(x) . x\, dx}{\int \mu_{\tilde{A}}(x) . dx}$$

Weighted Average Method

In this method, each membership function is weighted by its maximum membership value. Mathematically, the defuzzified output x∗x∗ will berepresented as –

$$x^* = \frac{\sum \mu_{\tilde{A}}\left(\overline{x_i}\right).\overline{x_i}}{\sum \mu_{\tilde{A}}\left(\overline{x_i}\right)}$$

Mean-Max Membership

This method is also known as the middle of the maxima. Mathematically, thedefuzzified output x∗x∗ will be represented as –

$$x^* = \frac{\sum_{i=1}^{n} \overline{x_i}}{n}$$

Traditional Fuzzy Refresher

Logic, which was originally just the study of what distinguishes sound argument from unsound argument, has now developed into a powerful and rigorous systemwhereby true statements can be discovered, given other statements that are already known to be true.

Predicate Logic

This logic deals with predicates, which are propositions containing variables. A predicate is an expression of one or more variables defined on some specific domain. A predicate with variables can be made a proposition by either assigninga value to the variable or by quantifying the variable.

Following are a few examples of predicates –

- Let E(x, y) denote "x = y"
- Let X(a, b, c) denote "a + b + c = 0"
- Let M(x, y) denote "x is married to y"

Propositional Logic

A proposition is a collection of declarative statements that have either a truth value "true" or a truth value "false". A propositional consists of propositional variables and connectives. The propositional variables are dented by capital letters (A, B, etc). The connectives connect the propositional variables.

A few examples of Propositions are given below –

- "Man is Mortal", it returns truth value "TRUE"
- "12 + 9 = 3 – 2", it returns truth value "FALSE"The following is not a Proposition –
- **"A is less than 2"** – It is because unless we give a specific value of A, wecannot say whether the statement is true or false.

Connectives

In propositional logic, we use the following five connectives –

- OR (∨∨)
- AND (∧∧)
- Negation/ NOT (¬¬)
- Implication / if-then (→→)
- If and only if (⇔⇔)

OR (∨∨)

The OR operation of two propositions A and B (written as A∨BA∨B) is true if atleast any of the propositional variable A or B is true.

The truth table is as follows –

A	B	A ∨ B
True	True	True
True	False	True
False	True	True
False	False	False

AND (∧∧)

The AND operation of two propositions A and B (written as AABAAB) is true ifboth the propositional variable A and B is true.
The truth table is as follows –

A	B	A ∧ B
True	True	True
True	False	False
False	True	False
False	False	False

Negation (¬¬)

The negation of a proposition A (written as ¬A¬A) is false when A is true and istrue when A is false.
The truth table is as follows –

A	¬A
True	False
False	True

Implication / if-then (→→)

An implication A→BA→B is the proposition "if A, then B". It is false if A is true andB is false. The rest cases are true.
The truth table is as follows –

A	B	A→B
True	True	True
True	False	False
False	True	True
False	False	True

If and only if (⇔⇔)
A⇔BA⇔B is a bi-conditional logical connective which is true when p and q aresame, i.e., both are false or both are true.
The truth table is as follows –

A	B	A⇔B
True	True	True
True	False	False
False	True	False
False	False	True

Well Formed Formula

Well Formed Formula (wff) is a predicate holding one of the following –

- All propositional constants and propositional variables are wffs.
- If x is a variable and Y is a wff, $\forall xY$ and $\exists xY$ are also wff.
- Truth value and false values are wffs.
- Each atomic formula is a wff.
- All connectives connecting wffs are wffs.

Quantifiers

The variable of predicates is quantified by quantifiers. There are two types of quantifier in predicate logic –

- Universal Quantifier
- Existential Quantifier

Universal Quantifier

Universal quantifier states that the statements within its scope are true for every value of the specific variable. It is denoted by the symbol $\forall$. **$\forall xP(x)$** is read as for every value of x, P(x) is true.

Example – "Man is mortal" can be transformed into the propositional form $\forall xP(x)$. Here, P(x) is the predicate which denotes that x is mortal and the universe of discourse is all men.

Existential Quantifier

Existential quantifier states that the statements within its scope are true for some values of the specific variable. It is denoted by the symbol $\exists$. **$\exists xP(x)$** for some values of x is read as, P(x) is true.

Example – "Some people are dishonest" can be transformed into the propositional form $\exists x\ P(x)$ where P(x) is the predicate which denotes x is dishonest and the universe of discourse is some people.

Nested Quantifiers

If we use a quantifier that appears within the scope of another quantifier, it is called a nested quantifier.

Example

- $\forall\ a\exists bP(x,y)$ where P(a,b) denotes a+b = 0
- $\forall\ a\forall b\forall cP(a,b,c)$ where P(a,b) denotes a+(b+c) = (a+b)+c

Note – $\forall a\exists bP(x,y) \neq \exists a\forall bP(x,y)$

Approximate Reasoning

Following are the different modes of approximate reasoning –

Categorical Reasoning

In this mode of approximate reasoning, the antecedents, containing no fuzzy quantifiers and fuzzy probabilities, are assumed to be in canonical form.

Qualitative Reasoning

In this mode of approximate reasoning, the antecedents and consequents have fuzzy linguistic variables; the input-output relationship of a system is expressed as a collection of fuzzy IF-THEN rules. This reasoning is mainly used in control system analysis.

Syllogistic Reasoning

In this mode of approximation reasoning, antecedents with fuzzy quantifiers are related to inference rules. This is expressed as –

$$x = S_1A\text{'s are B'sy} = S_2C\text{'s are D's}$$

$$z = S_3E\text{'s are F's}$$

Here A,B,C,D,E,F are fuzzy predicates.

- S_1 and S_2 are given fuzzy quantifiers.
- S_3 is the fuzzy quantifier which has to be decided.

Dispositional Reasoning

In this mode of approximation reasoning, the antecedents are dispositions thatmay contain the fuzzy quantifier "usually". The quantifier **Usually** links togetherthe dispositional and syllogistic reasoning; hence it pays an important role.

For example, the projection rule of inference in dispositional reasoning can begiven as follows −

Usually ((L,M) is R) ⇒ usually (L is [R ↓ L])

Here **[R ↓ L]** is the projection of fuzzy relation **R** on **LFuzzy Logic Rule Base**

It is a known fact that a human being is always comfortable making conversationsin natural language.

The representation of human knowledge can be done with the help of following natural language expression − **IF** antecedent **THEN** consequent

The expression as stated above is referred to as the Fuzzy IF-THEN rule base.Canonical Form Following is the canonical form of Fuzzy Logic Rule Base −

Rule 1 − If condition C1, then restriction R1

Rule 2 − If condition C1, then restriction R2

Rule n − If condition C1, then restriction RnInterpretations of Fuzzy IF-THEN Rules

Fuzzy IF-THEN Rules can be interpreted in the following four forms −

Assignment Statements

These kinds of statements use "=" (equal to sign) for the purpose of assignment.They are of the following form −

a = hello

climate = summer

Conditional Statements

These kinds of statements use the "IF-THEN" rule base form for the purpose ofcondition. They are of the following form −

IF temperature is high THEN Climate is hotIF food is fresh THEN eat.

Unconditional Statements

They are of the following form −

GOTO 10

turn the Fan off

Linguistic Variable

We have studied that fuzzy logic uses linguistic variables which are the words orsentences in a natural language. For example, if we say temperature, it is a linguistic variable; the values of which are very hot or cold, slightly hot or cold, very warm, slightly warm, etc. The words very, slightly are the linguistic hedges.

Characterization of Linguistic Variable

Following four terms characterize the linguistic variable −

- Name of the variable, generally represented by x.
- Term set of the variable, generally represented by t(x).
- Syntactic rules for generating the values of the variable x.
- Semantic rules for linking every value of x and its significance.

Propositions in Fuzzy Logic

As we know that propositions are sentences expressed in any language which aregenerally expressed in the following canonical form −

s as P

Here, s is the Subject and P is Predicate.

For example, "Delhi is the capital of India", this is a proposition where "Delhi" is the subject and "is the capital of India" is the predicate which shows the property of subject. We know that logic is the basis of reasoning and fuzzy logic extends the capability of reasoning by using fuzzy predicates, fuzzy-predicate modifiers, fuzzy quantifiers and fuzzy qualifiers in fuzzy propositions which creates the difference from classical logic.

Propositions in fuzzy logic include the following −

Fuzzy Predicate

Almost every predicate in natural language is fuzzy in nature hence, fuzzy logichas the predicates like tall, short, warm, hot, fast, etc.

Fuzzy-predicate Modifiers

We discussed linguistic hedges above; we also have many fuzzy-predicate modifiers which act as hedges. They are very essential for producing the values of a linguistic variable. For example, the words very, slightly are modifiers and the propositions can be like "water is slightly hot."

Fuzzy Quantifiers

It can be defined as a fuzzy number which gives a vague classification of the cardinality of one or more fuzzy or non-fuzzy sets. It can be used to influence probability within fuzzy logic. For example, the words many, most, frequently are used as fuzzy quantifiers and the propositions can be like "most people are allergic to it."

Fuzzy Qualifiers

Let us now understand Fuzzy Qualifiers. A Fuzzy Qualifier is also a proposition of Fuzzy Logic. Fuzzy qualification has the following forms –

Fuzzy Qualification Based on Truth

It claims the degree of truth of a fuzzy proposition.

Expression – It is expressed as x is t. Here, t is a fuzzy truth value.

Example – (Car is black) is NOT VERY True.Fuzzy Qualification Based on Probability It claims the probability, either numerical or an interval, of fuzzy proposition.

Expression – It is expressed as x is λ. Here, λ is a fuzzy probability.

Example – (Car is black) is Likely.

Fuzzy Qualification Based on Possibility It claims the possibility of fuzzy proposition.

Expression – It is expressed as x is π. Here, π is a fuzzy possibility.

Example – (Car is black) is Almost Impossible.

Inference System

Fuzzy Inference System is the key unit of a fuzzy logic system having decision making as its primary work. It uses the "IF…THEN" rules along with connectors"OR" or "AND" for drawing essential decision rules.

Characteristics of Fuzzy Inference System Following are some characteristics of FIS –

- The output from FIS is always a fuzzy set irrespective of its input which canbe fuzzy or crisp.
- It is necessary to have fuzzy output when it is used as a controller.
- A defuzzification unit would be there with FIS to convert fuzzy variables intocrisp variables.

Functional Blocks of FIS

The following five functional blocks will help you understand the construction of FIS –

- **Rule Base** – It contains fuzzy IF-THEN rules.
- **Database** – It defines the membership functions of fuzzy sets used in fuzzyrules.
- **Decision-making Unit** – It performs operation on rules.
- **Fuzzification Interface Unit** – It converts the crisp quantities into fuzzyquantities.
- **Defuzzification Interface Unit** – It converts the fuzzy quantities into crispquantities.

Following is a block diagram of fuzzy interference system.

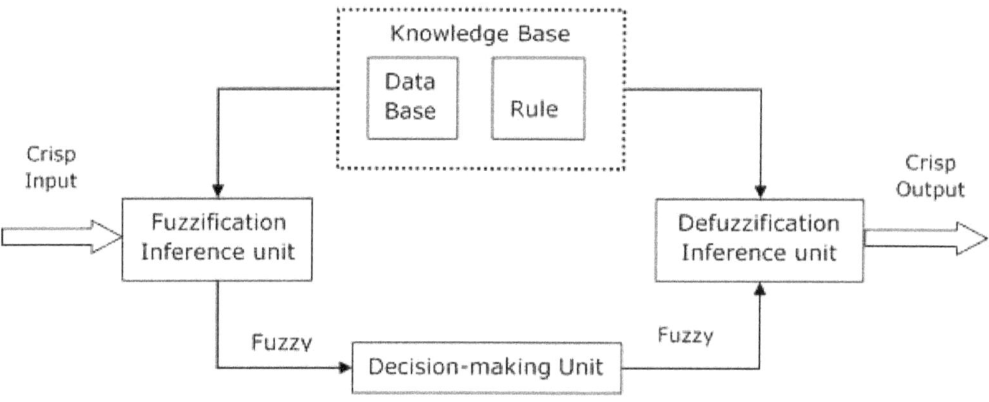

Working of FIS

The working of the FIS consists of the following steps –

- A fuzzification unit supports the application of numerous fuzzification methods, and converts the crisp input into fuzzy input.
- A knowledge base - collection of rule base and database is formed upon theconversion of crisp input into fuzzy input.
- The defuzzification unit fuzzy input is finally converted into crisp output.Methods of FIS

Let us now discuss the different methods of FIS. Following are the two importantmethods of FIS, having different consequent of fuzzy rules –

- Mamdani Fuzzy Inference System
- Takagi-Sugeno Fuzzy Model (TS Method)Mamdani Fuzzy Inference System

This system was proposed in 1975 by Ebhasim Mamdani. Basically, it was anticipated to control a steam engine and boiler combination by synthesizing aset of fuzzy rules obtained from people working on the system.

Steps for Computing the Output

Following steps need to be followed to compute the output from this FIS –

- **Step 1** – Set of fuzzy rules need to be determined in this step.
- **Step 2** – In this step, by using input membership function, the input wouldbe made fuzzy.
- **Step 3** – Now establish the rule strength by combining the fuzzified inputsaccording to fuzzy rules.
- **Step 4** – In this step, determine the consequent of rule by combining therule strength and the output membership function.
- **Step 5** – For getting output distribution combine all the consequents.
- **Step 6** – Finally, a defuzzified output distribution is obtained.

Following is a block diagram of Mamdani Fuzzy Interface System.

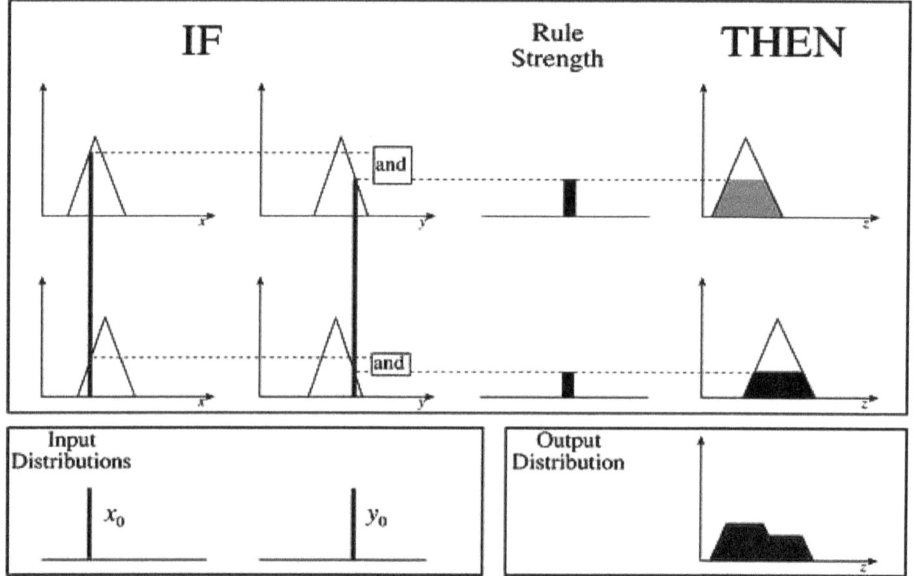

Takagi-Sugeno Fuzzy Model (TS Method)
This model was proposed by Takagi, Sugeno and Kang in 1985. Format of this ruleis given as –
IF x is A and y is B THEN Z = f(x,y)

Here, AB are fuzzy sets in antecedents and z = f(x,y) is a crisp function in theconsequent.

Fuzzy Inference Process
The fuzzy inference process under Takagi-Sugeno Fuzzy Model (TS Method) worksin the following way –

- **Step 1: Fuzzifying the inputs** – Here, the inputs of the system are madefuzzy.
- **Step 2: Applying the fuzzy operator** – In this step, the fuzzy operators mustbe applied to get the output.

Rule Format of the Sugeno Form
The rule format of Sugeno form is given by –if 7 = x and 9 = y then output is z = ax+by+c

Comparison between the two methods
Let us now understand the comparison between the Mamdani System and theSugeno Model.

- **Output Membership Function** – The main difference between them is on the basis of output membership function. The Sugeno output membershipfunctions are either linear or constant.
- **Aggregation and Defuzzification Procedure** – The difference between themalso lies in the consequence of fuzzy rules and due to the same their aggregation and defuzzification procedure also differs.
- **Mathematical Rules** – More mathematical rules exist for the Sugeno rulethan the Mamdani rule.
- **Adjustable Parameters** – The Sugeno controller has more adjustableparameters than the Mamdani controller.

Control System

Fuzzy logic is applied with great success in various control application. Almost allthe consumer products have fuzzy control. Some of the examples include controlling your room temperature with the help of air-conditioner, anti-brakingsystem used in vehicles, control on traffic lights, washing machines, large economic systems, etc.

Why Use Fuzzy Logic in Control Systems

A control system is an arrangement of physical components designed to alter another physical system so that this system exhibits certain desired characteristics. Following are some reasons of using Fuzzy Logic in ControlSystems –

- While applying traditional control, one needs to know about the model andthe objective function formulated in precise terms. This makes it very difficult to apply in many cases.
- By applying fuzzy logic for control we can utilize the human expertise andexperience for designing a controller.
- The fuzzy control rules, basically the IF-THEN rules, can be best utilized indesigning a controller.

Assumptions in Fuzzy Logic Control (FLC) Design

While designing fuzzy control system, the following six basic assumptions shouldbe made –

- **The plant is observable and controllable** – It must be assumed that the input, output as well as state variables are available for observation andcontrolling purpose.
- **Existence of a knowledge body** – It must be assumed that there exist a knowledge body having linguistic rules and a set of input-output data setfrom which rules can be extracted.
- **Existence of solution** – It must be assumed that there exists a solution.
- **'Good enough' solution is enough** – The control engineering must look for'good enough' solution rather than an optimum one.
- **Range of precision** – Fuzzy logic controller must be designed within anacceptable range of precision.
- **Issues regarding stability and optimality** – The issues of stability and optimality must be open in designing Fuzzy logic controller rather thanaddressed explicitly.

Architecture of Fuzzy Logic Control

The following diagram shows the architecture of Fuzzy Logic Control (FLC).

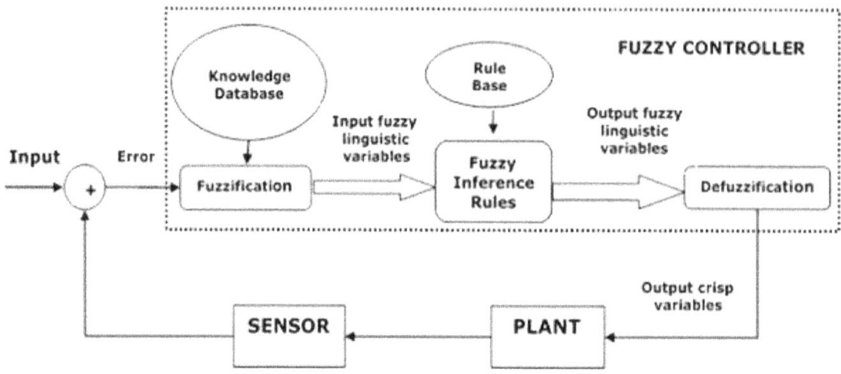

Major Components of FLC

Followings are the major components of the FLC as shown in the above figure –

- **Fuzzifier** – The role of fuzzifier is to convert the crisp input values into fuzzyvalues.
- **Fuzzy Knowledge Base** – It stores the knowledge about all the input-output fuzzy relationships. It also has the membership function which defines the input variables to the fuzzy rule base and the output variables to the plant under control.
- **Fuzzy Rule Base** – It stores the knowledge about the operation of theprocess of domain.
- **Inference Engine** – It acts as a kernel of any FLC. Basically it simulates human decisions by performing approximate reasoning.
- **Defuzzifier** – The role of defuzzifier is to convert the fuzzy values into crispvalues getting from fuzzy inference engine.

Steps in Designing FLC

Following are the steps involved in designing FLC –

- **Identification of variables** – Here, the input, output and state variables must be identified of the plant which is under consideration.
- **Fuzzy subset configuration** – The universe of information is divided into number of fuzzy subsets and each subset is assigned a linguistic label. Always make sure that these fuzzy subsets include all the elements of universe.
- **Obtaining membership function** – Now obtain the membership functionfor each fuzzy subset that we get in the above step.
- **Fuzzy rule base configuration** – Now formulate the fuzzy rule base byassigning relationship between fuzzy input and output.
- **Fuzzification** – The fuzzification process is initiated in this step.
- **Combining fuzzy outputs** – By applying fuzzy approximate reasoning, locatethe fuzzy output and merge them.
- **Defuzzification** – Finally, initiate defuzzification process to form a crispoutput.

Advantages of Fuzzy Logic Control

the advantages of Fuzzy Logic Control.

- **Cheaper** – Developing a FLC is comparatively cheaper than developing model based or other controller in terms of performance.
- **Robust** – FLCs are more robust than PID controllers because of their capability to cover a huge range of operating conditions.
- **Customizable** – FLCs are customizable.
- **Emulate human deductive thinking** – Basically FLC is designed to emulate human deductive thinking, the process people use to infer conclusion fromwhat they know.
- **Reliability** – FLC is more reliable than conventional control system.
- **Efficiency** – Fuzzy logic provides more efficiency when applied in controlsystem.

Disadvantages of Fuzzy Logic Control

We will now discuss what are the disadvantages of Fuzzy Logic Control.

- **Requires lots of data** – FLC needs lots of data to be applied.
- **Useful in case of moderate historical data** – FLC is not useful for programsmuch smaller or larger than historical data.

- **Needs high human expertise** – This is one drawback as the accuracy of the system depends on the knowledge and expertise of human beings.
- **Needs regular updating of rules** – The rules must be updated with time.

Fuzziness in Neural Networks

Artificial neural network (ANN) is a network of efficient computing systems the central theme of which is borrowed from the analogy of biological neural networks. ANNs are also named as "artificial neural systems," parallel distributed processing systems," "connectionist systems." ANN acquires large collection of units that are interconnected in some pattern to allow communications between units.

These units, also referred to as nodes or neurons, are simple processors which operate in parallel. Every neuron is connected with other neuron through a connection link. Each connection link is associated with a weight having the information about the input signal. This is the most useful information for neurons to solve a particular problem because the weight usually inhibits the signal that is being communicated.

Each neuron is having its internal state which is called the activation signal. Output signals, which are produced after combining the input signals and the activation rule, may be sent to other units. It also consists of a bias 'b' whose weight is always 1.

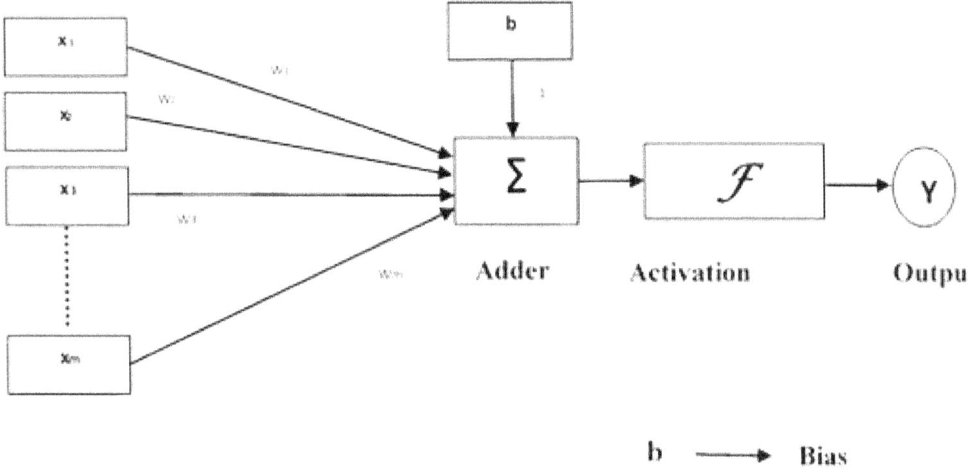

Neural Network Model

Why to use Fuzzy Logic in Neural Network

As we have discussed above that every neuron in ANN is connected with other neuron through a connection link and that link is associated with a weight having the information about the input signal. Hence we can say that weights have the useful information about input to solve the problems.

Following are some reasons to use fuzzy logic in neural networks –
- Fuzzy logic is largely used to define the weights, from fuzzy sets, in neural networks.
- When crisp values are not possible to apply, then fuzzy values are used.
- We have already studied that training and learning help neural networks perform better in unexpected situations. At that time fuzzy values would be more applicable than crisp values.
- When we use fuzzy logic in neural networks then the values must not be crisp and the processing can be done in parallel.

Fuzzy Cognitive Map

It is a form of fuzziness in neural networks. Basically FCM is like a dynamic state machine with fuzzy states (not just 1 or 0). Difficulty in using Fuzzy Logic in Neural Networks Despite having numerous advantages, there is also some difficulty while using fuzzy logic in neural networks.

The difficulty is related with membership rules, the need to build fuzzy system, because it is sometimes complicated to deduce it with the given set of complex data.

Neural-Trained Fuzzy Logic

The reverse relationship between neural network and fuzzy logic, i.e., neural network used to train fuzzy logic is also a good area of study. Following are twomajor reasons to build neuraltrained fuzzy logic –

- New patterns of data can be learned easily with the help of neural networks hence, it can be used to preprocess data in fuzzy systems.
- Neural network, because of its capability to learn new relationship with new input data, can be used to refine fuzzy rules to create fuzzy adaptivesystem.

Examples of Neural-Trained Fuzzy system

Neural-Trained Fuzzy systems are being used in many commercial applications.Let us now see a few examples where Neural-Trained Fuzzy system is applied –

- The Laboratory for International Fuzzy Engineering Research (LIFE) in Yokohama, Japan has a back-propagation neural network that derives fuzzy rules. This system has been successfully applied to foreign-exchange trade system with approximately 5000 fuzzy rules.
- Ford Motor Company has developed trainable fuzzy systems for automobileidle-speed control.
- NeuFuz, software product of National Semiconductor Corporation, supports the generation of fuzzy rules with a neural network for control applications.
- AEG Corporation of Germany uses neural-trained fuzzy control system forits water – and energy conserving machine. It is having total of 157 fuzzy rules.

Genetic Algorithm

Genetic algorithm (GAs) are a class of search algorithms designed on the naturalevolution process. Genetic Algorithms are based on the principles of **survival of the fittest**. A Genetic Algorithm method inspired in the world of Biology, particularly, the Evolution Theory by **Charles Darwin,** is taken as the basis of its working.

John Holland introduced the Genetic Algorithm in **1975**. Genetic Algorithms are utilizedto tackle optimization problems by copying the evolutionary behavior of species. From an initial random population of solutions, this population is advanced through selection, mutation, and crossover operators, inspired in natural evolution. By implementing the given set of operations, the population goes through an iterative procedure in which it reaches various states, and each one is called **generation**.

As a result of this procedure, the population is expected to reach a generation in which it contains a decent solution to the problem. In the Genetic Algorithm, the solution of the problem is coded as a **string of bits** or **real numbers**.

They have been shown in practice to be very efficient at functional optimization. It is used in searching for huge and sophisticated spaces. Genetic algorithms (GAs) are algorithms that are used for optimization and machine learning based on various features of biological evolution.

They need the given components:

- A process of coding solutions to solve the problem of chromosomes.
- An evaluation function that recovers a rating for each chromosome given toit.
- Operators that may be implemented to parents when they reproduce to alter their genetic composition. The standard operators are mutation andcrossover.
- Operators that may be implemented to parents when they reproduce to modify their genetic composition. The standard operators are mutation andcrossover.

Development of ANNs with Evolutionary Computation

The advancement of ANNs is a subject that has been broadly dealt with extremely different techniques. The world of evolutionary algorithms is no exemption, and evidence of that is the incredible amount of works that have been published about the various techniques in this area, even with genetic algorithms or GP. As a general rule, the field of ANNs generation using evolutionary algorithms is separated into three principal fields: **Evolution of weight, Architectures, Learningrules**.

Initially, the weight evolution begins from an ANN with a previously determinedtopology. The issue to be solved is the training of the association weights, attempting to limit the network error. With the utilization of an evolutionary algorithm, the weights can be represented either as the connection of binary orreal values.

Second, the evolution of architecture incorporates the generation of the topological structure. In order to utilize evolutionary algorithms to create ANNarchitectures, it is required to select how to encrypt the genotype of a given network for it to be used by the genetic operators.

At the first option, direct encoding, there is a balanced analogy between all of thegenes and their resulting phenotypes. The most typical encoding technique comprises a matrix that represents an architecture where each component reveals the presence or absence of association between two nodes.

In the encoding schemes, GP has been utilized to create both architecture and association weights at the same time, either for feed-forward or recurrent ANNs, with no limitations in their architecture. This new codification scheme also permits the acquiring of basic networks with a minimum number of neurons and associations, and the outcomes published are auspicious.

Apart from direct encoding, there are some indirect encoding techniques. In these techniques, just a few characteristics of the architecture are encoded in the chromosome. These techniques have various types of representation. First, the parametric representations portray the network as a group of parameters. For example, numbers of nodes for each layer, the number of associations between two layers,the number of hidden layers, etc.

Another no direct representation type dependson grammatical rules. In this system, the network is represented by a group of regulations, build as production rules that make a matrix that represents the network.

With respect to the evolution of the learning rule, there are various approaches, however, most of them are just based on how learning can alter or manage the evolution and also on the relationship between the architecture and the association weights.

ANNs working principle

The working principle of a standard Genetic Algorithm is illustrated in the given figure. The significant steps involved are the generation of a population of the solution, identifying the objective function and fitness function, and the application of genetic operators. These aspects are described with the assistanceof a fundamental genetic algorithm as below.

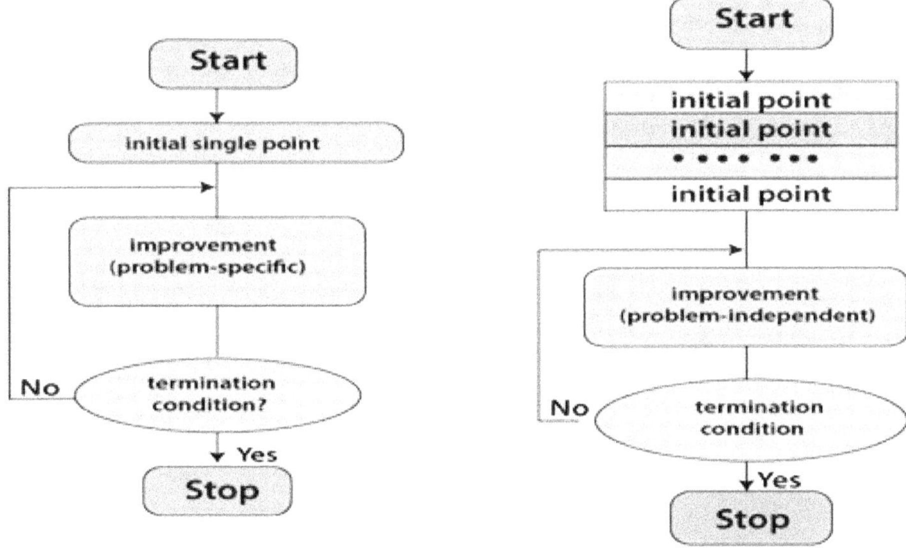

Start:
It generates a random population of n chromosomes.

Fitness:
It calculates the fitness f(x) of each chromosome x in the population.

New Population:
It generates a new population by repeating the following steps until the Newpopulation is finished.

Selection:
It chooses two parent chromosomes from a population as per their fitness. The better fitness, the higher the probability of

getting selected.

Crossover:

In crossover probability, cross over the parents to form new offspring (children). Ifno crossover was performed, the offspring is the exact copy of the parents.

Mutation:

In mutation probability, mutate new offspring at each locus.

Accepting:

It places new offspring in the new population.

Replace:

It uses the newly generated population for a further run of the algorithm.

Test:

If the end condition is satisfied, then it stops and returns the best solution in thecurrent population.

Loop:

In this step, we need to go to the second step for fitness evaluation.

The basic principle behind the genetic algorithms is that they generate and maintain a population of individuals represented by chromosomes. Chromosomes are a character string practically equivalent to the chromosomes appearing in DNA. These chromosomes are usually encoded solutions to a problem. It undergoes a process of evolution as per rules of selection, reproduction, and mutation.

Each individual in the environment (represented by chromosome) gets a measure of its fitness in the environment. Reproduction chooses individuals with high fitness values in the population. Through crossover and mutation of such individuals, a new population is determined in which individuals might be aneven better fit for their environment.

The process of crossover includes two chromosomes swapping chunks of data and is analogous to the process of reproduction. Mutation introduces slight changes into a little extant of the population, and it is representative of an evolutionary step.

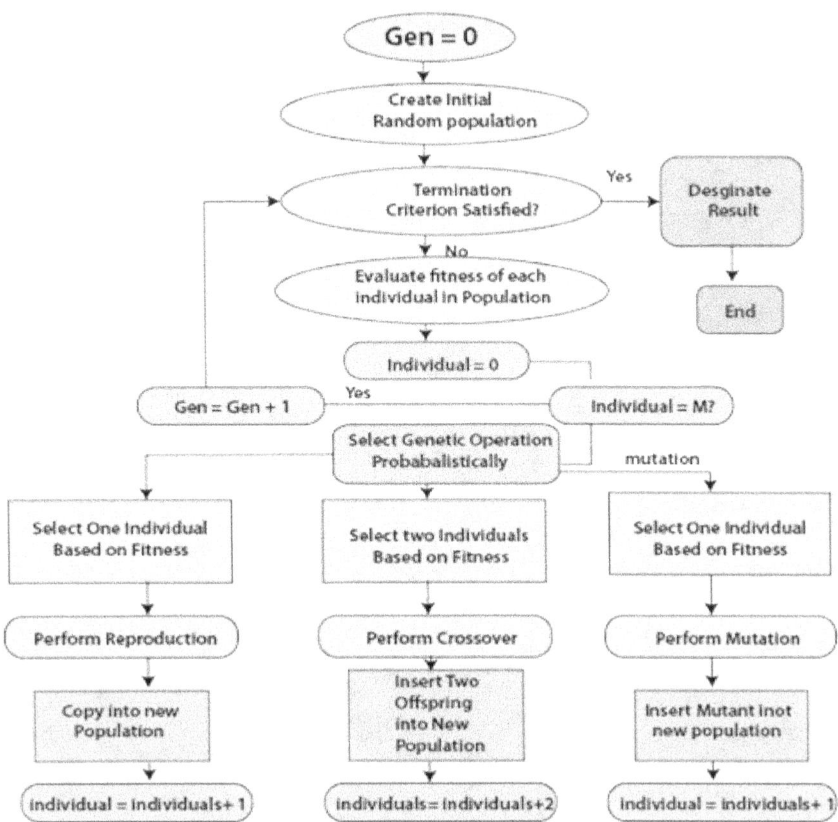

Difference between traditional and genetic approach

An algorithm is a progression of steps for solving a problem. A genetic algorithm is a problem-solving technique that uses genetics as its model of problem-solving. It is a search method to find approximate solutions to optimization and search issues. One can easily distinguish between a traditional and a genetic algorithm.

Traditional Algorithm	Genetic Algorithm
It selects the next point in the series by a deterministic computation.	It selects the next population by computation, which utilizes randomnumber generators.
It creates an individual point at eachiteration. The sequence of points approaches an optimal solution.	It creates a population of points at everyiteration. The best point in the population approaches an optimal solution.
Advancement in each iteration isproblem specific.	Concurrence in each iteration is aproblem independent.

Advantages of Genetic Algorithm:

- The genetic algorithm concept is easy to understand.
- The genetic algorithm supports multi-objective optimization.
- A genetic algorithm is suitable for noisy environments.
- The genetic algorithm is robust with respect to local minima/maxima.
- The genetic algorithm utilizes probabilistic transition rules.
- The genetic algorithm utilizes payoff (objective function) information, notderivatives.
- The genetic algorithm works well on mixed discrete functions.

Limitations of Genetic Algorithm:

Although Genetic algorithms have demonstrated to be a quick and powerful problem-solving approach, some limitations are found embedded in it. Some ofthese limitations are given below:

The first, and most significant, consideration in making a genetic algorithm is characterizing representation of the problem. The language used to determine candidate solutions must be robust. It must be able to endure random changessuch that fatal errors don't mistake.

One significant obstacle of genetic algorithms is the coding of the fitness (evaluation) function so that a higher fitness can be achieved, and better solutionsfor the problem are produced. A wrong decision of the fitness function may lead to significant consequences. For example, it is unable to find the solution for a problem and returning the wrong solution to the problem.

Along with making a decent choice of the fitness function, different parameters of a Genetic Algorithm like population size, mutation, and crossover rate must be chosen effectively. Small population size will not give enough solution to the genetic algorithm to produce precise results. A frequency of genetic change or poor selection scheme will result in disrupting the beneficial schema.

It is not recommended to utilize Genetic algorithms for analytical problems. Though Genetic algorithms can find exact solutions to these sorts of problems,traditional analytic techniques can find the same solutions in a short time with few computational data.

Applications of Genetic Algorithm:

Genetic Algorithm in Robotics:
Robotics is one of the most discussed fields in the computer industry today. It is used in various industries in order to increase profitability efficiency and accuracy.As the environment in which robots work with the time change, it becomes very tough for developers to figure out each possible behavior of the robot in order to cope with the changes.

This is the place where the Genetic Algorithm places a vital role. Hence a suitable method is required, which will lead the robot to its objective and will make it adaptive to new situations as it encounters them.

Genetic Algorithms are adaptive search techniques that are used to learn high-performance knowledge structures.
Genetic Algorithm in Financial Planning:
Models for **tactical asset distribution** and **international equity methodologies** have been enhanced with the use of Gas. Genetic algorithms are extremely efficient for financial modeling applications as they are driven by adjustments that can be used to improve the efficiency of predictions and returnover the benchmark set.

In addition, these methods are robust, permitting a greater range of extensions and constraints, which may not be accommodated intraditional techniques.

Encoding Methods in Genetic AlgorithmBiological Background:
1) **Chromosome** : All living organisms consists of cells. In each cell there is a same setof Chromosomes. Chromosomes are strings of DNA and consists of genes, blocks of DNA. Each gene encodes a trait, for example color of eyes.
2) **Reproduction** : During reproduction, combination (or crossover) occurs first. Genes from parents combine to form a whole new chromosome. The newly created offspring can then be mutated. The changes are mainly caused by errorsin copying genes from parents. The fitness of an organism is measured by the success of the organism in its life.

Operation of Genetic Algorithms:
Two important elements required for any problem before a genetic algorithm canbe used for a solution are-
- Method for representing a solution ex: a string of bits, numbers, characterex: determination total weight.
- Method for measuring the quality of any proposed solution, using fitnessfunction.

Basic principles :
- An individual is characterized by a set of parameters : **Genes**
- The genes are joined into a string : **Chromosome**
- The chromosome forms the **genotype**
- The genotype contains all information to construct an organism : Phenotype
- **Reproduction** is a "dumb" process on the chromosome of the **genotype**
- **Fitness** is measured in the real world ('Struggle for life') of thephenotype.

Algorithmic Phases :

    Calculate Fitness Function; while(Fitness Value != Optimal
    Value)
    {
        Selection; //Natural Selection, survival of fittest

        Crossover; //Reproduction, propagate favorable characteristicsMutation;
        Calculate Fitness Function;

    }
 }
Simple_Genetic_Algorithm()

{
Initialize the population;

Encoding using string :

Encoding of chromosomes is the first step in solving the problem and it dependsentirely on the problem heavily. The process of representing the solution in the form of a string of bits that conveys the necessary information. just as in a chromosome, each gene controls a particular characteristics of the individual, similarly, each bit in the string represents a characteristics of the solution.

Encoding Methods :

Binary Encoding : Most common methods of encoding. Chromosomes are string of 1s and 0s and each position in the chromosome represents a particular characteristics of the problem.

Chromosome A	10110010110011100101
Chromosome B	11111110000000011111

Permutation Encoding : Useful in ordering such as the Travelling Salesman Problem (TSP). In TSP, every chromosome is a string of numbers, each of which represents a city to be visited.

Chromosome A	1 5 3 2 6 4 7 9 8
Chromosome B	8 5 6 7 2 3 1 4 9

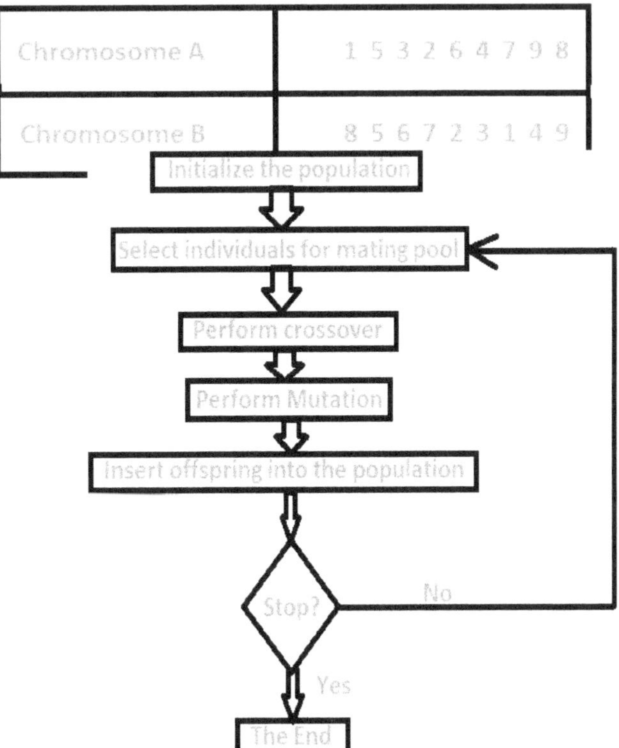

- **Value Encoding :** Used in problems where complicated values, such as realnumbers, are used and where binary encoding would not suffice. Good for some problems, nut often necessary to develop some specific crossover and mutation techniques for these chromosomes.

Fitness Function and Objective Function

In order to assess which of our genomes should go on into the next generation through reproduction or another means, we need a function to calculate their value in a way that allows us to compare values of two different genomes. This function is called a fitness function and we can denote it as f(x). Although it's notquite our f(x) from the clifftop picture, it's meant to

| Chromosome A | 1.235 5.323 0.454 2.321 2.454 |
| Chromosome B | (left), (back), (left), (right), (forward) |

approximate it.

It's usually always positive, and the larger the number the better the genome. When we use such a fitness function, we're performing maximization on the search space - looking for maximum value of fitness.

The objective function is quite similar to fitness function, and in a lot of cases they're the same, but sometimes the distinction is important. The objective function is used to calculate the fitness of the best genome in each generation (the one with the maximum fitness function value) in order to check whether itsatisfies a predetermined conditions.

Why use two different functions? Well, because the fitness function is performedon every genome in every generation, it's very important for it to be fast. It doesn't have to be very precise, as long as it more or less sorts the genomes by quality reasonably well.

On the other hand, the objective function is called only once per generation, so we can afford to use a more costly and more precise function, so we'd know forsure how good our result is. The objective function would be our f(x) on the clifftop picture, while the fitness function would be its close approximation.

The fitness function simply defined is a function which takes a **candidate solutionto the problem as input and produces as output** how "fit" our how "good" the solution is with respect to the problem in consideration.

Calculation of fitness value is done repeatedly in a GA and therefore it should be sufficiently fast. A slow computation of the fitness value can adversely affect a GAand make it exceptionally slow.

In most cases the fitness function and the objective function are the same as the objective is to either maximize or minimize the given objective function. However,for more complex problems with multiple objectives and constraints,

an **Algorithm Designer** might choose to have a different fitness function. A fitness function should possess the following characteristics –

- The fitness function should be sufficiently fast to compute.
- It must quantitatively measure how fit a given solution is or how fitindividuals can be produced from the given solution.

In some cases, calculating the fitness function directly might not be possible dueto the inherent complexities of the problem at hand. In such cases, we do fitnessapproximation to suit our needs.

The following image shows the fitness calculation for a solution of the 0/1 Knapsack. It is a simple fitness function which just sums the profit values of the items being picked (which have a 1), scanning the elements from left to right tillthe knapsack is full.

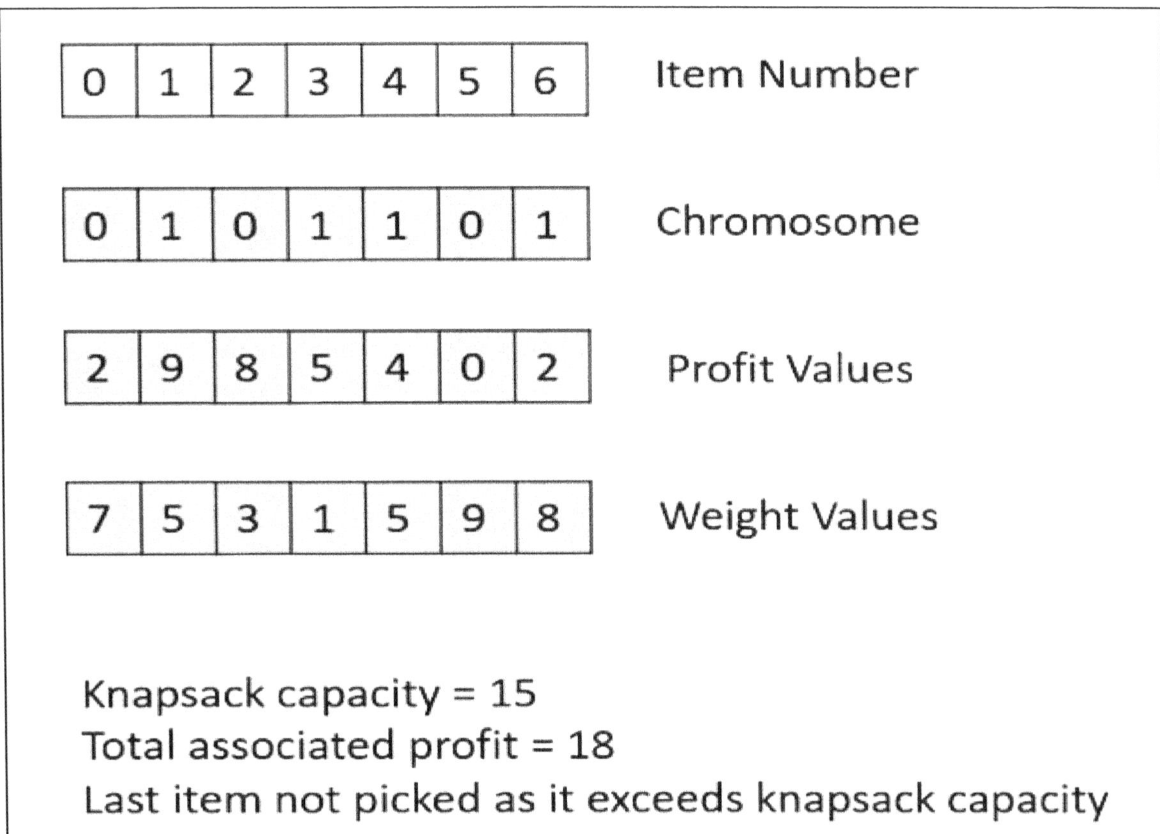

Crossover

The crossover operator is analogous to reproduction and biological crossover. In this more than one parent is selected and one or more off-springs are produced using the genetic material of the parents. Crossover is usually applied in a GA with a high probability – p_c.

Crossover Operators

In this section we will discuss some of the most popularly used crossover operators. It is to be noted that these crossover operators are very generic and the GA Designer might choose to implement a problem-specific crossover operator as well.

One Point Crossover

In this one-point crossover, a random crossover point is selected and the tails of its two parents are swapped to get new off-springs.

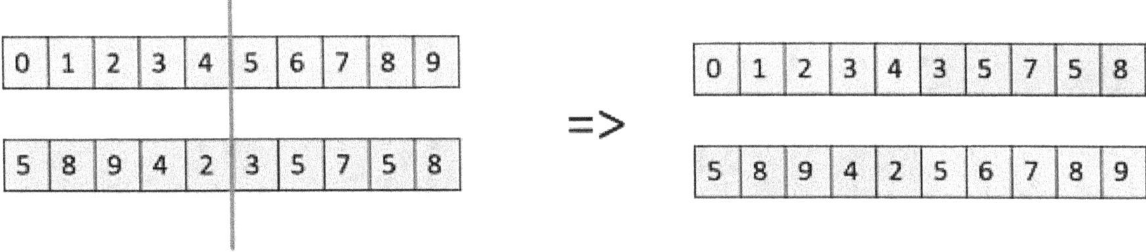

Multi Point Crossover

Multi point crossover is a generalization of the one-point crossover wherein alternating segments are swapped to get new off-springs.

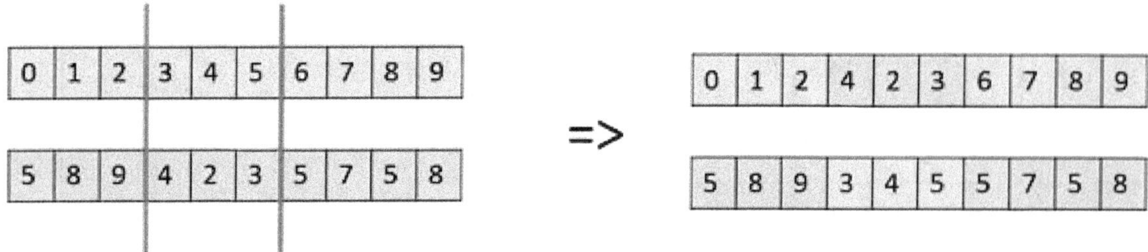

Uniform Crossover

In a uniform crossover, we don't divide the chromosome into segments, rather we treat each gene separately. In this, we essentially flip a coin for each chromosome to decide whether or not it'll be included in the off-spring. We canalso bias the coin to one parent, to have more genetic material in the child fromthat parent.

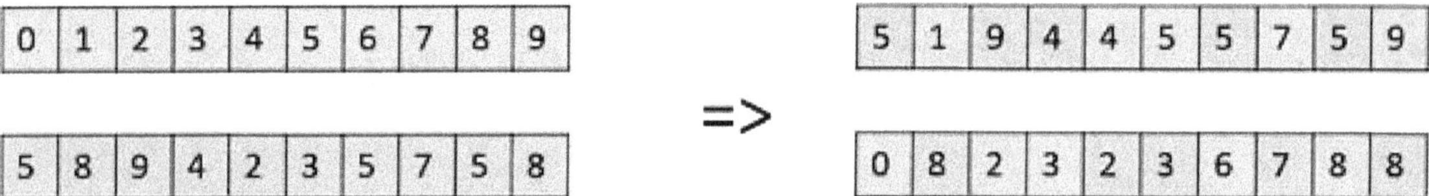

Whole Arithmetic Recombination

This is commonly used for integer representations and works by taking theweighted average of the two parents by using the following formulae –

- Child1 = $\alpha.x + (1-\alpha).y$
- Child2 = $\alpha.x + (1-\alpha).y$

Obviously, if $\alpha = 0.5$, then both the children will be identical as shown in thefollowing image.

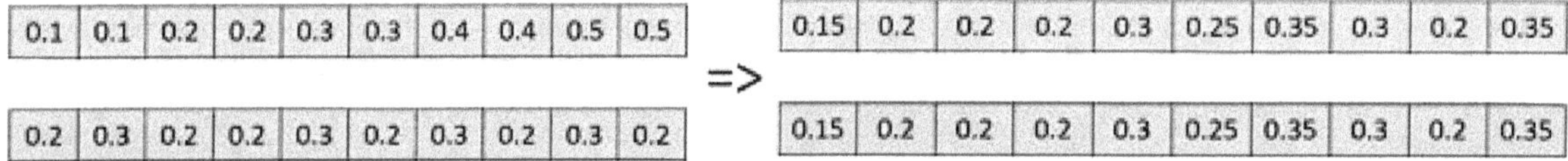

Davis' Order Crossover (OX1)

OX1 is used for permutation based crossovers with the intention of transmittinginformation about relative ordering to the off-springs. It works as follows –

- Create two random crossover points in the parent and copy the segmentbetween them from the first parent to the first offspring.
- Now, starting from the second crossover point in the second parent, copythe remaining unused numbers from the second parent to the first child, wrapping around the list.
- Repeat for the second child with the parent's role reversed.

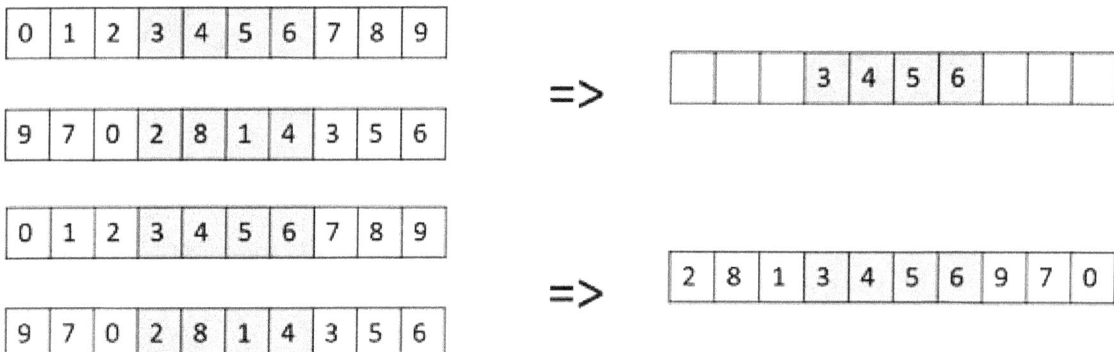

Repeat the same procedure to get the second child

There exist a lot of other crossovers like Partially Mapped Crossover (PMX), Order based crossover (OX2), Shuffle Crossover, Ring Crossover, etc.

Mutation

In simple terms, mutation may be defined as a small random tweak in the chromosome, to get a new solution. It is used to maintain and introduce diversity in the genetic population and is usually applied with a low probability – p_m. If the probability is very high, the GA gets reduced to a random search.

Mutation is the part of the GA which is related to the "exploration" of the search space. It has been observed that mutation is essential to the convergence of the GA while crossover is not.

Mutation Operators

In this section, we describe some of the most commonly used mutation operators. Like the crossover operators, this is not an exhaustive list and the GA designer might find a combination of these approaches or a problem-specific mutation operator more useful.

Bit Flip Mutation

In this bit flip mutation, we select one or more random bits and flip them. This is used for binary encoded GAs.

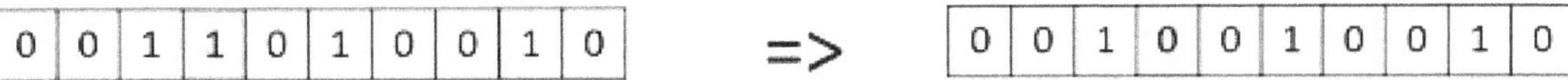

Random Resetting

Random Resetting is an extension of the bit flip for the integer representation. In this, a random value from the set of permissible values is assigned to a randomly chosen gene.

Swap Mutation

In swap mutation, we select two positions on the chromosome at random, and interchange the values. This is common in permutation based encodings.

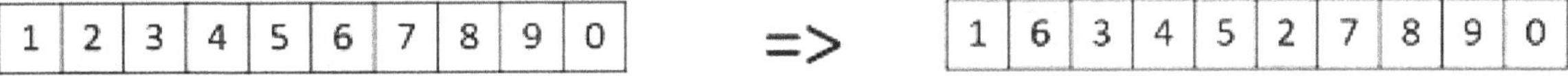

Scramble Mutation

Scramble mutation is also popular with permutation representations. In this, from the entire chromosome, a subset of genes is chosen and their values are scrambled or shuffled randomly.

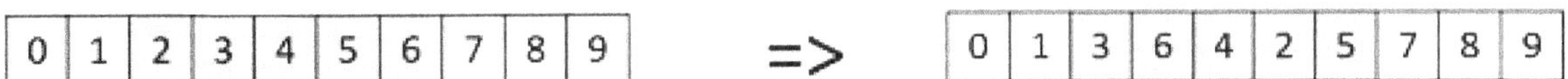

Inversion Mutation

In inversion mutation, we select a subset of genes like in scramble mutation, but instead of shuffling the subset, we merely invert the entire string in the subset.

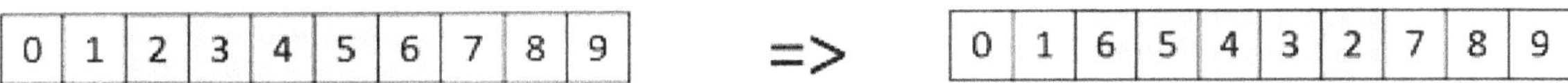

Problem Solving using GA Application Areas

Genetic Algorithms are primarily used in optimization problems of various kinds, but they are frequently used in other application areas as well.

In this section, we list some of the areas in which Genetic Algorithms are frequently used. These are –

- **Optimization** – Genetic Algorithms are most commonly used in optimization problems wherein we have to maximize or minimize a given objective function value under a given set of constraints. The approach to solve Optimization problems has been highlighted throughout the tutorial.
- **Economics** – GAs are also used to characterize various economic models like the cobweb model, game theory equilibrium

resolution, asset pricing,etc.

- **Neural Networks** – GAs are also used to train neural networks, particularlyrecurrent neural networks.
- **Parallelization** – GAs also have very good parallel capabilities, and prove to be very effective means in solving certain problems, and also provide a good area for research.
- **Image Processing** – GAs are used for various digital image processing (DIP)tasks as well like dense pixel matching.
- **Vehicle routing problems** – With multiple soft time windows, multipledepots and a heterogeneous fleet.
- **Scheduling applications** – GAs are used to solve various scheduling problems as well, particularly the time tabling problem.
- **Machine Learning** – as already discussed, genetics based machine learning(GBML) is a niche area in machine learning.
- **Robot Trajectory Generation** – GAs have been used to plan the path whicha robot arm takes by moving from one point to another.
- **Parametric Design of Aircraft** – GAs have been used to design aircrafts byvarying the parameters and evolving better solutions.
- **DNA Analysis** – GAs have been used to determine the structure of DNAusing spectrometric data about the sample.
- **Multimodal Optimization** – GAs are obviously very good approaches formultimodal optimization in which we have to find multiple optimum solutions.
- **Traveling salesman problem and its applications** – GAs have been used to solve the TSP, which is a well-known combinatorial problem using novel crossover and packing strategies.

Artificial Neural Network

The term "**Artificial Neural Network**" is derived from Biological neural networks that develop the structure of a human brain. Similar to the human brain that has neurons interconnected to one another, artificial neural networks also have neurons that are interconnected to one another in various layers of the networks.These neurons are known as nodes.

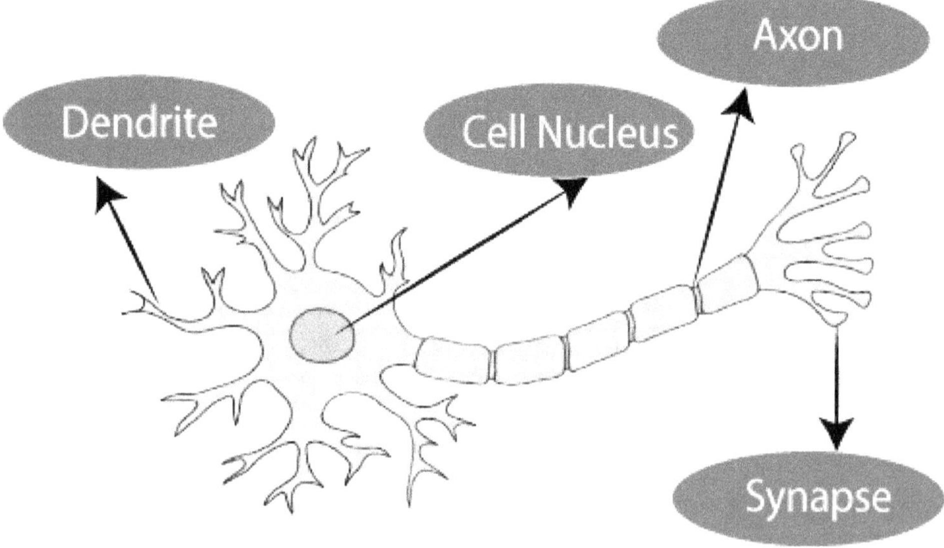

The given figure illustrates the typical diagram of Biological Neural Network. The typical Artificial Neural Network looks something like the given figure.

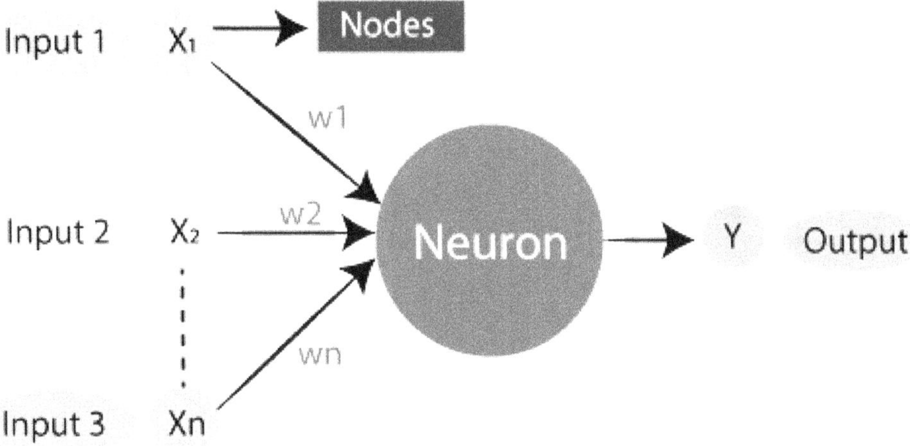

Dendrites from Biological Neural Network represent inputs in Artificial Neural Networks, cell nucleus represents Nodes, synapse represents Weights, and Axonrepresents Output.

Relationship between Biological neural network and artificial neural network:

Biological Neural Network	Artificial Neural Network
Dendrites	Inputs
Cell nucleus	Nodes
Synapse	Weights
Axon	Output

An **Artificial Neural Network** in the field of **Artificial intelligence** where it attempts to mimic the network of neurons makes up a human brain so thatcomputers will have an option to understand things and make decisions in a human-like manner. The artificial neural network is designed by programmingcomputers to behave simply like interconnected brain cells.

There are around 1000 billion neurons in the human brain. Each neuron has an association point somewhere in the range of 1,000 and 100,000. In the human brain, data is stored in such a manner as to be distributed, and we can extract more than one piece of this data when necessary from our memory parallelly. We can say that the human brain is made up of incredibly amazing parallel processors.

We can understand the artificial neural network with an example, consider an example of a digital logic gate that takes an input and gives an output. "OR" gate,which takes two inputs. If one or both the inputs are "On," then we get "On" in output. If both the inputs are "Off," then we get "Off" in output. Here the outputdepends upon input. Our brain does not perform the same task. The outputs to inputs relationship keep changing because of the neurons in our brain, which are"learning."

The architecture of an artificial neural network:
To understand the concept of the architecture of an artificial neural network, we have to understand what a neural network

consists of. In order to define a neural network that consists of a large number of artificial neurons, which are termed units arranged in a sequence of layers. Lets us look at various types of layers available in an artificial neural network.

Artificial Neural Network primarily consists of three layers:

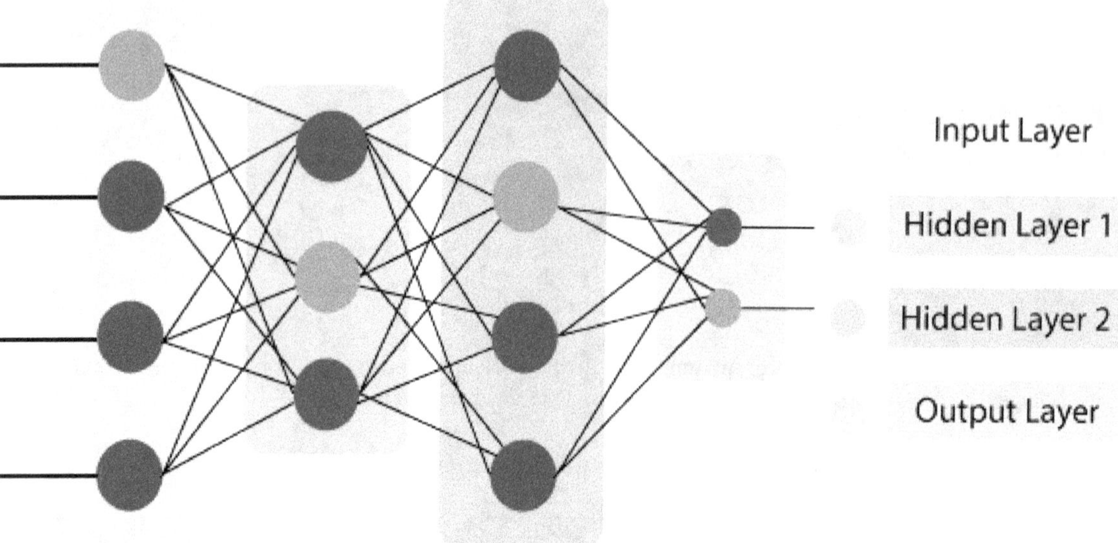

Input Layer:
As the name suggests, it accepts inputs in several different formats provided by the programmer.

Hidden Layer:
The hidden layer presents in-between input and output layers. It performs all the calculations to find hidden features and patterns.

Output Layer:
The input goes through a series of transformations using the hidden layer, whichfinally results in output that is conveyed using this layer.

The artificial neural network takes input and computes the weighted sum of theinputs and includes a bias. This computation is represented in the form of a transfer function.

$$\sum_{i=1}^{n} Wi * Xi + b$$

It determines weighted total is passed as an input to an activation function to produce the output. Activation functions choose whether a node should fire ornot. Only those who are fired make it to the output layer. There are distinctiveactivation functions available that can be applied upon the sort of task we are performing.

Advantages of Artificial Neural Network (ANN)Parallel processing capability:
Artificial neural networks have a numerical value that can perform more than onetask simultaneously.

Storing data on the entire network:
Data that is used in traditional programming is stored on the whole network, noton a database. The disappearance of a couple of pieces of data in one place doesn't prevent the network from working.

Capability to work with incomplete knowledge:
After ANN training, the information may produce output even with inadequate data. The loss of performance here relies upon the significance of missing data.

Having a memory distribution:
For ANN is to be able to adapt, it is important to determine the examples and toencourage the network according to the desired

output by demonstrating these examples to the network. The succession of the network is directly proportional to the chosen instances, and if the event can't appear to the network in all its aspects, it can produce false output.

Having fault tolerance:
Extortion of one or more cells of ANN does not prohibit it from generating output, and this feature makes the network fault-tolerance.

Disadvantages of Artificial Neural Network:

Assurance of proper network structure:
There is no particular guideline for determining the structure of artificial neural networks. The appropriate network structure is accomplished through experience, trial, and error.

Unrecognized behavior of the network:
It is the most significant issue of ANN. When ANN produces a testing solution, it does not provide insight concerning why and how. It decreases trust in the network.

Hardware dependence:
Artificial neural networks need processors with parallel processing power, as per their structure. Therefore, the realization of the equipment is dependent.

Difficulty of showing the issue to the network:
ANNs can work with numerical data. Problems must be converted into numerical values before being introduced to ANN. The presentation mechanism to be resolved here will directly impact the performance of the network. It relies on the user's abilities.

The duration of the network is unknown:
The network is reduced to a specific value of the error, and this value does not give us optimum results.
Science artificial neural networks that have steeped into the world in the mid- 20th century are exponentially developing. In the present time, we have investigated the pros of artificial neural networks and the issues encountered in the course of their utilization. It should not be overlooked that the cons of ANN networks, which are a flourishing science branch, are eliminated individually, and their pros are increasing day by day. It means that artificial neural networks will turn into an irreplaceable part of our lives progressively important.

How do artificial neural networks work?
Artificial Neural Network can be best represented as a weighted directed graph, where the artificial neurons form the nodes. The association between the neurons outputs and neuron inputs can be viewed as the directed edges with weights. The Artificial Neural Network receives the input signal from the external source in the form of a pattern and image in the form of a vector. These inputs are then mathematically assigned by the notations x(n) for every n number of inputs.

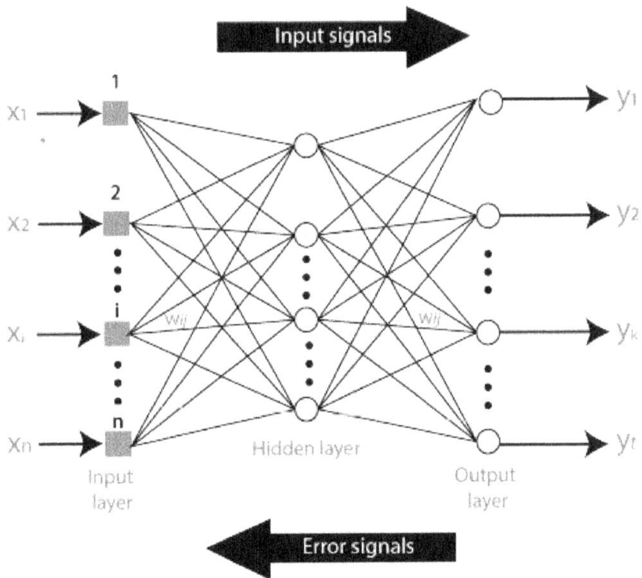

Afterward, each of the input is multiplied by its corresponding weights (these weights are the details utilized by the artificial neural networks to solve a specific problem). In general terms, these weights normally represent the strength of the interconnection between neurons inside the artificial neural network. All the weighted inputs are summarized inside the computing unit.

If the weighted sum is equal to zero, then bias is added to make the output non-zero or something else to scale up to the system's response. Bias has the same input, and weight equals to 1. Here the total of weighted inputs can be in the range of 0 to positive infinity. Here, to keep the response in the limits of the desired value, a certain maximum value is benchmarked, and the total of weighted inputs is passed through the activation function.

The activation function refers to the set of transfer functions used to achieve the desired output. There is a different kind of the activation function, but primarily either linear or non-linear sets of functions. Some of the commonly used sets of activation functions are the Binary, linear, and Tan hyperbolic sigmoidal activationfunctions. Let us take a look at each of them in details:

Binary:

In binary activation function, the output is either a one or a 0. Here, to accomplishthis, there is a threshold value set up. If the net weighted input of neurons is more than 1, then the final output of the activation function is returned as one or else the output is returned as 0.

Sigmoidal Hyperbolic:

The Sigmoidal Hyperbola function is generally seen as an "**S**" shaped curve. Here the tan hyperbolic function is used to approximate output from the actual net input. The function is defined as:

$$F(x) = (1/1 + \exp(-????x))$$

Where ???? is considered the Steepness parameter.

Types of Artificial Neural Network:

There are various types of Artificial Neural Networks (ANN) depending upon the human brain neuron and network functions, an artificial neural network similarlyperforms tasks. The majority of the artificial neural networks will have some similarities with a more complex biological partner and are very effective at their expected tasks. For example, segmentation or classification.

Feedback ANN:

In this type of ANN, the output returns into the network to accomplish the best- evolved results internally. As per the **University of Massachusetts**, Lowell Centre for Atmospheric Research. The feedback networks feed information back into itself and are well suited to solve optimization issues. The Internal system errorcorrections utilize feedback ANNs.

Feed-Forward ANN:

A feed-forward network is a basic neural network comprising of an input layer, an output layer, and at least one layer of a neuron. Through assessment of its outputby reviewing its input, the intensity of the network can be noticed based on group behavior of the associated neurons, and the output is decided. The primary advantage of this network is that it figures out how to evaluate and recognize input patterns.

Supervised learning

Supervised learning as the name indicates the presence of a supervisor as a teacher. Basically supervised learning is a learning in which we teach or train the machine using data which is well labeled that means some data is already tagged with the correct answer. After that, the machine is provided with a new set of examples(data) so that supervised learning algorithm analyses the training data(set of training examples) and produces a correct outcome from labeled data.

Supervised learning is the types of machine learning in which machines are trained using well "labelled" training data, and on basis of that data, machines predict the output. The labelled data means some input data is already tagged with the correct output.

In supervised learning, the training data provided to the machines work as thesupervisor that teaches the machines to predict the output correctly. It appliesthe same concept as a student learns in the supervision of the teacher.

Supervised learning is a process of providing input data as well as correct output data to the machine learning model. The aim of a supervised learning algorithm isto **find a mapping function to map the input variable(x) with the output variable(y)**.

In the real-world, supervised learning can be used for **Risk Assessment, Image classification, Fraud Detection, spam filtering**, etc.

How Supervised Learning Works?

In supervised learning, models are trained using labelled dataset, where the model learns about each type of data. Once the training process is completed, themodel is tested on the basis of test data (a subset of the training set), and then it predicts the output.

The working of Supervised learning can be easily understood by the belowexample and diagram:

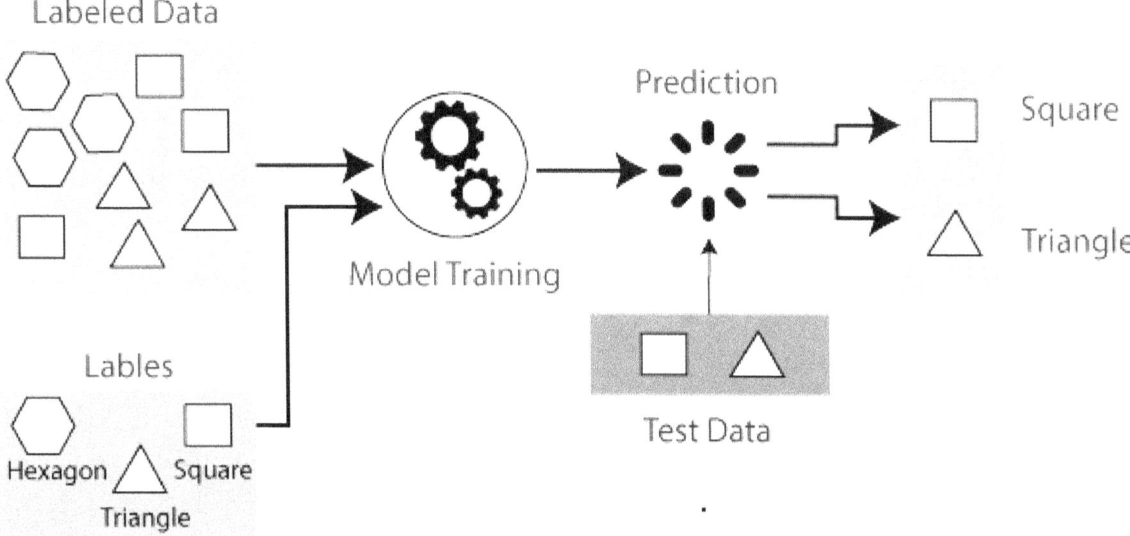

Suppose we have a dataset of different types of shapes which includes square,rectangle, triangle, and Polygon. Now the first step is that we need to train themodel for each shape.

- If the given shape has four sides, and all the sides are equal, then it will belabelled as a **Square**.
- If the given shape has three sides, then it will be labelled as a **triangle**.
- If the given shape has six equal sides then it will be labelled as **hexagon**.

Now, after training, we test our model using the test set, and the task of themodel is to identify the shape.

The machine is already trained on all types of shapes, and when it finds a new shape, it classifies the shape on the bases of a number of sides, and predicts theoutput.

Steps Involved in Supervised Learning:

- First Determine the type of training dataset
- Collect/Gather the labelled training data.
- Split the training dataset into training **dataset, test dataset, and validationdataset**.
- Determine the input features of the training dataset, which should have enough knowledge so that the model can accurately predict the output.
- Determine the suitable algorithm for the model, such as support vectormachine, decision tree, etc.
- Execute the algorithm on the training dataset. Sometimes we need validation sets as the control parameters, which are the subset of trainingdatasets.
- Evaluate the accuracy of the model by providing the test set. If the modelpredicts the correct output, which means our model is accurate.

Types of supervised Machine learning Algorithms:

Supervised learning can be further divided into two types of problems:

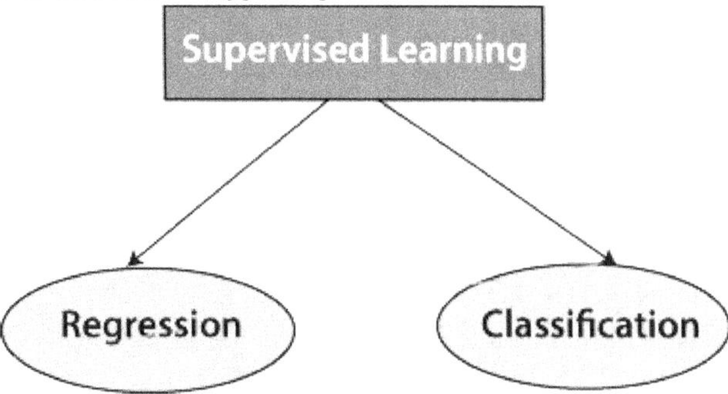

1. **Regression**

   Regression algorithms are used if there is a relationship between the input variable and the output variable. It is used for the prediction of continuous variables, such as Weather forecasting, Market Trends, etc. Below are somepopular Regression algorithms which come under supervised learning:
   - Linear Regression
   - Regression Trees
   - Non-Linear Regression
   - Bayesian Linear Regression
   - Polynomial Regression

2. **Classification**

   Classification algorithms are used when the output variable is categorical, whichmeans there are two classes such as Yes-No, Male-Female, True-false, etc.

Spam Filtering,
   - Random Forest
   - Decision Trees
   - Logistic Regression
   - Support vector Machines

Advantages of Supervised learning:
   - With the help of supervised learning, the model can predict the output onthe basis of prior experiences.
   - In supervised learning, we can have an exact idea about the classes ofobjects.
   - Supervised learning model helps us to solve various real-world problemssuch as **fraud detection, spam filtering**, etc.

Disadvantages of supervised learning:
   - Supervised learning models are not suitable for handling the complex tasks.
   - Supervised learning cannot predict the correct output if the test data isdifferent from the training dataset.
   - Training required lots of computation times.
   - In supervised learning, we need enough knowledge about the classes ofobject.

Unsupervised learning

Unsupervised learning is the training of machine using information that is neither classified nor labeled and allowing the algorithm to act on that information without guidance. Here the task of machine is to group unsorted information according to similarities, patterns and differences without any prior training of data.

Unlike supervised learning, no teacher is provided that means no training will be given to the machine. Therefore machine is restricted to find the hidden structurein unlabeled data by our-self.

For instance, suppose it is given an image having both dogs and cats which have not seen ever.

Thus the machine has no idea about the features of dogs and cat so we can't categorize it in dogs and cats. But it can categorize them according to their similarities, patterns, and differences i.e., we can easily categorize the above picture into two parts. First first may contain all pics having **dogs** in it and secondpart may contain all pics having **cats** in it. Here we didn't learn anything before, means no training data or examples.

Unsupervised learning classified into two categories of algorithms:
   - **Clustering**: A clustering problem is where you want to discover the inherent groupings in the data, such as grouping customers by purchasing behavior.

- **Association**: An association rule learning problem is where you want to discover rules that describe large portions of your data, such as people thatbuy X also tend to buy Y.

Unsupervised Learning

As the name suggests, unsupervised learning is a machine learning technique in which models are not supervised using training dataset. Instead, models itself findthe hidden patterns and insights from the given data. It can be compared to learning which takes place in the human brain while learning new things. It can bedefined as:

Unsupervised learning is a type of machine learning in which models are trainedusing unlabeled dataset and are allowed to act on that data without any supervision.

Unsupervised learning cannot be directly applied to a regression or classificationproblem because unlike supervised learning, we have the input data but no corresponding output data. The goal of unsupervised learning is to **find the underlying structure of dataset, group that data according to similarities, and represent that dataset in a compressed format**.

Example: Suppose the unsupervised learning algorithm is given an input dataset containing images of different types of cats and dogs. The algorithm is never trained upon the given dataset, which means it does not have any idea about thefeatures of the dataset. The task of the unsupervised learning algorithm is to identify the image features on their own. Unsupervised learning algorithm will perform this task by clustering the image dataset into the groups according to similarities between images.

Why use Unsupervised Learning?

Below are some main reasons which describe the importance of UnsupervisedLearning:

- Unsupervised learning is helpful for finding useful insights from the data.
- Unsupervised learning is much similar as a human learns to think by theirown experiences, which makes it closer to the real AI.
- Unsupervised learning works on unlabeled and uncategorized data which make unsupervised learning more important.
- In real-world, we do not always have input data with the corresponding output so to solve such cases, we need unsupervised learning.

Working of Unsupervised Learning

Working of unsupervised learning can be understood by the below diagram:

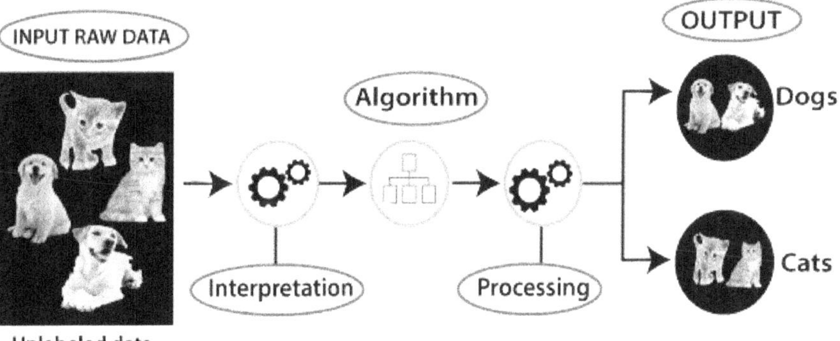

Here, we have taken an unlabeled input data, which means it is not categorized and corresponding outputs are also not given.

Now, this unlabeled input data is fed to the machine learning model in order to train it. Firstly, it will interpret theraw data to find the hidden patterns from the data and then will apply suitable algorithms such as k-means clustering, Decision tree, etc. Once it applies the suitable algorithm, the algorithm divides the data objects into groups according to the similarities and difference between the objects.

Types of Unsupervised Learning Algorithm:

The unsupervised learning algorithm can be further categorized into two types ofproblems:

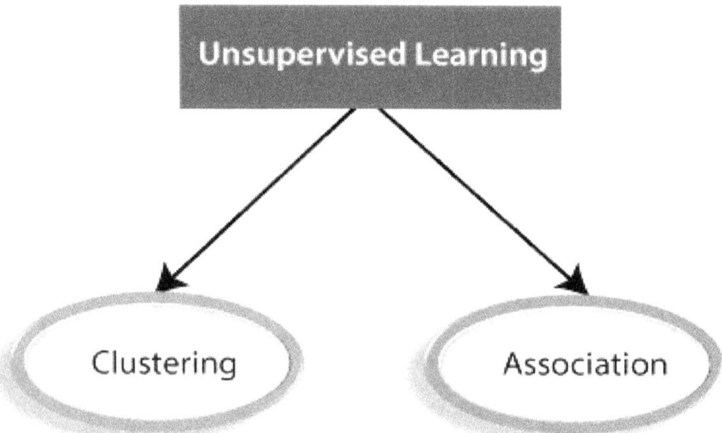

- **Clustering**: Clustering is a method of grouping the objects into clusters suchthat objects with most similarities remains into a group and has less or no similarities with the objects of another group. Cluster analysis finds the commonalities between the data objects and categorizes them as per the presence and absence of those commonalities.
- **Association**: An association rule is an unsupervised learning method which is used for finding the relationships between variables in the large database. It determines the set of items that occurs together in the dataset.Association rule makes marketing strategy more effective. Such as people who buy X item (suppose a bread) are also tend to purchase Y (Butter/Jam) item. A typical example of Association rule is Market Basket Analysis.

Unsupervised Learning algorithms:

Below is the list of some popular unsupervised learning algorithms:
- K-means clustering
- KNN (k-nearest neighbors)
- Hierarchal clustering
- Anomaly detection
- Neural Networks
- Principle Component Analysis
- Independent Component Analysis
- Apriori algorithm
- Singular value decomposition

Advantages of Unsupervised Learning
- Unsupervised learning is used for more complex tasks as compared tosupervised learning because, in unsupervised learning, we don't havelabeled input data.
- Unsupervised learning is preferable as it is easy to get unlabeled data incomparison to labeled data.

Disadvantages of Unsupervised Learning
- Unsupervised learning is intrinsically more difficult than supervised learningas it does not have corresponding output.
- The result of the unsupervised learning algorithm might be less accurate asinput data is not labeled, and algorithms do not know the exact output in advance.

Reinforcement Learning

Reinforcement learning is the training of machine learning models to make a sequence of decisions. The agent learns to achieve a goal in an uncertain, potentially complex environment. In reinforcement learning, an artificial intelligence faces a game-like situation. The computer employs trial and error to come up with a solution to the problem. To get the machine to do what the programmer wants, the artificial intelligence gets either rewards or penalties for the actions it performs. Its goal is to maximize the total reward.

Although the designer sets the reward policy–that is, the rules of the game–he gives the model no hints or suggestions for how to solve the game. It's up to the model to figure out how to perform the task to maximize the reward, starting from totally random trials and finishing with sophisticated tactics and superhuman skills. By leveraging the power of search and many trials, reinforcement learning is currently the most effective way to hint machine's creativity. In contrast to human beings, artificial intelligence can gather experience from thousands of parallel gameplays if a reinforcement learning algorithm is run on a sufficiently powerful computer infrastructure.

Reinforcement learning is an area of Machine Learning. It is about taking suitable action to maximize reward in a particular situation. It is employed by various software and machines to find the best possible behavior or path it should take in a specific situation. Reinforcement learning differs from the supervised learning in a way that in supervised learning the training data has the answer key with it so the model is trained with the correct answer itself whereas in reinforcement learning, there is no answer but the reinforcement agent decides what to do to perform the given task. In the absence of a training dataset, it is bound to learn from its experience.

Examples of reinforcement learning

Applications of reinforcement learning were in the past limited by weak computer infrastructure. However, as Gerard Tesauro's backgamon AI superplayer developed in 1990's shows, progress did happen. That early progress is now rapidly changing with powerful new computational technologies opening the way to completely new inspiring applications.
Training the models that control autonomous cars is an excellent example of a potential application of reinforcement learning. In an ideal situation, the computer should get no instructions on driving the car. The programmer would avoid hard-wiring anything connected with the task and allow the machine to learn from its own errors. In a perfect situation, the only hard-wired element would be the reward function.

For example, in usual circumstances we would require an autonomous vehicle to put safety first, minimize ride time, reduce pollution, offer passengers comfort and obey the rules of law. With an autonomous race car, on the other hand, we would emphasize speed much more than the driver's comfort. The programmer cannot predict everything that could happen on the road. Instead of building lengthy "if-then" instructions, the programmer prepares the reinforcement learning agent to be capable of learning from the system of rewards and penalties. The agent (another name for reinforcement learning algorithms performing the task) gets rewards for reaching specific goals.

Challenges with reinforcement learning

The main challenge in reinforcement learning lays in preparing the simulation environment, which is highly dependant on the task to be performed. When the model has to go superhuman in Chess, Go or Atari games, preparing the simulation environment is relatively simple. When it comes to building
a model capable of driving an autonomous car, building a realistic simulator is crucial before letting the car ride on the street. The model has to figure out how to brake or avoid a collision in a safe environment, where sacrificing even a thousand cars comes at a minimal cost. Transferring the model out of the training environment and into to the real world is where things get tricky. Scaling and tweaking the neural network controlling the agent is another challenge. There is no way to communicate with the network other than through the system of rewards and penalties. This in particular may lead to catastrophic forgetting, where acquiring new knowledge causes some of the old to be erased from the network (to read up on this issue, see this paper, published during the International Conference on Machine Learning).

Yet another challenge is reaching a local optimum – that is the agent performs the task as it is, but not in the optimal or required way. A "jumper" jumping like a kangaroo instead of doing the thing that was expected of it-walking-is a great example, and is also one that can be found in our recent blog post.
Finally, there are agents that will optimize the prize without performing the task it
was designed for. An interesting example can be found in the OpenAI video below, where the agent learned to gain rewards, but not to complete the race.

Main points in Reinforcement learning –

- Input: The input should be an initial state from which the model will start
- Output: There are many possible output as there are variety of solution to aparticular problem
- Training: The training is based upon the input, The model will return a state and the user will decide to reward or punish the model based on its output.
- The model keeps continues to learn.
- The best solution is decided based on the maximum reward.

Difference between Reinforcement learning and Supervised learning:

REINFORCEMENT LEARNING	SUPERVISED LEARNING
Reinforcement learning is all about making decisions sequentially. In simple words we can say that the output depends on the state of the current input and the next input depends on theoutput of the previous input	In Supervised learning the decision is made on the initial input or the input given at the start
In Reinforcement learning decision is dependent, So we give labels to sequences ofdependent decisions	Supervised learning the decisions are independent of each other so labels are given to each decision.
Example: Chess game	Example: Objectrecognition

Types of Reinforcement: There are two types of Reinforcement:

1. Positive –

Positive Reinforcement is defined as when an event, occurs due to a particular behavior, increases the strength and the frequency of thebehavior. In other words, it has a positive effect on behavior.

Advantages of reinforcement learning are:

- Maximizes Performance
- Sustain Change for a long period of time

Disadvantages of reinforcement learning:

- Too much Reinforcement can lead to overload of states which candiminish the results

2. Negative –

Negative Reinforcement is defined as strengthening of a behavior becausea negative condition is stopped or avoided.

Advantages of reinforcement learning:

- Increases Behavior
- Provide defiance to minimum standard of performance

Disadvantages of reinforcement learning:

- It Only provides enough to meet up the minimum behavior

Various Practical applications of Reinforcement Learning –

- RL can be used in robotics for industrial automation.
- RL can be used in machine learning and data processing
- RL can be used to create training systems that provide custom instructionand materials according to the requirement of students.

RL can be used in large environments in the following situations:
1. A model of the environment is known, but an analytic solution is notavailable;
2. Only a simulation model of the environment is given (the subject ofsimulation-based optimization)
3. The only way to collect information about the environment is to interactwith it.

Single Layer Perceptron

For understanding single layer perceptron, it is important to understand Artificial Neural Networks (ANN). Artificial neural networks is the information processing system the mechanism of which is inspired with the functionality of biological neural circuits. An artificial neural network possesses many processing units connected to each other. Following is the schematic representation of artificial neural network –

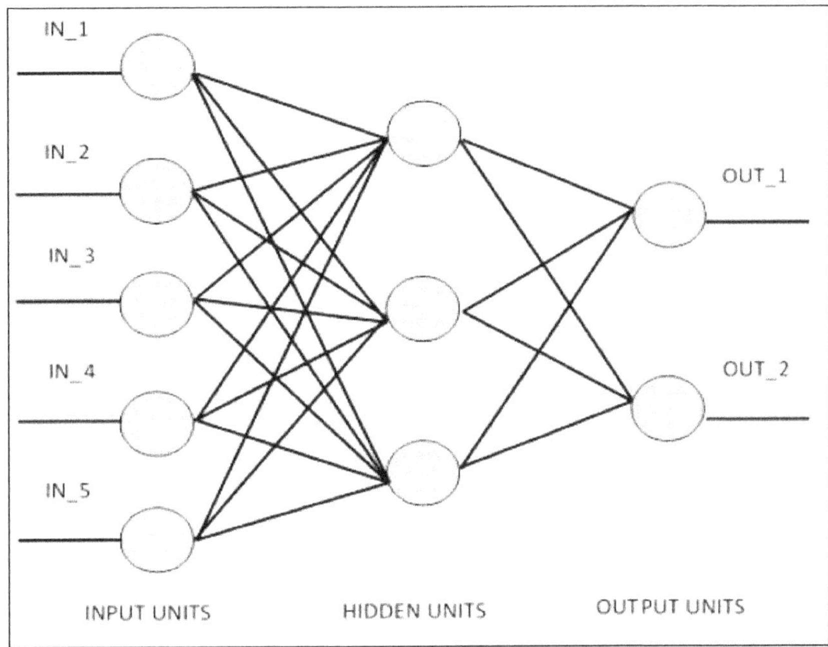

The diagram shows that the hidden units communicate with the external layer. While the input and output units communicate only through the hidden layer ofthe network.

The pattern of connection with nodes, the total number of layers and level of nodes between inputs and outputs with the number of neurons per layer definethe architecture of a neural network.

There are two types of architecture. These types focus on the functionalityartificial neural networks as follows –

- Single Layer Perceptron
- Multi-Layer Perceptron

Single Layer Perceptron

Single layer perceptron is the first proposed neural model created. The content ofthe local memory of the neuron consists of a vector of weights. The computation of a single layer perceptron is performed over the calculation of sum of the input vector each with the value multiplied by corresponding element of vector of the weights. The value which is displayed in the output will be the input of an activation function.

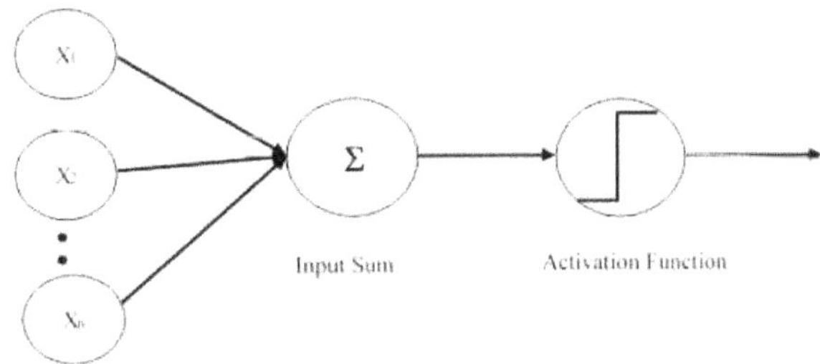

the implementation of single layer perceptron for an image classification problem using TensorFlow. The best example to illustrate the single layer perceptron is through representation of "Logistic Regression".

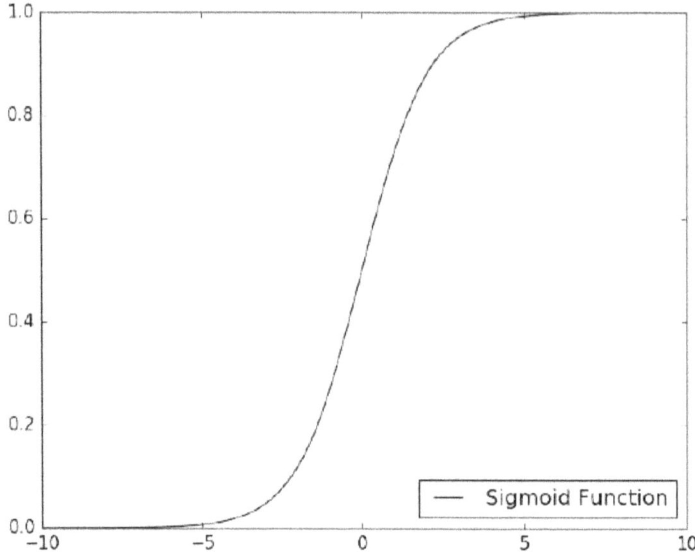

The following basic steps of training logistic regression –
- The weights are initialized with random values at the beginning of thetraining.
- For each element of the training set, the error is calculated with the difference between desired output and the actual output. The errorcalculated is used to adjust the weights.
- The process is repeated until the error made on the entire training set is not less than the specified threshold, until the maximum number of iterations is reached.

The complete code for evaluation of logistic regression is mentioned below –

```python
# Import MINST data

from tensorflow.examples.tutorials.mnist import input_data

mnist = input_data.read_data_sets("/tmp/data/", one_hot = True)

import tensorflow as tf

import matplotlib.pyplot as plt

# Parameters

learning_rate = 0.01

training_epochs = 25

batch_size = 100

display_step = 1

# tf Graph Input

x = tf.placeholder("float", [None, 784]) # mnist data image of shape 28*28 = 784

y = tf.placeholder("float", [None, 10]) # 0-9 digits recognition => 10 classes

# Create model
```

```python
# Set model weights

W = tf.Variable(tf.zeros([784, 10]))

b = tf.Variable(tf.zeros([10]))

# Construct model

activation = tf.nn.softmax(tf.matmul(x, W) + b) # Softmax

# Minimize error using cross entropy

cross_entropy = y*tf.log(activation)

cost = tf.reduce_mean\ (-tf.reduce_sum\ (cross_entropy,reduction_indices = 1))

optimizer = tf.train.\ GradientDescentOptimizer(learning_rate).minimize(cost)

#Plot settings

avg_set = []

epoch_set = []

# Initializing the variables init = tf.initialize_all_variables()

# Launch the graph

with tf.Session() as sess:

sess.run(init)

# Training cycle

for epoch in range(training_epochs):

avg_cost = 0.

total_batch = int(mnist.train.num_examples/batch_size)

# Loop over all batches

for i in range(total_batch):

batch_xs, batch_ys = \ mnist.train.next_batch(batch_size)

# Fit training using batch data sess.run(optimizer, \ feed_dict = {

x: batch_xs, y: batch_ys})

# Compute average loss avg_cost += sess.run(cost, \ feed_dict = {

x: batch_xs, \ y: batch_ys})/total_batch

# Display logs per epoch step

if epoch % display_step == 0:
```

print ("Epoch:", '%04d' % (epoch+1), "cost=", "{:.9f}".format(avg_cost))avg_set.append(avg_cost) epoch_set.append(epoch+1)
print ("Training phase finished")
plt.plot(epoch_set,avg_set, 'o', label = 'Logistic Regression Training phase')plt.ylabel('cost')
plt.xlabel('epoch')   plt.legend()
plt.show()
# Test model
correct_prediction = tf.equal(tf.argmax(activation, 1), tf.argmax(y, 1))# Calculate accuracy
accuracy = tf.reduce_mean(tf.cast(correct_prediction, "float")) print
("Model accuracy:", accuracy.eval({x: mnist.test.images, y: mnist.test.labels}))

Output

The above code generates the following output –

```
Use 'tf.global_variables_initializer' instead.
2018-07-09 11:41:19.920820: I T:\src\github\tensorflow\tensorflow\core\platform\cpu_feature_guard.cc:140] Your CPU supports instructions that this TensorFlow binary was
not compiled to use: AVX2
Epoch: 0001 cost= 1.176560601
Epoch: 0002 cost= 0.662504855
Epoch: 0003 cost= 0.550047454
Epoch: 0004 cost= 0.498801975
Epoch: 0005 cost= 0.463013413
Epoch: 0006 cost= 0.440974006
Epoch: 0007 cost= 0.423977672
Epoch: 0008 cost= 0.410615707
Epoch: 0009 cost= 0.399478001
Epoch: 0010 cost= 0.390970191
Epoch: 0011 cost= 0.383367628
Epoch: 0012 cost= 0.376823489
Epoch: 0013 cost= 0.371032368
Epoch: 0014 cost= 0.365939801
Epoch: 0015 cost= 0.361388407
Epoch: 0016 cost= 0.357217536
Epoch: 0017 cost= 0.353601805
Epoch: 0018 cost= 0.350117204
Epoch: 0019 cost= 0.347037825
Epoch: 0020 cost= 0.344160418
Epoch: 0021 cost= 0.341485278
Epoch: 0022 cost= 0.339003812
Epoch: 0023 cost= 0.336675840
Epoch: 0024 cost= 0.334456453
Epoch: 0025 cost= 0.332455397
Training phase finished
Model accuracy: 0.9115
```

The logistic regression is considered as a predictive analysis. Logistic regression is used to describe data and to explain the relationship between one dependent binary variable and one or more nominal or independent variables.

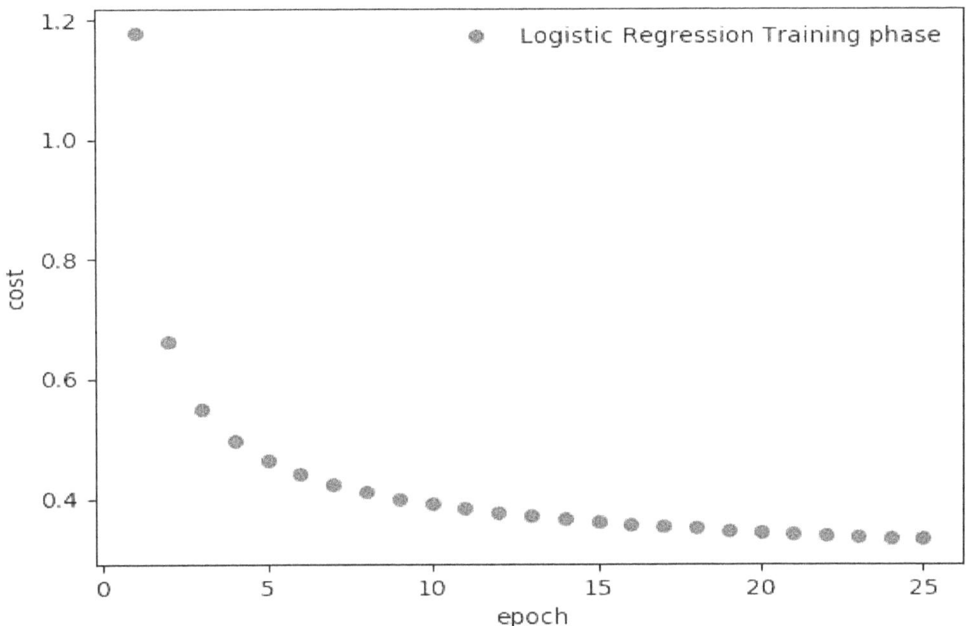

Multi-Layer Perceptron Learning

Multi-Layer perceptron defines the most complicated architecture of artificial neural networks. It is substantially formed from multiple layers of perceptron.

The diagrammatic representation of multi-layer perceptron learning is as shown below –

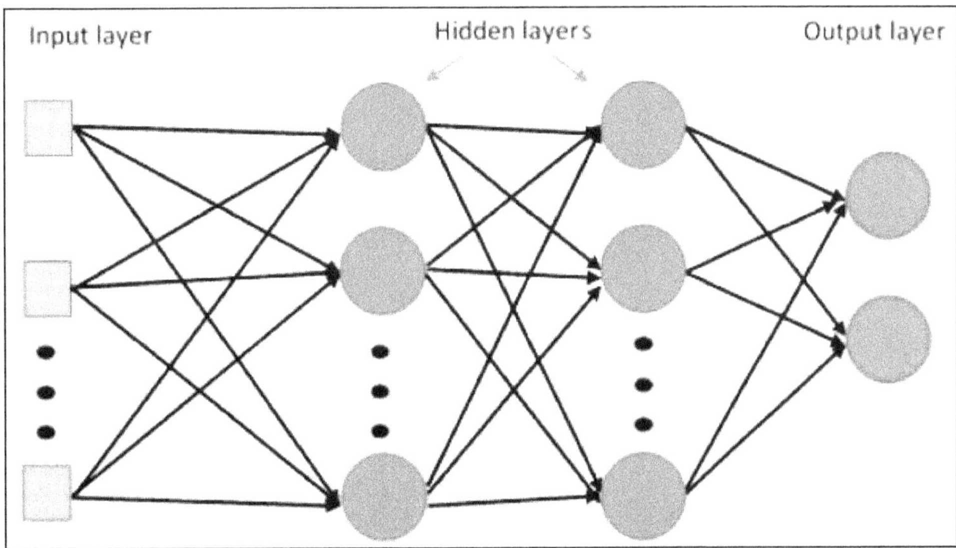

MLP networks are usually used for supervised learning format. A typical learningalgorithm for MLP networks is also called back propagation's algorithm.

The implementation with MLP for an image classification problem.

```
# Import MINST data
from        tensorflow.examples.tutorials.mnist        import        input_data        mnist        =
input_data.read_data_sets("/tmp/data/", one_hot = Truc)import tensorflow as tf
import matplotlib.pyplot as plt

# Parameters

learning_rate = 0.001
```

```python
training_epochs = 20

batch_size = 100

display_step = 1

# Network Parameters

n_hidden_1 = 256

# 1st layer num features

n_hidden_2 = 256 # 2nd layer num features

n_input = 784 # MNIST data input (img shape: 28*28) n_classes = 10

# MNIST total classes (0-9 digits)

# tf Graph input

x = tf.placeholder("float", [None, n_input])

y = tf.placeholder("float", [None, n_classes])

# weights layer 1

h = tf.Variable(tf.random_normal([n_input, n_hidden_1])) # bias layer 1

bias_layer_1 = tf.Variable(tf.random_normal([n_hidden_1]))

# layer 1 layer_1 = tf.nn.sigmoid(tf.add(tf.matmul(x, h), bias_layer_1))

# weights layer 2

w = tf.Variable(tf.random_normal([n_hidden_1, n_hidden_2]))

# bias layer 2

bias_layer_2 = tf.Variable(tf.random_normal([n_hidden_2]))

# layer 2

layer_2 = tf.nn.sigmoid(tf.add(tf.matmul(layer_1, w), bias_layer_2))

# weights output layer

output = tf.Variable(tf.random_normal([n_hidden_2, n_classes]))

# biar output layer

bias_output = tf.Variable(tf.random_normal([n_classes])) # output layer

output_layer = tf.matmul(layer_2, output) + bias_output

# cost function

cost = tf.reduce_mean(tf.nn.sigmoid_cross_entropy_with_logits(
```

```python
logits = output_layer, labels = y))

#cost  =   tf.reduce_mean(tf.nn.sigmoid_cross_entropy_with_logits(output_layer, y))

# optimizer

optimizer = tf.train.AdamOptimizer(learning_rate = learning_rate).minimize(cost)

# optimizer = tf.train.GradientDescentOptimizer(

learning_rate = learning_rate).minimize(cost)

# Plot settings

avg_set = []

epoch_set = []

# Initializing the variables

init = tf.global_variables_initializer()

# Launch the graph

with tf.Session() as sess:

sess.run(init)

# Training cycle

for epoch in range(training_epochs):

avg_cost = 0.

total_batch = int(mnist.train.num_examples / batch_size)

# Loop over all batches

for i in range(total_batch):

batch_xs, batch_ys = mnist.train.next_batch(batch_size)

# Fit training using batch data sess.run(optimizer, feed_dict = {

x: batch_xs, y: batch_ys})

# Compute average loss

avg_cost += sess.run(cost, feed_dict = {x: batch_xs, y: batch_ys}) /total_batch

# Display logs per epoch step

if epoch % display_step == 0:

print
```

Epoch:", '%04d' % (epoch + 1), "cost=", "{:.9f}".format(avg_cost)

avg_set.append(avg_cost)

epoch_set.append(epoch + 1)

print

"Training phase finished"

```
    plt.plot(epoch_set, avg_set, 'o', label = 'MLP Training phase')plt.ylabel('cost')
plt.xlabel('epoch')        plt.legend()
plt.show()
# Test model
```

```
correct_prediction = tf.equal(tf.argmax(output_layer, 1), tf.argmax(y, 1))# Calculate accuracy
accuracy = tf.reduce_mean(tf.cast(correct_prediction, "float"))print
"Model Accuracy:", accuracy.eval({x: mnist.test.images, y: mnist.test.labels})
```

The above line of code generates the following output –

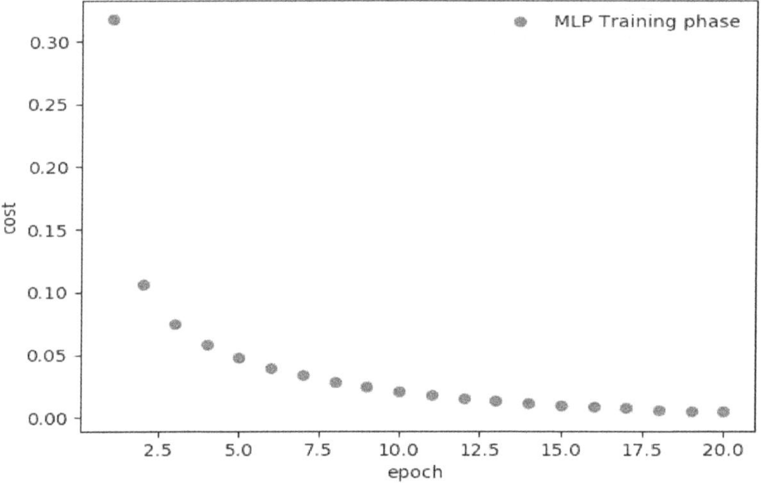

Organizing Feature Map

Kohonen Self-Organizing feature map (SOM) refers to a neural network, which is trained using competitive learning. Basic competitive learning implies that the competition process takes place before the cycle of learning. The competition process suggests that some criteria select a winning processing element. After the winning processing element is selected, its weight vector is adjusted according to the used learning law (Hecht Nielsen 1990).

The self-organizing map makes topologically ordered mappings between input data and processing elements of the map. Topological ordered implies that if two inputs are of similar characteristics, the most active processing elements answering to inputs that are located closed to each other on the map. The weight vectors of the processing elements are organized in ascending to descending order. $W_i < W_{i+1}$ for all values of i or W_{i+1} for all values of i (this definition is valid for one-dimensional self-organizing map only).

The self-organizing map is typically represented as a two-dimensional sheet of processing elements described in the figure given below. Each processing element has its own weight vector, and learning of SOM (self-organizing map) depends on the adaptation of these vectors. The processing elements of the network are made competitive in a self-organizing process, and specific criteria pick the winning processing element whose weights are updated. Generally, these criteria are used to limit the Euclidean distance between the input vector and the weight vector. SOM (self-organizing map) varies from basic competitive learning so that instead of adjusting only the weight vector of the winning processing element also weight vectors of neighboring processing elements are adjusted. First, the size of the neighborhood is largely making the rough ordering of SOM and size is diminished as time goes on. At last, only a winning processing element is adjusted, making the fine-tuning of SOM possible. The use of neighborhood makes topologically ordering procedure possible, and together with competitive learning makes process non-linear.

It is discovered by Finnish professor and researcher Dr. Teuvo Kohonen in 1982. The self-organizing map refers to an unsupervised learning model proposed for applications in which maintaining a topology between input and output spaces. The notable attribute of this algorithm is that the input vectors that are close and similar in high dimensional space are also mapped to close by nodes in the 2D space. It is fundamentally a method for dimensionality reduction, as it maps high-dimension inputs to a low dimensional discretized representation and preserves the basic structure of its input space.

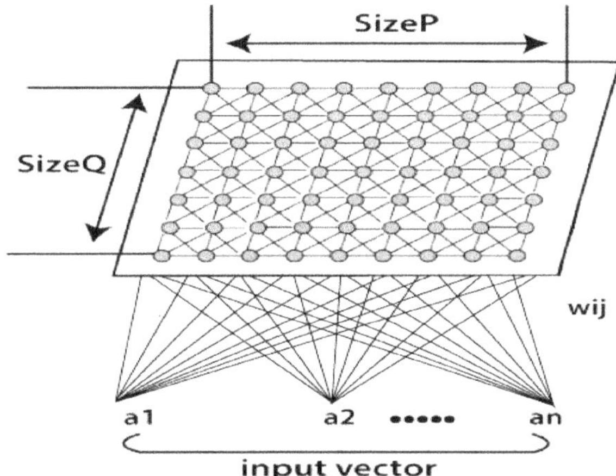

Kohonen Architecture

All the entire learning process occurs without supervision because the nodes are self-organizing. They are also known as feature maps, as they are basically retraining the features of the input data, and simply grouping themselves as indicated by the similarity between each other. It has practical value for visualizing complex or huge quantities of high dimensional data and showing the relationship between them into a low, usually two-dimensional field to check whether the given unlabeled data have any structure to it.

A self-Organizing Map (SOM) varies from typical artificial neural networks (ANNs) both in its architecture and algorithmic properties. Its structure consists of a single layer linear 2D grid of neurons, rather than a series of layers. All the nodes on this lattice are associated directly to the input vector, but not to each other. It means the nodes don't know the values of their neighbors, and only update the weight of their associations as a function of the given input. The grid itself is the map that coordinates itself at each iteration as a function of the input data. As such, after clustering, each node has its own coordinate (i.j), which enables one to calculate Euclidean distance between two nodes by means of the Pythagoras theorem.

A Self-Organizing Map utilizes competitive learning instead of error-correction learning, to modify its weights. It implies that only an individual node is activated at each cycle in which the features of an occurrence of the input vector are introduced to the neural network, as all nodes compete for the privilege to respond to the input.

The selected node- the Best Matching Unit (BMU) is selected according to the similarity between the current input values and all the other nodes in the network. The node with the fractional Euclidean difference between the input vector, all nodes, and its neighboring nodes is selected and within a specific radius, to have their position slightly adjusted to coordinate the input vector. By experiencing all the nodes present on the grid, the whole grid eventually matches the entire input dataset with connected nodes gathered towards one area, and dissimilar ones are isolated.

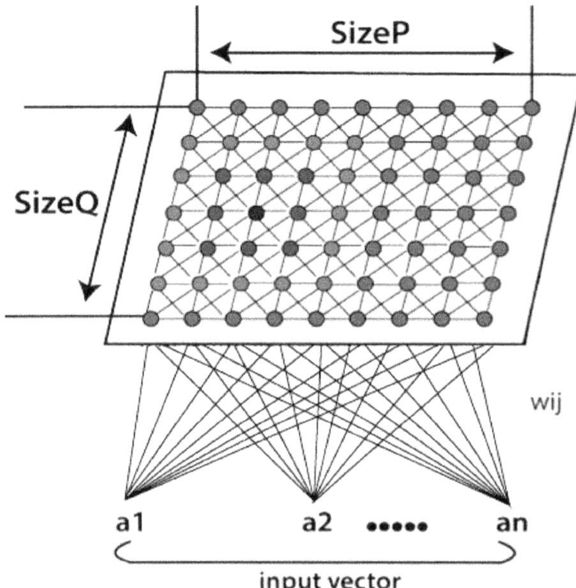

A Kohonen model with the BMW in blue, the layer inside the neighborhood radius in light blue and red, and the nodes outside are green.

Algorithm:

Step:1
Each node weight w_ij initialize to a random value.Step:2
Choose a random input vector x_k.

Step:3
Repeat steps 4 and 5 for all nodes on the map.

Step:4
Calculate the Euclidean distance between weight vector w_{ij} and the input vectorx(t) connected with the first node, where t, i, j =0.

Step:5
Track the node that generates the smallest distance t.

Step:6
Calculate the overall Best Matching Unit (BMU). It means the node with thesmallest distance from all calculated ones.

Step:7
Discover topological neighborhood βij(t) its radius σ(t) of BMU in Kohonen Map.

Step:8
Repeat for all nodes in the BMU neighborhood: Update the weight vector w_ij ofthe first node in the neighborhood of the BMU by including a fraction of the difference between the input vector x(t) and the weight w(t) of the neuron.

Step:9
Repeat the complete iteration until reaching the selected iteration limit t=n.
Here, step 1 represents initialization phase, while step 2 to 9 represents thetraining phase.
Where;
t = current iteration.
i = row coordinate of the nodes grid.
J = column coordinate of the nodes grid.
W= weight vector
w_ij = association weight between the nodes i,j in the grid.X = input vector
X(t)= the input vector instance at iteration t
β_ij = the neighborhood function, decreasing and representing node i,j distancefrom the BMU.
σ(t) = The radius of the neighborhood function, which calculates how far neighbornodes are examined in the 2D grid when

updating vectors. It gradually decreases over time.

Hopfield Networks

Hopfield network is a special kind of neural network whose response is different from other neural networks. It is calculated by converging iterative process. It has just one layer of neurons relating to the size of the input and output, which must be the same. When such a network recognizes, for example, digits, we present a list of correctly rendered digits to the network. Subsequently, the network can transform a noise input to the relating perfect output.

In 1982, **John Hopfield** introduced an artificial neural network to collect and retrieve memory like the human brain. Here, a neuron is either on or off the situation. The state of a neuron(on +1 or off 0) will be restored, relying on the input it receives from the other neuron. A Hopfield network is at first prepared to store various patterns or memories. Afterward, it is ready to recognize any of the learned patterns by uncovering partial or even some corrupted data about that pattern, i.e., it eventually settles down and restores the closest pattern. Thus, similar to the human brain, the Hopfield model has stability in pattern recognition.

A Hopfield network is a single-layered and recurrent network in which the neurons are entirely connected, i.e., each neuron is associated with other neurons. If there are two neurons i and j, then there is a connectivity weight w_{ij} lies between them which is symmetric $w_{ij} = w_{ji}$.

With zero self-connectivity, $W_{ii} = 0$ is given below. Here, the given three neurons having values $i = 1, 2, 3$ with values $X_i = \pm 1$ have connectivity weight W_{ij}.

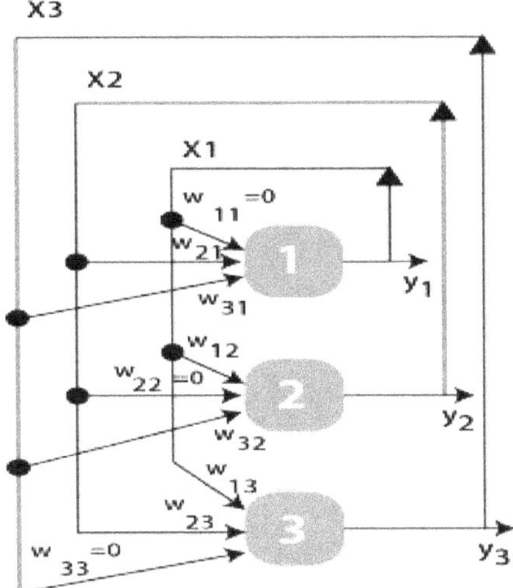

Updating rule:

Consider **N** neurons $= 1, \ldots, N$ with values $X_{i} = +1, -1$. The update rule is applied to the node i is given by:

$$\sum_{j=1}^{N} w_{ij}x_j$$

If $h_{i \geq 0}$ then $x_i \to 1$ otherwise $x_i \to -1$

Where $h_i =$ is called field at i, with $b \pounds R$ a bias.

Thus, $x_i \to sgn(h_i)$, where the value of $sgn(r)=1$, if $r \geq 0$, and the value of $sgn(r)=-1$, if $r < 0$.

We need to put $b_i=0$ so that it makes no difference in training the network with random patterns.

We, therefore, consider $h_i =$.

We have two different approaches to update the nodes:

$$\sum_{j=1}^{N} w_{ij}x_j$$

Synchronously:

In this approach, the update of all the nodes taking place simultaneously at each time.

Asynchronously:

In this approach, at each point of time, update one node chosen randomly or according to some rule. Asynchronous updating is more biologically realistic.

Hopfield Network as a Dynamical system:

Consider, $K = \{-1, 1\}^N$ so that each state $x \pounds X$ is given by $x_i \pounds \{-1,1\}$ for $1 \leq I \leq N$

Here, we get 2^N possible states or configurations of the network.

We can describe a metric on X by using the Hamming distance between any twostates:

P(x, y) = # {i: xi≠y$_i$}

N Here, **P** is a metric with **0≤H(x,y)≤ N**. It is clearly symmetric and reflexive.

With any of the asynchronous or synchronous updating rules, we get a discrete-time dynamical system.

The updating rule up: **X → X** describes a map.And Up: **X → X** is trivially continuous.

Example:

Suppose we have only two neurons: **N = 2**

There are two non-trivial choices for connectivities:

w$_{12}$ = w$_{21}$ = 1w$_{12}$= w$_{21}$ = -1

Asynchronous updating:

In the **first case,** there are two attracting fixed points termed as [-1,-1] and [-1,-1].All orbit converges to one of these. For a second, the fixed points are [-1,1] and [1,-1], and all orbits are joined through one of these. For any fixed point, swapping all the signs gives another fixed point.

Synchronous updating:

In the first and second cases, although there are fixed points, none can be attracted to nearby points, i.e., they are not attracting fixed points. Some orbitsoscillate forever.

Energy function evaluation:

Hopfield networks have an energy function that diminishes or is unchanged withasynchronous updating.

For a given state $X \in \{-1, 1\}$ N of the network and for any set of associationweights W_{ij} with $W_{ij} = w_{ji}$ and $w_{ii} = 0$ let,

Here, we need to update X_m to X'_m and denote the new energy by E' and showthat.

$$E = -1/2 \sum_{i,j=1}^{N} WijXiXj$$

E'-E = (X$_m$-X'$_m$) $\sum_{i\neq m}$WmiXi.

Using the above equation, if $X_m = X_m'$ then we have E' = E

If X_m = -1 and X_m' = 1 , then $X_m - X_m'$ = 2 and hm= $\sum_i$WmiXi ? 0Thus, E' - E ≤ 0

Similarly if X_m =1 and X_m'= -1 then $X_m - X_m'$ = 2 and h$_m$= $\sum_i$WmiXi < 0Thus, E - E' < 0.

Note:

If Xm flips, then E' - E = 2Xmhm

Neurons pull in or push away from each other:

Suppose the connection weight $W_{ij} = W_{ji}$ between two neurons I and j.If $W_{ij} > 0$, the updating rule implies:

- If X_j = **1**, then the contribution of j in the weighted sum, i.e., $W_{ij}X_j$, ispositive. Thus the value of X_i is pulled by j towards its value X_j= **1**

- If X_j= **-1** then $W_{ij}X_j$, is negative, and X_i is again pulled by j towards itsvalue X_j = **-1**

- Thus, if $W_{ij} > 0$, then the value of **i** is pulled by the value of **j**. By symmetry, thevalue of **j** is also pulled by the value of **i**.

If $W_{ij} < 0$, then the value of i is pushed away by the value of j.It follows that for a particular set of values $X_i \in \{-1, 1\}$ for; $1 \leq i \leq N$, the selection of weights taken as $W_{ij} = X_iX_j$ for;

1 ≤ i ≤ N correlates to the Hebbian rule. Training the network: One pattern (K$_i$=0)

Suppose the vector $x^{\rightarrow}$ = **(x$_1$,...,x$_i$,...,x$_N$) ∈ {-1,1}^{N}** is a pattern that we like to store inthe Hopfield network.

To build a Hopfield network that recognizes $x^{\rightarrow}$, we need to select connectionweight W_{ij} accordingly.

If we select W_{ij} =η X_iX_j for $1 \leq i , j \leq N$ (Here, **i≠j**), where η > 0 is the learning rate,then the value of X_i will not change under updating condition as we illustrate below.

We have

It implies that the value of X_i, whether **1** or **-1** will not change, so that $x^{\rightarrow}$ is a fixedpoint.

$$hi = \sum_{j=1}^{N} WijXj = \eta\sum_{j\neq i} XiXjXj = \eta\sum_{j\neq i} Xi = \eta(N-1)X_i$$

Note that - $x^{\rightarrow}$ also becomes a fixed point when we train the networkwith $x^{\rightarrow}$ validating that Hopfield networks are **sign blind**.

MCQ

1.   The technology that has the abilityto interact with the world.

a) AI
b) ML
c) IOT
d) IT

Answer: a

Explanation: AI which is artificial intelligence is the ability to interactwith the world. It is the ability to model the world and to learn and adapt.

2. The goal of AI is to build systemsthat exhibit intelligent behavior.
a) True
b) False

Answer: a

Explanation: The statement is true.There are 2 main goals in AI: to exhibit intelligent behavior and understand intelligence in order tomodel it.

3. The first neural network computer.
a) RFD
b) SNARC
c) AM
d) AN

Answer: b

Explanation: SNARC was the first neural network computer. it was builtby Minsky and Edmonds in 1956.

4. A hardware based system that hasautonomy, social ability and
reactivity.
a) AI
b) Autonomous Agent
c) Agency
d) Behavior Engineering

Answer: b

Explanation: The answer is Autonomous Agent. Autonomous agent has autonomy i.e. ability to operate without the direct intervention of humans or others.

5. A particular system that containsintelligent agents.
a) AI systems
b) Agency
c) Autonomous systems
d) Company

Answer: b

Explanation: It is called an agency. Aparticular system consisting of intelligent agents like computers or robots that cooperate to find the solution to a problem.

6. A methodology used to develop behavior-based autonomous agents.
a) Descriptors
b) Behavior engineering
c) Behavior modeling
d) Auto engineering

Answer: b

Explanation: The answer is behaviorengineering. Autonomous agent

implements autonomy, social abilityand reactivity.

7. An international research effort topromote autonomous robots.
a) Fresh Kitty
b) RoboCup
c) AICup
d) SPOT

Answer: b

Explanation: RoboCup is designed topromote autonomous robots. It is based on multi agent collaboration.

8. A type of non-monotonicreasoning.

a) Ordinary

b) Special

c) Duplicate

d) Default

Answer: d

Explanation: Default reasoning is a type of non-monotonic reasoning. Default logic is a non-monotonic logic proposed by Raymond Reiter to formalize reasoning with default assumptions.

9. The performance of an agent canbe improved based on this.

a) Observe

b) Learn

c) Improvise

d) Implement

Answer: b

Explanation: An AI system is designed to learn and improve. The same isimplemented on its agents.

10. Face recognition system is basedon

a) applied AI

b) parallel AI

c) serial AI

d) strong AI

Answer: a

Explanation: The answer is applied AI.It is based on applied artificial intelligence. It is an approach to develop commercially smart systems.

11. Which of the following is an extension of the semantic network?

a) Expert Systems

b) Rule Based Expert Systems

c) Decision Tree Based networks

d) Partitioned Networks

Answer: d Explanation: None.

12. Basic idea of an partitioned nets isto break network into spaces which consist of groups of nodes and arcs and regard each space as a node.

a) True

b) False

Answer: a Explanation: None.

13. Semantic Network represents

—

a) Syntactic relation betweenconcepts

b) Semantic relations betweenconcepts

c) All of the mentioned

d) None of the mentioned

Answer: b Explanation: None.

14. Which is not a desirable propertyof a logical rule-based system?

a) Locality

b) Attachment

c) Detachment

d) Truth-Functionality

Answer: b

Explanation: Rule-based system. Global attribute defines a particular problem space asuser specific and changes according to

user's plan to problem.

15. How is Fuzzy Logic different fromconventional control methods?
a) IF and THEN Approach
b) FOR Approach
c) WHILE Approach
d) DO Approach
Answer: a
Explanation: FL incorporates a simple, rule-based IF X AND Y THEN Z approach to a solving control problem rather than attempting to model a system mathematically.

16. In an Unsupervised learning
Explanation: Locality: In logical systems, whenever we have a rule of the form A => B, we can conclude B, given evidence A, without worrying about any other rules. Detachment: Once a logical proof is found for a proposition B, the proposition can be used regardless of how it was derived. That is, it can be detachment from itsjustification. Truth-functionality: In logic, the truth of complex sentences can be computed from the truth of the components. However, there are no Attachment properties lies in a
a) Specific output values are given
b) Specific output values are notgiven
c) No specific Inputs are given
d) Both inputs and outputs are given
Answer: b
Explanation: The problem of unsupervised learning involves learning patterns in the input whenno specific output values are supplied. We cannot expect the specific output to test your result.
Here the agent does not know whatto do, as he is not aware of the fact what propose system will come out. We can say an ambiguous un- proposed situation.

17. Inductive learning involves findinga
a) Consistent Hypothesis
b) Inconsistent Hypothesis
c) Regular Hypothesis
d) Irregular Hypothesis
Answer: a
Explanation: Inductive learning involves finding a consistent hypothesis that agrees with examples. The difficulty of the task depends on the chosen representation.

18. Computational learning theory analyzes the sample complexity andcomputational complexity of ____
a) Unsupervised Learning
b) Inductive learning
c) Forced based learning
d) Weak learning
Answer: b
Explanation: Computational learningtheory analyzes the sample complexity and computational
complexity of inductive learning. There is a tradeoff between the expressiveness of the hypothesis language and the ease of learning.

19. If a hypothesis says it should be positive, but in fact, it is negative, wecall it
a) A consistent hypothesis
b) A false negative hypothesis
c) A false positive hypothesis
d) A specialized hypothesis
Answer: c
Explanation: Consistent hypothesis gowith examples, If the hypothesis says it should be negative but infect it is positive, it is false negative. If a hypothesis says it should be positive, but in fact, it is negative, it is false positive. In a specialized hypothesis we need to have certain restrict or special conditions.

20. Neural Networks are complex __with manyparameters.
a) Linear Functions

b) Nonlinear Functions

c) Discrete Functions

d) Exponential Functions

Answer: b

Explanation: Neural networks parameters can be learned from noisy data and they have been used for thousands of applications, so it varies from problem to problem andthus use nonlinear functions.

21. A perceptron is a _______________

a) Feed-forward neural network

b) Backpropagation algorithm

c) Backtracking algorithm

d) Feed Forward-backward algorithm

Answer: a

Explanation: A perceptron is a Feed- forward neural network with no hidden units that can be representing only linear separable functions. If thedata are linearly separable, a simple weight updated rule can be used to fit the data exactly.

22. Which of the following statementis true?

a) Not all formal languages arecontext-free

b) All formal languages are Contextfree

c) All formal languages are likenatural language

d) Natural languages are context-oriented free

Answer: a

Explanation: Not all formal languagesare context-free.

23. Which of the following statementis not true?

a) The union and concatenation oftwo context-free languages is context-free

b) The reverse of a context-free language is context-free, but thecomplement need not be

c) Every regular language is context- free because it can be described by aregular grammar

d) The intersection two context-freelanguages is context-free

Answer: d

Explanation: The union and concatenation of two context-freelanguages are context-free; but intersection need not be.

24. A semantic network is used whenone has knowledge that is best understood as a set of concepts that are related to one another.

a) True

b) False

Answer: a

Explanation: None.

25. What are the limitations of thesemantic networks?

a) Intractability

b) Lack in expressing some of theproperties

c) Incomplete

d) Has memory constraints

Answer: b

Explanation: None.

26. What among the following is/arethe best example of semantic networks?

a) Wordnet

b) Human Food Chain

c) MYSIN

d) Autonomous car driver

Answer: a

Explanation: Wordnet is a lexicaldatabase of English.

27. Semantic Network is also knownas Frame networks.

a) True

b) False

Answer: a

Explanation: None.

28. What is Synonymy relation?

a) A is part of B

b) A denotes same as B

c) A is a kind of B

d) A is superordinate of B

Answer: b

Explanation: None.

29. What is Antonymy relation?

a) A is part of B

b) B has A as a part of itself

c) A denotes opposite of B

d) A is superordinate of B

Answer: c

Explanation: None.

30. Most semantic networks are notcognitive based.

a) True

b) False

Answer: b

Explanation: None.

31. In LISP, the function returns the list that results after the first elementis removed (the rest f the list), is _

a) car

b) last

c) cons

d) cdr

Answer: d

Explanation: None.

32. Which of the following containsthe output segments of Artificial Intelligence programming?

a) Printed language and synthesizedspeech

b) Manipulation of physical object

c) Locomotion

d) All of the mentioned

Answer: d

Explanation: None.

33. LISP was created by?

a) John McCarthy

b) Marvin Minsky

c) Alan Turing

d) Allen Newell and Herbert Simon

Answer: a

Explanation: None.

34. Expert Ease was developed underthe direction of_

a) John McCarthy

b) Donald Michie

c) Lofti Zadeh

d) Alan Turing

Answer: b

Explanation: None.

35. An Artificial Intelligence system developed by Terry A. Winograd to permit an interactive dialogue abouta domain he called blocks-world.

a) SHRDLU

b) SIMD

c) BACON

d) STUDENT

Answer: a

Explanation: None.

36. MLMenu, a natural language interface for the TI Explorer, is similar to

a) Ethernet

b) NaturalLink

c) PROLOG

d) The Personal Consultant

Answer: b

Explanation: None.

37. Strong Artificial Intelligence is _

a) the embodiment of human intellectual capabilities within acomputer

b) a set of computer programs that produce output that would be considered to reflect intelligence if itwere generated by humans

c) the study of mental faculties through the use of mental modelsimplemented on a computer

d) all of the mentioned

Answer: a

Explanation: None.

38. The traditional way to exit and LISP system is to enter_

a) quit

b) exit

c) bye

d) ok

Answer: b

Explanation: None.

39. In which of the following situations might a blind search beacceptable?

a) real-life situation

b) complex game

c) small search space

d) all of the mentioned

Answer: c

Explanation: None.

40. What is Artificial intelligence?

a) Putting your intelligence intoComputer

b) Programming with your ownintelligence

c) Making a Machine intelligent

d) Playing a Game

Answer: c

Explanation: Because AI is to make the system or machine will act as perthe requirement.

41. The performance of an agent canbe improved by_

a) Learning

b) Observing

c) Perceiving

d) None of the mentioned

Answer: a

Explanation: An agent can improve bysaving the previous states on which itwas earlier, hence in future it can learn to respond in the same situation better.

42. External actions of the agent isselected by
a) Perceive
b) Performance
c) Learning
d) Actuator
Answer: b
Explanation: It depends on how youwant to improve and what the performance measures are.

43. The action of the Simple reflexagent completely depends upon
things work automatically through _
machine without using human effort.Machine will give the result with just giving input from human. That means
a) Perception history
b) Current perception
c) Learning theory
d) Utility functions
Answer: b
Explanation: These agents select actions based on the current perception, ignoring the rest of theperception history.

44. Which of the following could bethe approaches to Artificial Intelligence?
a) Strong Artificial Intelligence
b) Weak Artificial Intelligence
c) Applied Artificial Intelligence
d) All of the mentioned
Answer: d
Explanation: Strong Artificial Intelligence aims to build machines that can truly reason and solve problems. Weak Artificial Intelligence deals withthe creation of some form of computer-based artificial intelligence that cannot truly reason and solve problems but can act as if it were intelligent. Applied Artificial Intelligence aims to produce commercially viable "smart" systems.
In the Cognitive Artificial Intelligenceapproach, a computer is used to test theories about how the human mindworks.

45. An Artificial Neural Network Isbased on?
a) Strong Artificial Intelligenceapproach
b) Weak Artificial Intelligenceapproach
c) Cognitive Artificial Intelligenceapproach
d) Applied Artificial Intelligenceapproach
Answer: c
Explanation: In the Cognitive ArtificialIntelligence approach, a computer is used to test theories about how the human mind works, for example, theories about how we recognize faces and other objects, or about how we solve abstract problems.

46. The Face Recognition system isbased on?
a) Strong Artificial Intelligenceapproach
b) Weak Artificial Intelligenceapproach
c) Cognitive Artificial Intelligenceapproach
d) Applied Artificial Intelligenceapproach
Answer: d
Explanation: Applied Artificial Intelligence approach aims to produce commercially viable "smart" systems such as, for example, a security system that is able to recognize the faces of people who permitted to enter a particular building. Applied Artificial Intelligencehas already enjoyed considerable success.

47. A completely automated chess engine (Learn from previous games)is based on?
a) Strong Artificial Intelligenceapproach
b) Weak Artificial Intelligenceapproach
c) Cognitive Artificial Intelligenceapproach
d) Applied Artificial Intelligenceapproach

Answer: a

Explanation: Strong Artificial Intelligence aims to build machines that can truly reason and solve problems. These machines must be self-aware and their overall intellectual ability needs to be indistinguishable from that of a human being. Strong Artificial Intelligence maintains that suitably programmed machines are capable ofcognitive mental states.

48. A basic line following robot isbased on
a) Strong Artificial Intelligenceapproach
b) Weak Artificial Intelligenceapproach
c) Cognitive Artificial Intelligenceapproach
d) Applied Artificial Intelligenceapproach

Answer: b

Explanation: Weak Artificial Intelligence deals with the creation ofsome form of computer-based artificial intelligence that cannot truly reason and solve problems, but can act as if it were intelligent. Weak Artificial Intelligence holds that suitably programmed machines can simulate human cognition.

49. Which of the following task/tasksArtificial Intelligence could not do yet?
a) Understand natural languagerobustly
b) Web mining
c) Construction of plans in real time dynamic systems
d) All of the mentioned

Answer: d

Explanation: These are the areas inwhich need more focus for improvements.

50. What among the following is/arethe example of the intelligent agent/agents?
a) Human
b) Robot
c) Autonomous Spacecraft
d) All of the mentioned

Answer: d

Explanation: Humans can be looked upon as agents. They have eyes, ears,skin, taste buds, etc. for sensors; and hands, fingers, legs, mouth for effectors. Robots are agents. Robots may have camera, sonar, infrared, bumper, etc. for sensors. They can have grippers, wheels, lights, speakers, etc. for actuators. Autonomous Spacecraft takesdecision on its own based on perceptions.

51. When talking to a speech recognition program, the program divides each second of your speechinto 100 separate
a) Codes
b) Phonemes
c) Samples
d) Words

Answer: c

Explanation: None.

52. Which term is used for describingthe judgmental or commonsense partof problem solving?
a) Heuristic
b) Critical
c) Value based
d) Analytical

Answer: a

Explanation: None.

53. Which stage of the manufacturingprocess has been described as "the mapping of function onto form"?
a) Design
b) Distribution
c) Project management
d) Field service

Answer: a

Explanation: None.

54. Which kind of planning consists ofsuccessive representations of different levels of a plan?

a) hierarchical planning

b) non-hierarchical planning

c) project planning

d) all of the mentioned

Answer: a

Explanation: None.

55. What was originally called the"imitation game" by its creator?

a) The Turing Test

b) LISP

c) The Logic Theorist

d) Cybernetics

Answer: a

Explanation: None.

56. Decision support programs aredesigned to help managers make _

a) budget projections

b) visual presentations

c) business decisions

d) vacation schedules

Answer: c

Explanation: None.

57. PROLOG is an AI programming language, which solves problems witha form of symbolic logic known as predicate calculus. It was developed in 1972 at the University of Marseilles by a team of specialists. Can you name the person who headed this team?

a) Alain Colmerauer

b) Niklaus Wirth

c) Seymour Papert

d) John McCarthy

Answer: a

Explanation: None.

58. Programming a robot by physically moving it through the trajectory you want it to follow becalled

a) contact sensing control

b) continuous-path control

c) robot vision control

d) pick-and-place control

Answer: b

Explanation: None.

59. To invoke the LISP system, youmust enter_

a) AI

b) LISP

c) CL (Common Lisp)

d) Both LISP and CL

Answer: b

Explanation: None.

60. In LISP, what is the function (list-length <list>)?

a) returns a new list that is equal to<:list> by copying the top-level element of <list>

b) returns the length of <list>

c) returns t if <list> is empty

d) all of the mentioned

Answer: b

Explanation: None.

61. What is the primary interactivemethod of communication used byhumans?

a) reading

b) writing

c) speaking

d) all of the mentioned

Answer: c

Explanation: None.

62. Elementary linguistic units thatare smaller than words are?

a) allophones

b) phonemes

c) syllables

d) all of the mentioned

Answer: d

Explanation: None.

63. In LISP, the atom that stands for"true" is

a) t

b) ml

c) y

d) time

Answer: a

Explanation: None.

64. A mouse device may be _

a) electro-chemical

b) mechanical

c) optical

d) both mechanical and optical

Answer: d

Explanation: None.

65. An expert system differs from adatabase program in that only an expert system

a) contains declarative knowledge

b) contains procedural knowledge

c) features the retrieval of storedinformation

d) expects users to draw their ownconclusions

Answer: b

Explanation: None.

66. Arthur Samuel is linked inextricably with a program thatplayed

a) checkers

b) chess

c) cricket

d) football

Answer: a

Explanation: None.

67. Natural language understanding isused in

a) natural language interfaces

b) natural language front ends

c) text understanding systems

d) all of the mentioned

Answer: d

Explanation: None.

68. Which of the following searchbelongs to totally ordered plan search?

a) Forward state-space search

b) Hill-climbing search

c) Depth-first search

d) Breadth-first search

Answer: a

Explanation: Forward and backward state-space search are particular forms of totally ordered plan search.

69. Which cannot be taken as advantage for totally ordered plansearch?

a) Composition

b) State search

c) Problem decomposition

d) None of the mentioned

Answer: c

Explanation: As the search explore only linear sequences of actions, Sothey cannot take advantage of problem decomposition.

70. What is the advantage of totallyordered plan in constructing the plan?

a) Reliability

b) Flexibility

c) Easy to use

d) All of the mentioned

Answer: b

Explanation: Totally ordered plan hasthe advantage of flexibility in the order in which it constructs the plan.

71. Which strategy is used for delaying a choice during search?

a) First commitment

b) Least commitment

c) Both First & Least commitment

d) None of the mentioned

Answer: b

Explanation: The general strategy of delaying a choice during search is called the least commitment strategy.

72. Which algorithm places two actions into a plan without specifyingwhich should come first?

a) Full-order planner

b) Total-order planner

c) Semi-order planner

d) Partial-order planner

Answer: d

Explanation: Any planning algorithm that can place two actions into a planwithout specifying which should come first is called partial-order planner.

73. How many possible plans are available in partial-order solution?

a) 3

b) 4

c) 5

d) 6

Answer: d

Explanation: The partial-order solution corresponds to six possibletotal-order plans.

74. What is the other name of eachand every total-order plans?

a) Polarization

b) Linearization

c) Solarization

d) None of the mentioned

Answer: b

Explanation: Each and every total order plan is also called as linearization of the partial-order plan.

75. What are present in the emptyplan?

a) Start

b) Finish

c) Modest

d) Both Start & Finish

Answer: d

Explanation: The 'empty' plan contains just the start and finishactions.

76. What are not present in startactions?

a) Preconditions

b) Effect

c) Finish

d) None of the mentioned

Answer: a

Explanation: Start has no precondition and has as its effects allthe literals in the initial state of the planning problem.

77. What are not present in finishactions?

a) Preconditions

b) Effect

c) Finish

d) None of the mentioned

Answer: b

Explanation: Finish has no effects and has as its preconditions the goal literals of the planning algorithm.

78. Which can be adapted forplanning algorithms?

a) Most-constrained variable

b) Most-constrained literal

c) Constrained

d) None of the mentioned

Answer: a

Explanation: The most-constrained variable heuristic from CSPs can be adapted for planning algorithm andseems to work well.

79. Which of the following are examples of software developmenttools?

a) debuggers

b) editors

c) assemblers, compilers andinterpreters

d) all of the mentioned

Answer: d

Explanation: None.

80. Which is the first AI programminglanguage?

a) BASIC

b) FORTRAN

c) IPL(Inductive logic programming)

d) LISP

Answer: d

Explanation: None.

81. The Personal Consultant is basedon?

a) EMYCIN

b) OPS5+

c) XCON

d) All of the mentioned

Answer: d

Explanation: None.

82. What is Machine learning?

a) The autonomous acquisition ofknowledge through the use of computer programs

b) The autonomous acquisition ofknowledge through the use of manual programs

c) The selective acquisition of knowledge through the use ofcomputer programs

d) The selective acquisition ofknowledge through the use ofmanual programs

Answer: a

Explanation: Machine learning is theautonomous acquisition of knowledge through the use of computer programs.

83. Which of the factors affect the performance of learner system does not include?

a) Representation scheme used

b) Training scenario

c) Type of feedback

d) Good data structures

Answer: d

Explanation: Factors that affect the performance of learner system doesnot include good data structures.

84. Different learning methods doesnot include?

a) Memorization

b) Analogy

c) Deduction

d) Introduction

Answer: d

Explanation: Different learningmethods does not include the introduction.

85. In language understanding, thelevels of knowledge that does not include.

a) Phonological

b) Syntactic

c) Empirical

d) Logical

Answer: c

Explanation: In language understanding, the levels of knowledge that does not includeempirical knowledge.

86. A model of language consists ofthe categories which does not include?

a) Language units

b) Role structure of units

c) System constraints

d) Structural units

Answer: d

Explanation: A model of language consists of the categories which doesnot include structural units.

87. What is a top-down parser?

a) Begins by hypothesizing a sentence (the symbol S) and successively predicting lower level constituents until individual preterminal symbols are written

b) Begins by hypothesizing a sentence (the symbol S) and successively predicting upper level constituents until individual preterminal symbols are written

c) Begins by hypothesizing lower-levelconstituents and successively predicting a sentence (the symbol S)

d) Begins by hypothesizing upper-level constituents and successively predicting a sentence (the symbol S)

Answer: a

Explanation: A top-down parser begins by hypothesizing a sentence (the symbol S) and successively predicting lower-level constituents until individual preterminal symbolsare written.

88. Among the following which is nota horn clause?

a) p

b) Øp V q

c) p → q

d) p → Øq

Answer: d

Explanation: p → Øq is not a hornclause.

89. The action 'STACK(A, B)' of arobot arm specify to

a) Place block B on Block A

b) Place blocks A, B on the table inthat order

c) Place blocks B, A on the table inthat order

d) Place block A on block B

Answer: d

Explanation: The action 'STACK(A,B)'of a robot arm specify to Place blockA on block B.

90. Which instruments are used forperceiving and acting upon the environment?

a) Sensors and Actuators

b) Sensors

c) Perceiver

d) None of the mentioned

Answer: a

Explanation: An agent is anything thatcan be viewed as perceiving and acting upon the environment through the sensors and actuators.

91. What is meant by agent's perceptsequence?

a) Used to perceive the environment

b) Complete history of actuator

c) Complete history of perceivedthings

d) None of the mentioned

Answer: c

Explanation: An agent's percept sequence is the complete history ofeverything that the agent has ever perceived.

92. How many types of agents arethere in artificial intelligence?

a) 1

b) 2

c) 3

d) 4

Answer: d

Explanation: The four types of agentsare Simple reflex, Model based, Goalbased and Utility based agents.

93. What is the rule of simple reflexagent?

a) Simple-action rule

b) Condition-action rule

c) Simple & Condition-action rule

d) None of the mentioned

Answer: b

Explanation: Simple reflex agent is based on the present condition andso it is condition action rule.

94. What are the composition foragents in artificial intelligence?

a) Program

b) Architecture

c) Both Program & Architecture

d) None of the mentioned

Answer: c

Explanation: An agent program willimplement function mapping percepts to actions.

95. In which agent does the problemgenerator is present?

a) Learning agent

b) Observing agent

c) Reflex agent

d) None of the mentioned

Answer: a

Explanation: Problem generator willgive the suggestion to improve the output for learning agent.

96. Which is used to improve the agent's performance?

a) Perceiving
b) Learning
c) Observing
d) None of the mentioned

Answer: b

Explanation: An agent can improve itsperformance by storing its previous actions.

97. Which agent deals with happyand unhappy states?

a) Simple reflex agent
b) Model based agent
c) Learning agent
d) Utility based agent

Answer: d

Explanation: A utility function maps astate onto a real number which describes the associated degree of happiness.

98. In Hopfield network with symmetric weights, energy at eachstate may?

a) increase
b) decrease
c) decrease or remain same
d) decrease or increase

Answer: c

Explanation: Energy of the networkcan't increase as it may then lead toinstability.

99. In Hopfield model with symmetricweights, network can move to?

a) lower
b) higher
c) lower or higher
d) lower or same

Answer: d

Explanation: In Hopfield model withsymmetric weights, network can move to lower or same state.

100. Can error in recall due to falseminima be reduced?

a) yes
b) no

Answer: a

Explanation: There are generally two methods to reduce error in recall dueto false minima.

101. How can error in recall due tofalse minima be reduced?

a) deterministic update for states
b) stochastic update for states
c) not possible
d) none of the mentioned

Answer: b

Explanation: Error in recall due tofalse minima can be reduced by stochastic update for states.

102. Energy at each state in hopfield with symmetric weights network mayincrease or decrease?

a) yes
b) no

Answer: b

Explanation: Energy of the networkcant increase as it may then lead toinstability.

103. Pattern storage problem which cannot be represented by a feedbacknetwork of given size can be called as?

a) easy problems
b) hard problems
c) no such problem exist

d) none of the mentioned

Answer: b

Explanation: Pattern storage problem which cannot be represented by a feedback network of given size are known as hard problems.

104. What is the other way to reduce error in recall due to false minima apart from stochastic update?

a) no other method exist

b) by storing desired patterns at lowest energy minima

c) by storing desired patterns at energy maxima

d) none of the mentioned

Answer: b

Explanation: Error in recall due to false minima can be reduced by stochastic update or by storing desired patterns at lowest energy minima.

105. How can error in recall due to false minima be further reduced?

a) using suitable activation dynamics

b) cannot be further reduced

c) by storing desired patterns at energy maxima

d) none of the mentioned

Answer: a

Explanation: Error in recall due to false minima can further be reduced by using suitable activation dynamics.

106. As temperature increase, what happens to stochastic update?

a) increase in update

b) decrease in update

c) no change

d) none of the mentioned

Answer: c

Explanation: Temperature doesn't affect stochastic update.

107. Why does change in temperature doesn't affect stochastic update?

a) shape landscape depends on the network and its weights which varies accordingly and compensates the effect

b) shape landscape depends on the network and its weights which is fixed

c) shape landscape depends on the network, its weights and the output function which varies accordingly and compensates the effect

d) shape landscape depends on the network, its weights and the output function which is fixed

Answer: d

Explanation: Change in temperature doesn't affect stochastic update because shape landscape depends on the network, its weights and the output function which is fixed.

108. Which action sequences are used to achieve the agent's goal?

a) Search

b) Plan

c) Retrieve

d) Both Search & Plan

Answer: d

Explanation: When the environment becomes more tricky means, the agent needs plan and search action sequence to achieve the goal.

109. Which element in the agent are used for selecting external actions?

a) Perceive

b) Performance

c) Learning

d) Actuator

Answer: b

Explanation: None.

110. Given a stream of text, Named Entity Recognition determines whichpronoun maps to which noun.

a) False

b) True

Answer: a

Explanation: Given a stream of text,Named Entity Recognition determines which items in the text maps to proper names.

111. Natural Language generation isthe main task of Natural language processing.

a) True

b) False

Answer: a

Explanation: Natural Language Generation is to Convert informationfrom computer databases into readable human language.

112. OCR (Optical CharacterRecognition) uses NLP.

a) True

b) False

Answer: a

Explanation: Given an image representing printed text, determinesthe corresponding text.

113. Parts-of-Speech taggingdetermines

a) part-of-speech for each word dynamically as per meaning of thesentence

b) part-of-speech for each word dynamically as per sentence structure

c) all part-of-speech for a specificword given as input

d) all of the mentioned

Answer: d

Explanation: A Bayesian network provides a complete description ofthe domain.

114. Parsing determines Parse Trees(Grammatical Analysis) for a given sentence.

a) True

b) False

Answer: a

Explanation: Determine the parse tree (grammatical analysis) of a given sentence. The grammar for natural languages is ambiguous and typical sentences have multiple possible analyses. In fact, perhaps surprisingly,for a typical sentence there may be thousands of potential parses (most of which will seem completely nonsensical to a human).

115. Ambiguity may be caused by________

a) syntactic ambiguity

b) multiple word meanings

c) unclear antecedents

d) all of the mentioned

Answer: d

Explanation: None.

116. Which company offers the LISPmachine considered "the most powerful symbolic processor available"?

a) LMI

b) Symbolics

c) Xerox

d) Texas Instruments

Answer: b

Explanation: None.

117. What of the following is considered a pivotal event in thehistory of Artificial Intelligence?

a) 1949, Donald O, The organizationof Behavior

b) 1950, Computing Machinery andIntelligence

c) 1956, Dartmouth UniversityConference Organized by JohnMcCarthy

d) 1961, Computer and ComputerSense
Answer: c
Explanation: None.

118. What are the two subfields ofNatural language processing?
a) symbolic and numeric
b) time and motion
c) algorithmic and heuristic
d) understanding and generation
Answer: c
Explanation: None.

119. High-resolution, bit-mappeddisplays are useful for displaying _
a) clearer characters
b) graphics
c) more characters
d) all of the mentioned
Answer: c
Explanation: None.

120. A bidirectional feedback looplinks computer modeling with _
a) artificial science
b) heuristic processing
c) human intelligence
d) cognitive science
Answer: c
Explanation: None.

121. Which of the following have people traditionally done better thancomputers?
a) recognizing relative importance
b) finding similarities
c) resolving ambiguity
d) all of the mentioned
Answer: c
Explanation: None.

122. In LISP, the function evaluatesboth and is
a) set
b) setq
c) add
d) eva
Answer: a
Explanation: None.

123. Which type of actuator generates a good deal of power buttends to be messy?
a) electric
b) hydraulic
c) pneumatic
d) both hydraulic & pneumatic
Answer: b
Explanation: None.

124. Research scientists all over the world are taking steps towards building computers with circuits patterned after the complex interconnections existing among thehuman brain's nerve cells. What name is given to such type of computers?
a) Intelligent computers
b) Supercomputers
c) Neural network computers

d) Smart computers

Answer: c

Explanation: None.

125. The integrated circuit wasinvented by Jack Kilby of _

a) MIT

b) Texas Instruments

c) Xerox

d) All of the mentioned

Answer: b

Explanation: None.

126. The Cedar, BBN Butterfly, Cosmic Cube and Hypercube machinecan be characterized as_

a) SISD

b) MIMD

c) SIMD

d) MISD

Answer: b

Explanation: None.

127. A series of AI systems, developed by Pat Langley to explorethe role of heuristics in scientific discovery is

a) RAMD

b) BACON

c) MIT

d) DU

Answer: b

Explanation: None.

128. IR (information Retrieval) and IE(Information Extraction) are the two same thing.

a) True

b) False

Answer: b

Explanation: Information retrieval (IR)

– This is concerned with storing, searching and retrieving information.It is a separate field within computerscience (closer to databases), but IR relies on some NLP methods (for example, stemming). Some current research and applications seek to bridge the gap between IR and NLP. Information extraction (IE) – This is concerned in general with the extraction of semantic information from text. This covers tasks such as named entity recognition, Coreference resolution, relationship extraction, etc.

129. Many words have more than one meaning; we have to select the meaning which makes the most sensein context. This can be resolved by

a) Fuzzy Logic

b) Word Sense Disambiguation

c) Shallow Semantic Analysis

d) All of the mentioned

Answer: b

Explanation: Shallow Semantic Analysis doesn't cover word sensedisambiguation.

130. Given a sound clip of a person orpeople speaking, determine the textual representation of the speech.

a) Text-to-speech

b) Speech-to-text

c) All of the mentioned

d) None of the mentioned

Answer: b

Explanation: NLP is required tolinguistic analysis.

131. Speech Segmentation is asubtask of Speech Recognition.

a) True

b) False
Answer: a
Explanation: None.

132. In linguistic morphology _ is the process for reducing inflected words to their rootform.
a) Rooting
b) Stemming
c) Text-Proofing
d) Both Rooting & Stemming
Answer: b
Explanation: None.

133. Which depends on the perceptsand actions available to the agent?
a) Agent
b) Sensor
c) Design problem
d) None of the mentioned
Answer: c
Explanation: The design problem depends on the percepts and actionsavailable to the agent, the goals thatthe agent's behavior should satisfy.

134. Which were built in such a way that humans had to supply the inputsand interpret the outputs?
a) Agents
b) AI system
c) Sensor
d) Actuators
Answer: b
Explanation: AI systems were built insuch a way that humans had to supply the inputs and interpret the outputs.

135. Which technology uses miniaturized accelerometers andgyroscopes?
a) Sensors
b) Actuators
c) MEMS
d) None of the mentioned
Answer: c
Explanation: Micro Electromechanically System uses miniaturized accelerometers and gyroscopes and is used to produce actuators.

136. What is used for trackinguncertain events?
a) Filtering algorithm
b) Sensors
c) Actuators
d) None of the mentioned
Answer: a
Explanation: Filtering algorithm is used for tracking uncertain events because in this the real perception isinvolved.

137. What is not represented byusing propositional logic?
a) Objects
b) Relations
c) Both Objects & Relations
d) None of the mentioned
Answer: c
Explanation: Objects and relationsare not represented by using propositional logic explicitly.

138. What will take place as the agent observes its interactions withthe world?
a) Learning
b) Hearing

c) Perceiving

d) Speech

Answer: a

Explanation: Learning will take place as the agent observes its interactionswith the world and its own decision-making process.

139. Which modifies the performanceelement so that it makes better decision?

a) Performance element

b) Changing element

c) Learning element

d) None of the mentioned

Answer: c

Explanation: A learning element modifies the performance element sothat it can make better decision.

140. How many things are concernedin the design of a learning element?

a) 1

b) 2

c) 3

d) 4

Answer: c

Explanation: The three main issues are affected in design of a learning element are components, feedbackand representation.

141. What is used in determining thenature of the learning problem?

a) Environment

b) Feedback

c) Problem

d) All of the mentioned

Answer: b

Explanation: The type of feedback is used in determining the nature of thelearning problem that the agent faces.

142. How many types are available inmachine learning?

a) 1

b) 2

c) 3

d) 4

Answer: c

Explanation: The three types of machine learning are supervised,unsupervised and reinforcement.

143. Which is used for utility functions in game playing algorithm?

a) Linear polynomial

b) Weighted polynomial

c) Polynomial

d) Linear weighted polynomial

Answer: d

Explanation: Linear weighted polynomial is used for learning element in the game playingprograms.

144. Which is used to choose amongmultiple consistent hypotheses?

a) Razor

b) Ockham razor

c) Learning element

d) None of the mentioned

Answer: b

Explanation: Ockham razor prefersthe simplest hypothesis consistentwith the data intuitively.

145. What will happen if the hypothesis space contains the truefunction?

a) Realizable

b) Unrealizable

c) Both Realizable & Unrealizable

d) None of the mentioned

Answer: b

Explanation: A learning problem isrealizable if the hypothesis space contains the true function.

146. What takes input as an objectdescribed by a set of attributes?

a) Tree

b) Graph

c) Decision graph

d) Decision tree

Answer: d

Explanation: Decision tree takes inputas an object described by a set of attributes and returns a decision.

147. How the decision tree reachesits decision?

a) Single test

b) Two test

c) Sequence of test

d) No test

Answer: c

Explanation: A decision tree reaches its decision by performing a sequenceof tests.

148. Which functions are used aspreferences over state history?

a) Award

b) Reward

c) Explicit

d) Implicit

Answer: b

Explanation: Reward functions maybe that preferences over states arereally compared from preferences over state histories.

149. Which kind of agent architectureshould an agent an use?

a) Relaxed

b) Logic

c) Relational

d) All of the mentioned

Answer: d

Explanation: Because an agent may experience any kind of situation, Sothat an agent should use all kinds ofarchitecture.

150. Specify the agent architecture name that is used to capture all kindsof actions.

a) Complex

b) Relational

c) Hybrid

d) None of the mentioned

Answer: c

Explanation: A complete agent mustbe able to do anything by using hybrid architecture.

151. Which agent enables the deliberation about the computationalentities and actions?

a) Hybrid

b) Reflective

c) Relational

d) None of the mentioned

Answer: b

Explanation: Because it enables theagent to capture within itself.

152. What can operate over the jointstate space?

a) Decision-making algorithm

b) Learning algorithm

c) Complex algorithm

d) Both Decision-making & Learningalgorithm

Answer: d

Explanation: Decision-making and learning algorithms can operate overthe joint state space and thereby serve to implement and used to improve the computational activities.

153. What is the main task of aproblem-solving agent?
a) Solve the given problem and reachto goal
b) To find out which sequence ofaction will get it to the goal state
c) All of the mentioned
d) None of the mentioned
Answer: c
Explanation: The problem-solvingagents are one of the goal-based agents.

154. What is state space?
a) The whole problem
b) Your Definition to a problem
c) Problem you design
d) Representing your problem withvariable and parameter
Answer: d
Explanation: Because state space is mostly concerned with a problem, when you try to solve a problem, we have to design a mathematical structure to the problem, which can only be through variables and parameters. eg. You have given a 4- gallon jug and another 3-gallon jug. Neither has measuring marker on it. You have to fill the jugs with water. How can you get exactly 2 gallons of water in to 4 gallons. Here the state space can defined as set of ordered pairs integers(x,y), such that x=0,1,2,3 or 4 and y=0,1,2 or 3; X represents the number of gallons in 4 gallon jug and y represents the quantity of water in the 3-gallon jug.

155. The problem-solving agent withseveral immediate options of unknown value can decide what to do by just examining different possible sequences of actions that lead to states of known value, and then choosing the best sequence. This process of looking for such a sequence is called Search.
a) True
b) False
Answer: a
Explanation: Refer to the definition ofproblem-solving agent.

156. A search algorithm takes ___as an input and returns ___as an output.
a) Input, output
b) Problem, solution
c) Solution, problem
d) Parameters, sequence of actions
Answer: b
Explanation: A search algorithm takesinput as a problem and returns a solution to the problem as an output.

157. A problem in a search space isdefined by one of these state.
a) Initial state
b) Last state
c) Intermediate state
d) All of the mentioned
Answer: a
Explanation: A problem has four components initial state, goal test,set of actions, path cost.

158. The Set of actions for a problemin a state space is formulated by a
a) Intermediate states
b) Initial state
c) Successor function, which takescurrent action and returns next immediate state
d) None of the mentioned
Answer: c
Explanation: The most common formulation for actions uses a successor function. Given a particularstate x, SUCCESSOR-FN(x) returns a set of (action, successor) ordered pairs, where each action is one of thelegal actions in state x and each successor is a state that can be reached from x by applying the action.

159. A solution to a problem is a path from the initial state to a goal state. Solution quality is measured by the path cost function, and an optimal solution has the highest path cost among all solutions.
a) True
b) False
Answer: a
Explanation: A solution to a problem is a path from the initial state to a goal state. Solution quality is measured by the path cost function, and an optimal solution has the lowest path cost among all solutions.

160. The process of removing detail from a given state representation is called__
a) Extraction
b) Abstraction
c) Information Retrieval
d) Mining of data
Answer: b
Explanation: The process of removing detail from a representation is called abstraction.

161. A problem-solving approach works well for
a) 8-Puzzle problem
b) 8-queen problem
c) Finding a optimal path from a given source to a destination
d) Mars Hover (Robot Navigation)
Answer: d
Explanation: Problem-solving approach works well for toy problems and real-world problems.

162. The_ is a touring problem in which each city must be visited exactly once. The aim is to find the shortest tour.
a) Finding shortest path between a source and a destination
b) Travelling Salesman problem
c) Map coloring problem
d) Depth first search traversal on a given map represented as a graph
Answer: b
Explanation: Refer the TSP problem.

163. Web Crawler is a/an
a) Intelligent goal-based agent
b) Problem-solving agent
c) Simple reflex agent
d) Model based agent
Answer: a
Explanation: Web Crawling is type of search for a relevant document from given seed documents. Focused crawlers exists, helps to improvise the search efficiency.

164. What is the major component/components for measuring the performance of problem solving?
a) Completeness
b) Optimality
c) Time and Space complexity
d) All of the mentioned
Answer: d
Explanation: For best performance consideration of all component is necessary.

165. A production rule consists of
____
a) A set of Rule
b) A sequence of steps
c) Set of Rule & sequence of steps
d) Arbitrary representation to problem

Answer: c

Explanation: When you are trying to solve a problem, you should design how to get a step-by-step solution with constraints condition to your problem, e.g Chess board problem.

166. Which search method takes lessmemory?

a) Depth-First Search

b) Breadth-First search

c) Linear Search

d) Optimal search

Answer: a

Explanation: Depth-First Search takes less memory since only the nodes on the current path are stored, but in Breadth First Search, all of the tree that has generated must be stored.

167. Which is the best way to go forGame playing problem?

a) Linear approach

b) Heuristic approach (Someknowledge is stored)

c) Random approach

d) An Optimal approach

Answer: b

Explanation: We use a Heuristic approach, as it will find out brute force computation, looking at hundreds of thousands of positions. G Chess competition betweenHuman and AI based Computer.

168. General games involves

a) Single-agent

b) Multi-agent

c) Neither Single-agent nor Multi-agent

d) Only Single-agent and Multi-agent

Answer: d

Explanation: Depending upon gamesit could be single agent (Sudoku) or multi-agent (Chess).

169. Adversarial search problemsuses _

a) Competitive Environment

b) Cooperative Environment

c) Neither Competitive norCooperative Environment

d) Only Competitive and CooperativeEnvironment

Answer: a

Explanation: Since in cooperative environment agents' goals are I conflicts. They compete for goal.

170. Mathematical game theory, a branch of economics, views any multi-agent environment as a game provided that the impact of each agent on the others is "significant," regardless of whether the agents arecooperative or competitive.

a) True

b) False

Answer: a

Explanation: None.

171. Zero sum games are the one inwhich there are two agents whose actions must alternate and in whichthe utility values at the end of the game are always the same.

a) True

b) False

Answer: b

Explanation: Utility values are alwayssame and opposite.

172. Zero sum game has to be a _____game.

a) Single player

b) Two player

c) Multiplayer

d) Three player

Answer: c

Explanation: Zero sum games couldbe multiplayer games as long as thecondition for zero sum game is satisfied.

173. A game can be formally definedas a kind of search problem with thefollowing components.
a) Initial State
b) Successor Function
c) Terminal Test
d) All of the mentioned
Answer: d

Explanation: The initial state includesthe board position and identifies the player to move. A successor functionreturns a list of (move, state) pairs, each indicating a legal move and the resulting state. A terminal test determines when the game is over. States where the game has ended are called terminal states. A utility function (also called an objective function or payoff function), which gives a numeric value for the terminalstates. In chess, the outcome is a win,lose, or draw, with values +1, -1, or 0.

174. The initial state and the legalmoves for each side define the_ for the game.
a) Search Tree
b) Game Tree
c) State Space Search
d) Forest
Answer: b

Explanation: An example of gametree for Tic-Tac-Toe game.

175. General algorithm applied ongame tree for making decision of win/lose is
a) DFS/BFS Search Algorithms
b) Heuristic Search Algorithms
c) Greedy Search Algorithms
d) MIN/MAX Algorithms
Answer: d

Explanation: Given a game tree, the optimal strategy can be determined by examining the min/max value of each node, which we write as MINIMAX- VALUE(n). The min/max value of a node is the utility (for MAX) of being in the corresponding state, assuming that both players playoptimally from there to the end of the game. Obviously, the min/max value of a terminal state is just its utility. Furthermore, given a choice, MAX will prefer to move to a state of maximum value, whereas MIN prefers a state of minimum value.

176. The minimax algorithm computes the minimax decision fromthe current state. It uses a simple recursive computation of the minimax values of each successor state, directly implementing the defining equations. The recursion proceeds all the way down to the leaves of the tree, and then the minimax values are backed up through the tree as the recursion unwinds.
a) True
b) False
Answer: a

Explanation: Refer definition ofminimax algorithm.

177. What is the complexity ofminimax algorithm?
a) Same as of DFS
b) Space – bm and time – bm
c) Time – bm and space – bm
d) Same as BFS
Answer: a

Explanation: Same as DFS.

178. Which is the most straightforward approach forplanning algorithm?
a) Best-first search
b) State-space search
c) Depth-first search
d) Hill-climbing search
Answers: b

Explanation: The straightforward approach for planning algorithm is state space search because it takes into account of everything for findinga solution.

179. What are taken into account ofstate-space search?
a) Postconditions
b) Preconditions
c) Effects
d) Both Preconditions & Effects
Answer: d
Explanation: The state-space searchtakes both precondition and effectsinto account for solving a problem.

180. How many ways are available tosolve the state-space search?
a) 1
b) 2
c) 3
d) 4
Answer: b
Explanation: There are two ways available to solve the state-space search. They are forward from the initial state and backward from thegoal.

181. What is the other name forforward state-space search?
a) Progression planning
b) Regression planning
c) Test planning
d) None of the mentioned
Answer: a
Explanation: It is sometimes called asprogression planning, because it moves in the forward direction.

182. How many states are available instate-space search?
a) 1
b) 2
c) 3
d) 4
Answer: d
Explanation: There are four states available in state-space search. They are initial state, actions, goal test andstep cost.

183. What is the main advantage ofbackward state-space search?
a) Cost
b) Actions
c) Relevant actions
d) All of the mentioned
Answer: c
Explanation: The main advantage of backward search will allow us toconsider only relevant actions.

184. What is the other name of thebackward state-space search?
a) Regression planning
b) Progression planning
c) State planning
d) Test planning
Answer: a
Explanation: Backward state-space search will find the solution from goalto the action, So it is called as Regression planning.

185. What is meant by consistent instate-space search?
a) Change in the desired literals
b) Not any change in the literals
c) No change in goal state
d) None of the mentioned

Answer: b
Explanation: Consistent means that the completed actions will not undoany desired literals.

186. What will happen if a predecessor description is generatedthat is satisfied by the initial state of the planning problem?
a) Success
b) Error
c) Compilation
d) Termination
Answer: d
Explanation: None.

187. Which approach is to pretendthat a pure divide and conquer algorithm will work?
a) Goal independence
b) Subgoal independence
c) Both Goal & Subgoal independence
d) None of the mentioned
Answer: b
Explanation: Subgoal independenceapproach is to pretend that a pure divide and conquer algorithm will work for admissible heuristics.

188. Which search is equal to minimax search but eliminates the branches that can't influence the finaldecision?
a) Depth-first search
b) Breadth-first search
c) Alpha-beta pruning
d) None of the mentioned
Answer: c
Explanation: The alpha-beta search computes the same optimal moves as minimax, but eliminates the branches that can't influence the final decision.

189. Which values are independent inminimax search algorithm?
a) Pruned leaves x and y
b) All states are dependent
c) Root is independent
d) None of the mentioned
Answer: a
Explanation: The minimax decision are independent of the values of thepruned values x and y because of theroot values.

190. To which depth does the alpha-beta pruning can be applied?
a) 10 states
b) 8 States
c) 6 States
d) Any depth
Answer: d
Explanation: Alpha–beta pruning canbe applied to trees of any depth andit is possible to prune entire subtree rather than leaves.

191. Which search is similar tominimax search?
a) Hill-climbing search
b) Depth-first search
c) Breadth-first search
d) All of the mentioned
Answer: b
Explanation: The minimax search is depth-first search, So at one time wejust have to consider the nodes alonga single path in the tree.

192. Which value is assigned to alphaand beta in the alpha-beta pruning?
a) Alpha = max

b) Beta = min

c) Beta = max

d) Both Alpha = max & Beta = min

Answer: d

Explanation: Alpha and beta are the values of the best choice we have found so far at any choice point along the path for MAX and MIN.

193.   Where does the values of alpha-beta search get updated?

a) Along the path of search

b) Initial state itself

c) At the end

d) None of the mentioned

Answer: a

Explanation: Alpha-beta search updates the value of alpha and beta as it gets along and prunes the remaining branches at node.

194.   How the effectiveness of the alpha-beta pruning gets increased?

a) Depends on the nodes

b) Depends on the order in which they are executed

c) All of the mentioned

d) None of the mentioned

Answer: a

Explanation: None.

195.   What is called as transposition table?

a) Hash table of next seen positions

b) Hash table of previously seen positions

c) Next value in the search

d) None of the mentioned

Answer: b

Explanation: Transposition is the occurrence of repeated states frequently in the search.

196.   Which is identical to the closed list in Graph search?

a) Hill climbing search algorithm

b) Depth-first search

c) Transposition table

d) None of the mentioned

Answer: c

Explanation: None.

197.   Which function is used to calculate the feasibility of whole game tree?

a) Evaluation function

b) Transposition

c) Alpha-beta pruning

d) All of the mentioned

Answer: a

Explanation: Because we need to cut the search off at some point and apply an evaluation function that gives an estimate of the utility of the state.

198.   Which is created by using single propositional symbol?

a) Complex sentences

b) Atomic sentences

c) Composition sentences

d) None of the mentioned

Answer: b

Explanation: Atomic sentences are indivisible syntactic elements consisting of single propositional symbol.

199.   Which is used to construct the complex sentences?

a) Symbols
b) Connectives
c) Logical connectives
d) All of the mentioned
Answer: c Explanation: None.

200. How many proposition symbolsare there in artificial intelligence?
a) 1
b) 2
c) 3
d) 4
Answer: b
Explanation: The two propositionsymbols are true and false.

201. How many logical connectivesare there in artificial intelligence?
a) 2
b) 3
c) 4
d) 5
Answer: d
Explanation: The five logical symbolsare negation, conjunction, disjunction, implication and biconditional.

202. Which is used to compute thetruth of any sentence?
a) Semantics of propositional logic
b) Alpha-beta pruning
c) First-order logic
d) Both Semantics of propositionallogic & Alpha-beta pruning
Answer: a
Explanation: Because the meaning ofthe sentences is really needed to compute the truth.

203. Which are needed to computethe logical inference algorithm?
a) Logical equivalence
b) Validity
c) Satisfiability
d) All of the mentioned
Answer: d
Explanation: Logical inference algorithm can be solved be usinglogical equivalence, Validity and satisfiability.

204. From which rule does the modusponens are derived?
a) Inference rule
b) Module rule
c) Both Inference & Module rule
d) None of the mentioned
Answer: a
Explanation: Inference rule containsthe standard pattern that leads to desired goal. The best form of inference rule is modus ponens.

205. Which is also called singleinference rule?
a) Reference
b) Resolution
c) Reform
d) None of the mentioned
Answer: b
Explanation: Because resolution yields a complete inference rulewhen coupled with any search algorithm.

206. Which form is called as a conjunction of disjunction of literals?
a) Conjunctive normal form

b) Disjunctive normal form

c) Normal form

d) All of the mentioned

Answer: a

Explanation: None

207. An algorithm is complete if

a) It terminates with a solution when one exists

b) It starts with a solution

c) It does not terminate with a solution

d) It has a loop

Answer: a

Explanation: An Algorithm is complete if It terminates with a solution when one exists.

208. What can be viewed as a singlelateral of disjunction?

a) Multiple clause

b) Combine clause

c) Unit clause

d) None of the mentioned

Answer: c

Explanation: A single literal can be viewed as a disjunction or one literalalso, called a unit clause.

209. What is the goal of artificialintelligence?

a) To solve real-world problems

b) To solve artificial problems

c) To explain various sorts ofintelligence

d) To extract scientific causes

Answer: c

Explanation: Artificial Intelligence's goal is to explain various sorts of intelligence.

210. Which is true regarding BFS(Breadth First Search)?

a) BFS will get trapped exploring asingle path

b) The entire tree so far been generated must be stored in BFS

c) BFS is not guaranteed to find asolution if exists

d) BFS is nothing but Binary FirstSearch

Answer: b

Explanation: Regarding BFS-The entire tree so far been generatedmust be stored in BFS.

211. What is a heuristic function?

a) A function to solve mathematicalproblems

b) A function which takes parametersof type string and returns an integer value

c) A function whose return type isnothing

d) A function that maps fromproblem state descriptions tomeasures of desirability

Answer: d

Explanation: Heuristic function is afunction that maps from problem state descriptions to measures of desirability.

212. The traveling salesman probleminvolves n cities with paths connecting the cities. The time takenfor traversing through all the cities, without knowing in advance the length of a minimum tour, is

a) O(n)

b) O(n2)

c) O(n!)

d) O(n/2)

Answer: c

Explanation: The traveling salesman problem involves n cities with paths connecting the cities. The time taken for traversing through all the cities,without knowing in advance the length of a minimum tour, is O(n!).

213. What is the problem space ofmeans-end analysis?

a) An initial state and one or moregoal states

b) One or more initial states and onegoal state

c) One or more initial states and oneor more goal state

d) One initial state and one goal state

Answer: a

Explanation: The problem space ofmeans-end analysis has an initial state and one or more goal states.

214. An algorithm A is admissible if______

a) It is not guaranteed to return anoptimal solution when one exists

b) It is guaranteed to return an optimal solution when one exists

c) It returns more solutions, but notan optimal one

d) It guarantees to return moreoptimal solutions

Answer: b

Explanation: An algorithm A is admissible if It is guaranteed to return an optimal solution when oneexists.

215. Knowledge may be

I.   Declarative.

II.   Procedural.

III.   Non-procedural.

a) Only (I)

b) Only (II)

c) Only (III)

d) Both (I) and (II)

Answer: d

Explanation: Knowledge may bedeclarative and procedural.

216. What is the frame?

a) A way of representing knowledge

b) Data Structure

c) Data Type

d) None of the mentioned

Answer: a

Explanation: None.

217. Frames in artificial intelligence isderived from semantic nets.

a) True

b) False

Answer: a

Explanation: A frame is an artificial intelligence data structure used to divide knowledge into substructures by representing "stereotypedsituations.".

218. Which of the following elementsconstitutes the frame structure?

a) Facts or Data

b) Procedures and default values

c) Frame names

d) Frame reference in hierarchy

Answer: a

Explanation: None.

219. Like semantic networks, framescan be queried using spreading activation.

a) True

b) False

Answer: a

Explanation: None.

220. What is Hyponymy relation?

a) A is part of B

b) B has A as a part of itself

c) A is subordinate of B

d) A is superordinate of B

Answer: c

Explanation: In linguistics, a hyponym is a word or phrase whose semantic field is included within that of another word, its hypernym (sometimes spelled hypernym outside of the natural language processing community). In simpler terms, a hyponym shares a type-of relationship with its hypernym.

221. The basic inference mechanism in semantic network in which knowledge is represented as Frames is to follow the links between the nodes.

a) True

b) False

Answer: a

Explanation: None.

222. There exists two way to infer using semantic networks in which knowledge is represented as Frames.

1) Intersection Search

2) Inheritance Search

a) True

b) False

Answer: a

Explanation: None.

223. What is perceptron?

a) a single layer feed-forward neural network with pre-processing

b) an auto-associative neural network

c) a double layer auto-associative neural network

d) a neural network that contains feedback

Answer: a

Explanation: The perceptron is a single layer feed-forward neural network. It is not an auto-associative network because it has no feedback and is not a multiple layer neural network because the pre-processing stage is not made of neurons.

224. What is an auto-associative network?

a) a neural network that contains no loops

b) a neural network that contains feedback

c) a neural network that has only one loop

d) a single layer feed-forward neural network with pre-processing

Answer: b

Explanation: An auto-associative network is equivalent to a neural network that contains feedback. The number of feedback paths(loops) does not have to be one.

225. A 4-input neuron has weights 1,2, 3 and 4. The transfer function is linear with the constant of proportionality being equal to 2. The inputs are 4, 10, 5 and 20 respectively. What will be the output?

a) 238

b) 76

c) 119

d) 123

Answer: a

Explanation: The output is found by multiplying the weights with their respective inputs, summing the results and multiplying with the transfer function. Therefore: Output = 2 * (1*4 + 2*10 + 3*5 + 4*20) = 238.

226. Which of the following is true?

(i) On average, neural networks have higher computational rates than conventional computers.

(ii) Neural networks learn by example.

(iii) Neural networks mimic the way the human brain works.

a) All of the mentioned are true

b) (ii) and (iii) are true

c) (i), (ii) and (iii) are true

d) None of the mentioned

Answer: a

Explanation: Neural networks have higher computational rates than conventional computers because a lot of the operation is done in parallel. That is not the case when the neural network is simulated on a computer. The idea behind neural nets is based on the way the humanbrain works. Neural nets cannot be programmed, they can only learn byexamples.

227. Which of the following is true forneural networks?

(i)   The training time depends on thesize of the network.

(ii)   Neural networks can be simulatedon a conventional computer.

(iii)   Artificial neurons are identical inoperation to biological ones.

a) All of the mentioned

b) (ii) is true

c) (i) and (ii) are true

d) None of the mentioned

Answer: c

Explanation: The training time depends on the size of the network;the number of neuron is greater andtherefore the number of possible'states' is increased. Neural networks can be simulated on a conventional computer but the main advantage ofneural networks – parallel execution– is lost. Artificial neurons are notidentical in operation to the biological ones.

228. What are the advantages of neural networks over conventional computers?

(i)   They have the ability to learn byexample

(ii)   They are more fault tolerant

(iii)   They are more suited for real timeoperation due to their high 'computational' rates

a) (i) and (ii) are true

b) (i) and (iii) are true

c) Only (i)

d) All of the mentioned

Answer: d

Explanation: Neural networks learn by example. They are more fault tolerant because they are always able to respond and small changes in inputdo not normally cause a change in output. Because of their parallel architecture, high computational rates are achieved.

229. Which of the following is true?Single layer associative neural networks do not have the ability to:

(i)   perform pattern recognition

(ii)   find the parity of a picture

(iii)   (iii)determine whether two or more shapes in a picture are connected ornot

a) (ii) and (iii) are true

b) (ii) is true

c) All of the mentioned

d) None of the mentioned

Answer: a

Explanation: Pattern recognition is what single layer neural networks arebest at but they don't have the abilityto find the parity of a picture or to determine whether two shapes are connected or not.

230. Which is true for neuralnetworks?

a) It has set of nodes and connections

b) Each node computes it's weightedinput

c) Node could be in excited state ornon-excited state

d) All of the mentioned

Answer: d

Explanation: All mentioned are thecharacteristics of neural network.

231. What is Neuro software?

a) A software used to analyzeneurons

b) It is powerful and easy neuralnetwork

c) Designed to aid experts in realworld

d) It is software used byNeurosurgeon

Answer: b

Explanation: None.

232. What is Artificial intelligence?

a) Putting your intelligence intoComputer

b) Programming with your ownintelligence

c) Making a Machine intelligent

d) Playing a Game

Answer: c

Explanation: Because AI is to make things work automatically through machine without using human effort.Machine will give the result with just giving input from human. That meansthe system or machine will act as perthe requirement.

233. Which is not the commonly usedprogramming language for AI?

a) PROLOG

b) Java

c) LISP

d) Perl

Answer: d

Explanation: Because Perl is used as ascript language, and not of much use for AI practice. All others are used to generate an artificial program.

234. Artificial Intelligence has itsexpansion in the following application.

a) Planning and Scheduling

b) Game Playing

c) Diagnosis

d) All of the mentioned

Answer: d

Explanation: All sectors require intelligence and automation for itsworking.

235. What is an 'agent'?

a) Perceives its environment throughsensors and acting upon that environment through actuators

b) Takes input from the surroundings and uses its intelligence and performsthe desired operations

c) A embedded program controllingline following robot

d) All of the mentioned

Answer: d

Explanation: An agent is anything thatcan be viewed as perceiving and acting upon the environment throughthe sensors and actuators. Mean it takes input from its environment through sensors, performs operation and gives output through actuators.

236. Agents behavior can be bestdescribed by

a) Perception sequence

b) Agent function

c) Sensors and Actuators

d) Environment in which agent isperforming

Answer: b

Explanation: An agent's behavior is described by the agent function that maps any given percept sequence to an action, which can be implemented by agent program. The agent function is an abstract mathematical description; the agent program is a concrete implementation, running onthe agent architecture.

237. Rational agent is the one whoalways does the right thing.

a) True

b) False

Answer: a

Explanation: Rational agent is the one who always does the right thing Right in a sense that it makes the agent the most successful.

238. Performance Measures are fixedfor all agents.

a) True
b) False
Answer: a
Explanation: As a general rule, it isbetter to design performance
measures according to what one actually wants in the environment,rather than according to how one thinks the agent should behave.

239. What is rational at any giventime depends on?
a) The performance measure thatdefines the criterion of success
b) The agent's prior knowledge of theenvironment
c) The actions that the agent canperform
d) All of the mentioned
Answer: d
Explanation: For each possible percept sequence, a rational agent should select an action that is expected to maximize its performance measure, given the evidence provided by the percept sequence and whatever built-in knowledge the agent has.

240. An omniscient agent knows the actual outcome of its actions and can act accordingly; but omniscience is impossible in reality. Rational Agent always does the right thing; but Rationality is possible in reality.
a) True
b) False
Answer: a
Explanation: Refer the definition ofrational and omniscient agents.

241. The Task Environment of anagent consists of_
a) Sensors
b) Actuators
c) Performance Measures
d) All of the mentioned
Answer: d
Explanation: The task environment of an agent is described by four parts performance measures, sensors, actuators and environment, generallyknown as the PEAS descriptions.

242. What could possibly be the environment of a Satellite ImageAnalysis System?
a) Computers in space and earth
b) Image categorization techniques
c) Statistical data on image pixelintensity value and histograms
d) All of the mentioned
Answer: d
Explanation: An environment is something which agent stays in.

243. Categorize Crossword puzzle inFully Observable / Partially Observable.
a) Fully Observable
b) partially Observable
c) All of the mentioned
d) None of the mentioned
Answer: a
Explanation: In crossword puzzle an agent knows the complete state of the environment through its sensors.

244. The game of Poker is a singleagent.
a) True
b) False
Answer: b
Explanation: The game of poker involves multiple player, hence its works in Multi-agent environment.

245. Satellite Image Analysis Systemis (Choose the one that is not applicable).
a) Episodic
b) Semi-Static

c) Single agent

d) Partially Observable

Answer: d

Explanation: System knows the current status of the analysis thoughtits inputs.

246. An agent is composed of

a) Architecture

b) Agent Function

c) Perception Sequence

d) Architecture and Program

Answer: d

Explanation: An agent is anything thatcan be viewed as perceiving and acting upon the environment through the sensors and actuators.

247. Why is the XOR problem exceptionally interesting to neuralnetwork researchers?

a) Because it can be expressed in a way that allows you to use a neuralnetwork

b) Because it is complex binary operation that cannot be solved usingneural networks

c) Because it can be solved by a singlelayer perceptron

d) Because it is the simplest linearlyinseparable problem that exists.

Answer: d

Explanation: None.

248. What is back propagation?

a) It is another name given to thecurvy function in the perceptron

b) It is the transmission of error backthrough the network to adjust the inputs

c) It is the transmission of error back through the network to allow weightsto be adjusted so that the network can learn

d) None of the mentioned

Answer: c

Explanation: Back propagation is thetransmission of error back through the network to allow weights to be adjusted so that the network can learn.

249. Why are linearly separableproblems of interest of neural network researchers?

a) Because they are the only class ofproblem that network can solve successfully

b) Because they are the only class ofproblem that Perceptron can solve successfully

c) Because they are the only mathematical functions that arecontinue

d) Because they are the only mathematical functions you can draw

Answer: b

Explanation: Linearly separable problems of interest of neural network researchers because theyare the only class of problem that Perceptron can solve successfully.

250. Which of the following is not thepromise of artificial neural network?

a) It can explain result

b) It can survive the failure of somenodes

c) It has inherent parallelism

d) It can handle noise

Answer: a

Explanation: The artificial Neural Network (ANN) cannot explain result.

251. Neural Networks are complex __with manyparameters.

a) Linear Functions

b) Nonlinear Functions

c) Discrete Functions

d) Exponential Functions

Answer: a

Explanation: Neural networks are complex linear functions with manyparameters.

252. A perceptron adds up all the weighted inputs it receives, and if itexceeds a certain value, it outputs a1, otherwise it just outputs a 0.

a) True

b) False

c) Sometimes – it can also outputintermediate values as well

d) Can't say

Answer: a

Explanation: Yes the perceptronworks like that.

253. What is the name of the function in the following statement"A perceptron adds up all the weighted inputs it receives, and if itexceeds a certain value, it outputs a1, otherwise it just outputs a 0"?

a) Step function

b) Heaviside function

c) Logistic function

d) Perceptron function

Answer: b

Explanation: Also known as the step function – so answer 1 is also right. Itis a hard thresholding function, eitheron or off with no in-between.

254. Having multiple perceptrons can actually solve the XOR problem satisfactorily: this is because each perceptron can partition off a linear part of the space itself, and they can then combine their results.

a) True – this works always, and thesemultiple perceptrons learn to classify even complex problems

b) False – perceptrons are mathematically incapable of solvinglinearly inseparable functions, no matter what you do

c) True – perceptrons can do this butare unable to learn to do it – they have to be explicitly hand-coded

d) False – just having a singleperceptron is enough

Answer: c

Explanation: None.

255. The network that involves backward links from output to theinput and hidden layers is called

a) Self organizing maps

b) Perceptrons

c) Recurrent neural network

d) Multi layered perceptron

Answer: c

Explanation: RNN (Recurrent neural network) topology involves backwardlinks from output to the input and hidden layers.

256. Which of the following is an application of NN (Neural Network)?

a) Sales forecasting

b) Data validation

c) Risk management

d) All of the mentioned

Answer: d

Explanation: All mentioned optionsare applications of Neural Network.

257. What is the field of NaturalLanguage Processing (NLP)?

a) Computer Science

b) Artificial Intelligence

c) Linguistics

d) All of the mentioned

Answer: d

Explanation: None.

258. NLP is concerned with the interactions between computers andhuman (natural) languages.

a) True

b) False

Answer: a

Explanation: NLP has its focus on understanding the human spoken/written language and converts that interpretation into machine understandable language.

259. What is the main challenge/s ofNLP?
a) Handling Ambiguity of Sentences
b) Handling Tokenization
c) Handling POS-Tagging
d) All of the mentioned
Answer: a
Explanation: There are enormousambiguity exists when processingnatural language.

260. Modern NLP algorithms are based on machine learning, especiallystatistical machine learning.
a) True
b) False
Answer: a
Explanation: None.

261. Choose form the following areaswhere NLP can be useful.
a) Automatic Text Summarization
b) Automatic Question-AnsweringSystems
c) Information Retrieval
d) All of the mentioned
Answer: d
Explanation: None.

262. What is Coreference Resolution?
a)　Anaphora Resolution
b)　Given a sentence or larger chunkof text, determine which words ("mentions") refer to the same objects ("entities")
c)　All of the mentioned
d)　None of the mentioned
Answer: b
Explanation: Anaphora resolution is aspecific type of coreference resolution.

263. What is Machine Translation?
a) Converts one human language toanother
b) Converts human language tomachine language
c) Converts any human language toEnglish
d) Converts Machine language tohuman language
Answer: a
Explanation: The best-known exampleof machine translation is googled translator.

264. The more general task of coreference resolution also includesidentifying so-called "bridging relationships" involving referringexpressions.
a) True
b) False
Answer: a
Explanation: Refer the definition ofCoreference Resolution.

265. What is MorphologicalSegmentation?
a) Does Discourse Analysis
b) Separate words into individual morphemes and identify the class ofthe morphemes
c) Is an extension of propositional logic
d) None of the mentioned
Answer: b
Explanation: None.

266. Autonomous Question/Answering systems are _
a) Expert Systems

b) Rule Based Expert Systems
c) Decision Tree Based Systems
d) All of the mentioned
Answer: d
Explanation: None.

267. Which of the following are theapplications of Expert systems?
a) Disease Diagnosis
b) Planning and Scheduling
c) Decision making
d) All of the mentioned
Answer: d Explanation: None.

268. What are the main componentsof the expert systems?
a) Inference Engine
b) Knowledge Base
c) Inference Engine & KnowledgeBase
d) None of the mentioned
Answer: c
Explanation: Look at the general architecture of rule based expertsystems.

269. There are primarily two modesfor an inference engine: forward chaining and backward chaining.
a) True
b) False
Answer: a
Explanation: None.

270. What among the following constitutes the representation of theknowledge in different forms?
a) Relational method where each factis set out systematically in columns
b) Inheritable knowledge where relational knowledge is made up ofobjects
c) Inferential knowledge
d) All of the mentioned
Answer: d Explanation: None.

271. What are Semantic Networks?
a) A way of representing knowledge
b) Data Structure
c) Data Type
d) None of the mentioned
Answer: a
Explanation: None.

272. Graph used to represent semantic network is_
a) Undirected graph
b) Directed graph
c) Directed Acyclic graph (DAG)
d) Directed complete graph
Answer: b
Explanation: Semantic Network is a directed graph consisting of vertices,which represent concepts and edges,which represent semantic relations between the concepts.

273. Which of the following are the Semantic Relations used in SemanticNetworks?
a) Meronymy
b) Holonymy
c) Hyponymy
d) All of the mentioned
Answer: d

Explanation: None.

274. What is Meronymy relation?
a) A is part of B
b) B has A as a part of itself
c) A is a kind of B
d) A is superordinate of B
Answer: a
Explanation: A meronym denotes aconstituent part of or a member ofsomething. That is,
"X" is a meronym of "Y" if Xs areparts of Y(s), or
"X" is a meronym of "Y" if Xs aremembers of Y(s).

275. What is Hypernym relation?
a) A is part of B
b) B has A as a part of itself
c) A is a kind of B
d) A is superordinate of B
Answer: d
Explanation: In linguistics, a hyponym is a word or phrase whose semantic field is included within that of another word, its hypernym (sometimes spelled hypernym outside of the natural language processing community). In simpler terms, a hyponym shares a type-of relationship with its hypernym.

276. What is Holonymy relation?
a) A is part of B
b) B has A as a part of itself
c) A is a kind of B
d) A is superordinate of B
Answer: b
Explanation: Holonymy (in Greek holon = whole and onoma = name) isa semantic relation. Holonymy defines the relationship between a term denoting the whole and a term denoting a part of, or a member of, the whole. That is,'X' is a holonym of 'Y' if Ys are partsof Xs, or 'X' is a holonym of 'Y' if Ys aremembers of Xs.

277. The basic inference mechanismin semantic network is to follow thelinks between the nodes.
a) True
b) False
Answer: a
Explanation: None.

278. There exists two way to inferusing semantic networks.
1) Intersection Search
2) Inheritance Search
a) True
b) False
Answer: a
Explanation: None.

279. The process by which the brain incrementally orders actions needed to complete a specific task is referredas_
a) Planning problem
b) Partial order planning
c) Total order planning
d) Both Planning problem & Partialorder planning
Answer: b
Explanation: Definition of partialorder planning.

280. To complete any task, the brainneeds to plan out the sequence by which to execute the behavior. One way the brain does this is with a partial-order plan.
a) True

b) False

Answer: a Explanation: None.

281. In partial order plan

A. Relationships between the actionsof the behavior are set prior to the actions

B. Relationships between the actionsof the behavior are not set until absolutely necessary

Choose the correct option.

a) A is true

b) B is true

c) Either A or B can be truedepending upon situation

d) Neither A nor B is true

Answer: a

Explanation: Relationship betweenbehavior and actions is establisheddynamically.

282. Partial-order planning exhibits the Principle of Least Commitment, which contributes to the efficiency ofthis planning system as a whole.

a) True

b) False

Answer: a

Explanation: None.

283. Following is/are the componentsof the partial order planning.

a) Bindings

b) Goal

c) Causal Links

d) All of the mentioned

Answer: d

Explanation: Bindings: The bindings ofthe algorithm are the connections between specific variables in the action. Bindings, as ordering, only occur when it is absolutely necessary. Causal Links: Causal links in the algorithm are those that categorically order actions. They are not the specific order (1,2,3) of the actions, rather the general order as in Action 2 must come somewhere after Action1, but before Action 2.

Plan Space: The plan space of the algorithm is constrained between itsstart and finish. The algorithm starts,producing the initial state and finishes when all parts of the goal is been achieved.

284. Partial-order planning is theopposite of total-order planning.

a) True

b) False

Answer: a

Explanation: Partial-order planning isthe opposite of total-order planning,in which actions are sequenced all atonce and for the entirety of the task at hand.

285. Sussman Anomaly illustrates aweakness of interleaved planning algorithm.

a) True

b) False

Answer: b

Explanation: Sussman Anomalyillustrates a weakness of non interleaved planning algorithm.

286. One the main drawback of thistype of planning system is that it requires a lot of computational powers at each node.

a) True

b) False

Answer: a

Explanation: None.

287. What are you predicating by thelogic: $\forall$x: $\exists$y: loyalto(x, y).

a) Everyone is loyal to someone

b) Everyone is loyal to all

c) Everyone is not loyal to someone

d) Everyone is loyal

Answer: a

Explanation: ᵛx denotes Everyone or all, and €y someone and loyal to is the proposition logic making map x toy.

288. A plan that describe how to takeactions in levels of increasing refinement and specificity is

a) Problem solving

b) Planning

c) Non-hierarchical plan

d) Hierarchical plan

Answer: d

Explanation: A plan that describes how to take actions in levels of increasing refinement and specificityis Hierarchical (e.g., "Do something" becomes the more specific "Go to work," "Do work," "Go home.") Mostplans are hierarchical in nature.

289. A constructive approach in which no commitment is made unlessit is necessary to do so, is

a) Least commitment approach

b) Most commitment approach

c) Nonlinear planning

d) Opportunistic planning

Answer: a

Explanation: Because we are not sureabout the outcome.

290. Uncertainty arises in the Wumpus world because the agent'ssensors give only_

a) Full & Global information

b) Partial & Global Information

c) Partial & local Information

d) Full & local information

Answer: c

Explanation: The Wumpus world is a grid of squares surrounded by walls, where each square can contain agents and objects. The agent (you) always starts in the lower left corner,a square that will be labeled [1, 1].

The agent's task is to find the gold, return to [1, 1] and climb out of the cave. Therefore, uncertainty is there as the agent gives partial and local information only. Global variable arenot goal specific problem solving.

291. What is the form of Fuzzy logic?

a) Two-valued logic

b) Crisp set logic

c) Many-valued logic

d) Binary set logic

Answer: c

Explanation: With fuzzy logic set membership is defined by certainvalue. Hence it could have many values to be in the set.

292. Traditional set theory is alsoknown as Crisp Set theory.

a) True

b) False

Answer: a

Explanation: Traditional set theory set membership is fixed or exact either the member is in the set or not. There is only two crisp values true or false. In case of fuzzy logic there are many values. With weightsay x the member is in the set.

293. The truth values of traditional set theory is_and thatof fuzzy set is_

a) Either 0 or 1, between 0 & 1

b) Between 0 & 1, either 0 or 1

c) Between 0 & 1, between 0 & 1

d) Either 0 or 1, either 0 or 1

Answer: a

Explanation: Refer the definition ofFuzzy set and Crisp set.

294. Fuzzy logic is extension of Crisp set with an extension of handling theconcept of Partial Truth.

a) True

b) False

Answer: a
Explanation: None.

295. The room temperature is hot. Here the hot (use of linguistic variable is used) can be representedby
a) Fuzzy Set
b) Crisp Set
c) Fuzzy & Crisp Set
d) None of the mentioned
Answer: a
Explanation: Fuzzy logic deals withlinguistic variables.

296. The values of the set membership is represented by
a) Discrete Set
b) Degree of truth
c) Probabilities
d) Both Degree of truth &Probabilities
Answer: b
Explanation: Both Probabilities and degree of truth ranges between 0 – 1.

297. Japanese were the first to utilizefuzzy logic practically on high-speed trains in Sendai.
a) True
b) False
Answer: a
Explanation: None.

298. Fuzzy Set theory defines fuzzyoperators. Choose the fuzzy operators from the following.
a) AND
b) OR
c) NOT
d) All of the mentioned
Answer: d
Explanation: The AND, OR, and NOToperators of Boolean logic exist in fuzzy logic, usually defined as the minimum, maximum, and complement;

299. There are also other operators,more linguistic in nature, called _ that can be applied tofuzzy set theory.
a) Hedges
b) Lingual Variable
c) Fuzz Variable
d) None of the mentioned
Answer: a
Explanation: None.

300. Fuzzy logic is usually represented as
a) IF-THEN-ELSE rules
b) IF-THEN rules
c) Both IF-THEN-ELSE rules & IF-THENrules
d) None of the mentioned
Answer: b
Explanation: Fuzzy set theory definesfuzzy operators on fuzzy sets. The problem in applying this is that the appropriate fuzzy operator may not be known. For this reason, fuzzy logicusually uses IF-THEN rules, or constructs that are equivalent, such as fuzzy associative matrices.
Rules are usually expressed in theform: IF variable IS property THEN action

301. _ is/are theway/s to represent uncertainty.
a) Fuzzy Logic
b) Probability
c) Entropy

d) All of the mentioned

Answer: d

Explanation: Entropy is amount ofuncertainty involved in data.

Represented by H(data).

302. _are algorithms that learn from their more complex environments (hence eco) to generalize, approximate and simplify solution logic.

a) Fuzzy Relational DB

b) Ecorithms

c) Fuzzy Set

d) None of the mentioned

Answer: c

Explanation: Local structure is usuallyassociated with linear rather than exponential growth in complexity.

303. Which of the following is an advantage of using an expert systemdevelopment tool?

a) imposed structure

b) knowledge engineering assistance

c) rapid prototyping

d) all of the mentioned

Answer: d

Explanation: None.

304. An AI system developed by Daniel Bobrow to read and solvealgebra word problems.

a) SHRDLU

b) SIMD

c) BACON

d) STUDENT

Answer: d

Explanation: None.

305. The "Turing Machine" showed that you could use a/an_ system to program any algorithmic task.

a) binary

b) electro-chemical

c) recursive

d) semantic

Answer: a Explanation: None.

306. MCC is investigating the improvement of the relationshipbetween people and computers through a technology called

a) computer-aided design

b) human factors

c) parallel processing

d) all of the mentioned

Answer: b

Explanation: None.

307. The first widely-used commercial form of Artificial Intelligence (Al) is being used in many popular products like microwave ovens, automobiles and plug in circuitboards for desktop PCs. It allows machines to handle vague information with a deftness that mimics human intuition. What is the name of this Artificial Intelligence?

a) Boolean logic

b) Human logic

c) Fuzzy logic

d) Functional logic

Answer: c

Explanation: None.

308. In his landmark book Cybernetics, Norbert Wiener suggested a way of modeling scientific phenomena using notenergy, but_

a) mathematics

b) intelligence

c) information

d) history

Answer: c

Explanation: None.

309. Input segments of AIprogramming contain(s)?

a) sound

b) smell

c) touch

d) none of the mentioned

Answer: d

Explanation: None.

310. Which of the following applications include in the StrategicComputing Program?

a) battle management

b) autonomous systems

c) pilot's associate

d) all of the mentioned

Answer: d

Explanation: None.

311. In LISP, the function evaluates <object> and assigns this value to theunevaluated <sconst>.

a) (constant <sconst> <object>)

b) (defconstant <sconst> <object>)

c) (eva <sconst> <object>)

d) (eva <object> <sconst>)

Answer: b

Explanation: None.

312. Factors which affect the performance of learner system doesnot include?

a) Representation scheme used

b) Training scenario

c) Type of feedback

d) Good data structures

Answer: d

Explanation: Factors which affect theperformance of learner system does not include good data structures.

313. Which of the following does notinclude different learning methods?

a) Memorization

b) Analogy

c) Deduction

d) Introduction

Answer: d

Explanation: Different learning methods include memorization,analogy and deduction.

314. Which of the following is themodel used for learning?

a) Decision trees

b) Neural networks

c) Propositional and FOL rules

d) All of the mentioned

Answer: d

Explanation: Decision trees, Neural networks, Propositional rules and FOLrules all are the models of learning.

315. Automated vehicle is anexample of_

a) Supervised learning

b) Unsupervised learning

c) Active learning

d) Reinforcement learning

Answer: a

Explanation: In automatic vehicle set of vision inputs and corresponding actions are available to learner henceit's an example of supervised learning.

316. Which of the following is anexample of active learning?

a) News Recommender system

b) Dust cleaning machine

c) Automated vehicle

d) None of the mentioned

Answer: a

Explanation: In active learning, not only the teacher is available but thelearner can ask suitable perception-action pair examples to improve performance.

317. In which of the following learning the teacher returns rewardand punishment to learner?

a) Active learning

b) Reinforcement learning

c) Supervised learning

d) Unsupervised learning

Answer: b

Explanation: Reinforcement learningis the type of learning in which teacher returns reward or punishment to learner.

318. Decision trees are appropriate for the problems where_

a) Attributes are both numeric andnominal

b) Target function takes on a discretenumber of values.

c) Data may have errors

d) All of the mentioned

Answer: d

Explanation: Decision trees can beused in all the conditions stated.

319. Which of the following is not anapplication of learning?

a) Data mining

b) WWW

c) Speech recognition

d) None of the mentioned

Answer: d

Explanation: All mentioned optionsare applications of learning.

320. Which of the following is thecomponent of learning system?

a) Goal

b) Model

c) Learning rules

d) All of the mentioned

Answer: d

Explanation: Goal, model, learningrules and experience are the components of learning system.

321. Which of the following is also called as exploratory learning?

a) Supervised learning

b) Active learning

c) Unsupervised learning

d) Reinforcement learning

Answer: c

Explanation: In unsupervised learning, no teacher is available hence it is also called unsupervisedlearning.

322. When talking to a speech recognition program, the program divides each second of your speechinto 100 separates

a) Codes
b) Phonemes
c) Samples
d) Words
Answer: c
Explanation: None.

323. Which term is used for describing the judgmental or commonsense part of problemsolving?
a) Heuristic
b) Critical
c) Value based
d) Analytical
Answer: a
Explanation: None.

324. described as "the mapping offunction onto form"?
a) Design
b) Distribution
c) Project management
d) Field service
Answer: a
Explanation: None.

325. Which kind of planning consistsof successive representations of different levels of a plan?
a) hierarchical planning
b) non-hierarchical planning
c) project planning
d) all of the mentioned
Answer: a
Explanation: None.

326. What was originally called the"imitation game" by its creator?
a) The Turing Test
b) LISP
c) The Logic Theorist
d) Cybernetics
Answer: a
Explanation: None.

327. ART (Automatic Reasoning Tool)is designed to be used on _
a) LISP machines
b) Personal computers
c) Microcomputers
d) All of the mentioned
Answer: a
Explanation: None.

328. Which particular generation of computers is associated with artificial intelligence?
a) Second
b) Fourth
c) Fifth
d) Third
Answer: c
Explanation: None.

329. Shaping teaching techniques tofit the learning patterns of individualstudents is the goal of
a) decision support

b) automatic programming

c) intelligent computer-assisted instruction

d) expert systems

Answer: c

Explanation: None.

330. Which of the following functionreturns t If the object is a symbol m LISP?

a) (* <object>)

b) (symbolp <object>)

c) (nonnumeric <object>)

d) (constantp <object>)

Answer: b

Explanation: None.

331. The symbols used in describingthe syntax of a programming language are_

a) 0

b) {}

c) ""

d) <>

Answer: d

Explanation: None.

332. How many kinds of mutation arefound in DNA which includes mutation of only one base?

a) 1

b) 2

c) 3

d) 4

Answer: b

Explanation: There are two kinds of mutation which is observed in the DNA that include only one base and are also known as point mutation. These mutations are transition where the mutation occurs chancing a purine to purine and pyrimidine to pyrimidine, and transversion where there purine is converted to purine and vice versa.

333. What is the overall rate at whichnew mutations arise spontaneously at any given site on the chromosome per round of replication?

a) ≈ 10-8 – 10-12

b) ≈ 10-7 – 10-9

c) ≈ 10-6 – 10-11

d) ≈ 10-5 – 10-10

Answer: c

Explanation: The overall rate at whichnew mutations arise spontaneously at any given site on the chromosome ranges from ≈ 10-6 – 10-11 per round of DNA replication. With some sites on the chromosomes being hot spots, mutations arise at a high frequency inthese sites.

334. The mutation occurs at a random basis within a genome.

a) True

b) False

Answer: b

Explanation: The mutation occurs at aparticular mutation prone region known as the hot spots. The hot spots are rich in di- or tri- nucleotide repeat sequences known as microsatellites.

335. What is the dinucleotidesequence of microsatellites?

a) CA

b) AT

c) CC

d) GC

Answer: a

Explanation: Microsatellites involves the repeats of the dinucleotide sequence of CA. the CA repeat is found at many widely scattered sitesin the genome of humans and other eukaryotes.

336. By which process miss- incorporated base can change into apermanent mutation?
a) Replication
b) Transcription
c) Translation
d) Transposition
Answer: a
Explanation: A potential mutation may be introduced by misincorporation in any round of replication. In the next round of replication if the mutation is not repaired it gets permanently incorporated in the DNA sequence.

337. Detection of mismatches and fidelity of replication is maintained bymutation repair system.
a) True
b) False
Answer: a
Explanation: Proofreading by the polymerase is not always perfect andsome mismatches may escape the detection which can become a permanent mutation if not corrected. This fidelity check is done by the mutation repair system; more precisely mismatch repair system, of the cell itself ensuring that perfect matches occur in the complementarystrands.

338. How many steps are required toattain mismatch repair?
a) 1
b) 3
c) 2
d) 4
Answer: c
Explanation: The mismatch repair system involves two steps. The first step involves the scanning of the genome for mismatches. The secondstep ensures the correction of mismatch that has occurred in the genome.

339. What is the name of the computer program that simulates thethought processes of human beings?
a) Human logic
b) Expert reason
c) Expert system
d) Personal information
Answer: c
Explanation: None.

340. What is the name of the computer program that contains the distilled knowledge of an expert?
a) Database management system
b) Management information System
c) Expert system
d) Artificial intelligence
Answer: c
Explanation: None.

341. Claude Shannon described theoperation of electronic switching circuits with a system of mathematical logic called _
a) LISP
b) XLISP
c) Neural networking
d) Boolean algebra
Answer: c
Explanation: None.

342. A computer program that contains expertise in a particulardomain is called?
a) intelligent planner
b) automatic processor
c) expert system
d) operational symbolizer

Answer: c
Explanation: None.

343. What is the term used fordescribing the judgmental or commonsense part of problemsolving?
a) Heuristic
b) Critical
c) Value based
d) Analytical
Answer: a
Explanation: None.

344. What was originally called the"imitation game" by its creator?
a) The Turing Test
b) LISP
c) The Logic Theorist
d) Cybernetics
Answer: a
Explanation: None.

345. A series of Artificial Intelligence systems, developed by Pat Langley toexplore the role of heuristics in scientific discovery is_
a) RAMD
b) BACON
c) MIT
d) DU
Answer: b
Explanation: None.

346. A.M. turing developed a technique for determining whether a computer could or could not demonstrate the artificial Intelligence, Presently, this techniqueis called
a) Turing Test
b) Algorithm
c) Boolean Algebra
d) Logarithm
Answer: a
Explanation: None.

347. Which of the following, is a component of an expert system?
a) inference engine
b) knowledge base
c) user interface
d) all of the mentioned
Answer: d
Explanation: None.

348. A computer vision techniquethat relies on image templates is knowledge base contain information _ in the form of
a) parameters
b) contexts
c) production rules
d) all of the mentioned
Answer: d
Explanation: None.

349. The explanation facility of an
a) edge detection
b) binocular vision
c) model-based vision

d) robot vision
Answer: c
Explanation: None.

350. In LISP, the function (copy-list<list>)
a) returns a new list that is equal to <list> by copying the top-levelelement of <list>
b) returns the length of <list>
c) returns t if <list> is empty
d) all of the mentioned
Answer: a
Explanation: None.

351. Who is the "father" of artificialintelligence?
a) Fisher Ada
b) John McCarthy
c) Allen Newell
d) Alan Turning
Answer: a
Explanation: None.

352. In 1985, the famous chess player David Levy beat a world champion chess program in four straight games by using orthodox moves that confused the program. What was thename of the chess program?
a) Kaissa
b) CRAY BLITZ
c) Golf
d) DIGDUG
Answer: b
Explanation: None.

353. A process that is repeated,evaluated, and refined is called _
a) diagnostic
b) descriptive
c) interpretive
d) iterative
Answer: d
Explanation: None.

354. Visual clues that are helpful in computer vision include
a) color and motion
b) depth and texture
c) height and weight
d) color and motion, depth andtexture
Answer: d
Explanation: None.

355. A heuristic is a way of trying expert system may be used to _
a) construct a diagnostic model
b) expedite the debugging process
c) explain the system's reasoningprocess
d) expedite the debugging process &explain the system's reasoning process
Answer: d
Explanation: None.

356. A* algorithm is based on
a) Breadth-First-Search
b) Depth-First –Search
c) Best-First-Search

d) Hill climbing

Answer: c

Explanation: Best-first-search is givingthe idea of optimization and quick choose of path, and all these characteristic lies in A* algorithm.

357. The search strategy the uses a problem specific knowledge is knownas_

a) Informed Search

b) Best First Search

c) Heuristic Search

d) All of the mentioned

Answer: d

Explanation: The problem specific knowledge is also known as Heuristics and Best-First search usessome heuristic to choose the best node for expansion.

358. Uninformed search strategiesare better than informed search strategies.

a) True

b) False

Answer: a

Explanation: Informed search strategies uses some problem specificknowledge, hence more efficient to finding goals.

359. Best-First search is a type ofinformed search, which uses _ to choose thebest next node for expansion.

a) Evaluation function returninglowest evaluation

b) Evaluation function returninghighest evaluation

c) Evaluation function returninglowest & highest evaluation

d) None of them is applicable

Answer: a

Explanation: Best-first search is an instance of the general TREE-SEARCH or GRAPH-SEARCH algorithm in which a node is selected for expansion based on an evaluation function, f (n). Traditionally, the node with the lowest evaluation is selected for expansion, because the evaluation measures distance to the goal.

360. Best-First search can be

a) Queue

b) Stack

c) Priority Queue

d) Circular Queue

Answer: c

Explanation: Best-first search can beimplemented within our general search framework via a priority queue, a data structure that will maintain the fringe in ascending order of f-values.

361. The name "best-first search" is avenerable but inaccurate one. After all, if we could really expand the bestnode first, it would not be a search atall; it would be a straight march to the goal. All we can do is choose the node that appears to be best according to the evaluation function.

a) True

b) False

Answer: a

Explanation: If the evaluation function is exactly accurate, then this will indeed be the best node; in reality, the evaluation function will sometimes be off, and can lead the search astray.

362. Greedy search strategy choosesthe node for expansion in

a) Shallowest

b) Deepest

c) The one closest to the goal node

d) Minimum heuristic cost

Answer: c

Explanation: Sometimes minimum heuristics can be used, sometimes maximum heuristics function can be used. It depends upon the applicationon which the algorithm is applied.

363. What is the evaluation functionin greedy approach?
a) Heuristic function
b) Path cost from start node tocurrent node
c) Path cost from start node to current node + Heuristic cost
d) Average of Path cost from start node to current node and Heuristiccost
Answer: a
Explanation: Greedy best-first search3 tries to expand the node thatis closest to the goal, on the grounds that this is likely to lead to a solution quickly. Thus, it evaluates nodes by using just the heuristic function: f (n) = h(n).

364. What is the space complexity of Greedy search?
a) O(b)
b) O(bl)
c) O(m)
d) O(bm)
Answer: d
Explanation: O(bm) is the space complexity where b is the branchingfactor and m is the maximum depthof the search tree. Since this algorithm resembles the DFS.

365. What is the evaluation functionin A* approach?
a) Heuristic function
b) Path cost from start node tocurrent node
c) Path cost from start node to current node + Heuristic cost
d) Average of Path cost from start node to current node and Heuristiccost
Answer: c
Explanation: The most widely-knownform of best-first search is called A* search. It evaluates nodes by combining g(n), the cost to reach thenode, and h(n.), the cost to get from the node to the goal: f(n) = g(n) + h(n). Since g(n) gives the path cost from the start node to node n, and h(n) is the estimated cost of the cheapest path from n to the goal.

366. A* is optimal if h(n) is an admissible heuristic-that is, providedthat h(n) never underestimates the cost to reach the goal.
a) True
b) False
Answer: a
Explanation: A* is optimal if h(n) is anadmissible heuristic-that is, provided that h(n) never overestimates the cost to reach the goal. Refer both theexample from the book for better understanding of the algorithms.

367. The process by which the brain orders actions needed to complete a specific task is referred as ________________
a) Planning problem
b) Partial order planning
c) Total order planning
d) Both Planning problem & Partialorder planning
Answer: d
Explanation: None.

368. The famous spare tire problemor Scheduling classes for bunch of students or Air cargo transport are the best example of
a) Planning problem
b) Partial Order planning problem
c) Total order planning
d) None of the mentioned
Answer: a Explanation: None.

369. To eliminate the inaccuracy problem in planning problem or partial order planning problem we can use __data structure/s.
a) Stacks
b) Queue
c) BST (Binary Search Tree)
d) Planning Graphs
Answer: d

Explanation: A planning graph can be used to give better heuristicestimates.

370. Planning graphs consists of
a) a sequence of levels
b) a sequence of levels which corresponds to time steps in the plan
c) a sequence of actions which corresponds to the state of the system
d) none of the mentioned
Answer: b
Explanation: Planning graphs is a sequence of levels, which corresponds to time steps in the planwhere level 0 is the initial state at start.

371. Planning graphs works only forprepositional planning problems.
a) True
b) False
Answer: a
Explanation: Planning graphs work only for propositional planning problems-ones with no variables. Both STRIPS and ADL representationscan be propositionalized. For problems with large numbers and objects, this could result in a very substantial blowup in the number ofaction schemata.

372. _algorithms is used to extract the plan directly fromthe planning graph, rather than usinggraph to provide heuristic.
a) BFS/DFS
b) A*
c) Graph-Plan
d) Greedy
Answer: c
Explanation: None.

373. Planning problem can be described as a propositional logic.
a) True
b) False
Answer: a
Explanation: Yes, The approach we take is based on testing the satisfiability of a logical sentence rather than on proving a theorem. We will be finding models of propositional sentences that look likethis: Initial state $/\backslash$ all possible actiondescriptions $/\backslash$ goal.

374. What is the other name of eachplan resulted in partial order planning?
a) Polarization
b) Linearization
c) Solarization
d) None of the mentioned
Answer: b
Explanation: Each and every total order plan is also called as linearization of the partial-order plan.

375. What are the two major aspectswhich combines AI Planning problem?
a) Search & Logic
b) Logic & Knowledge Based Systems
c) FOL & Logic
d) Knowledge Based Systems
Answer: a
Explanation: None.

376. _algorithm translatesa planning problem in to prepositional axioms.
a) GraphPlan
b) SatPlan
c) Greedy
d) None of the mentioned
Answer: b

Explanation: The SATPLAN algorithm translates a planning problem into propositional axioms and applies a satisfiability algorithm to find a modelthat corresponds a valid plan.

377. _planning allowsthe agent to take advice from the domain designer in the form of decomposition rules.
a) GraphPlan
b) Hierarchical task network (HTN)
c) SatPlan
d) None of the mentioned
Answer: b
Explanation: None.

378. Standard planning algorithmsassumes environment to be
a) Deterministic
b) Fully observable
c) Single agent
d) Stochastic
Answer: a
Explanation: It assumes complete and correct information, deterministic and fully-observable environment, which many domains violates.

379. A re-planning agent uses execution monitoring and splices inrepairs as needed.
a) True
b) False
Answer: a
Explanation: None.

380. Incorrect information results inunsatisfied preconditions for actionsand plans_detects violations of the preconditions for successful completion of the plan.
a) Conditional Plan
b) Conformant Planning
c) Execution monitoring
d) Both Conditional Plan & Executionmonitoring
Answer: c
Explanation: None.

381. What is the extraction of themeaning of utterance?
a) Syntactic
b) Semantic
c) Pragmatic
d) None of the mentioned
Answer: b
Explanation: Semantic analysis is used to extract the meaning from thegroup of

382. What is used to augment a grammar for arithmetic expressionwith semantics?
a) Notation
b) DCG notation
c) Constituent
d) All of the mentioned
Answer: b
Explanation: DCG notation is used to augment a grammar for arithmetic expression with semantics and it is used to build a parse tree.

383. What can't be done in thesemantic interpretation?
a) Logical term
b) Complete logical sentence
c) Both Logical term & Completelogical sentence
d) None of the mentioned

Answer: c

Explanation: Some kind of sentencein the semantic interpretation can't be logical term nor a complete logicalsentence.

384. How many verb tenses are therein the English language?

a) 1

b) 2

c) 3

d) 4

Answer: c

Explanation: There are three types oftenses available in english language are past, present and future.

385. Which is used to mediate between syntax and semantics?

a) Form

b) Intermediate form

c) Grammer

d) All of the mentioned

Answer: b

Explanation: None.

386. What is meant by quasi-logicalform?

a) Sits between syntactic and logicalform

b) Logical connectives

c) All of the mentioned

d) None of the mentioned

Answer: a

Explanation: It can be translated intoa regular first-order logical sentence, so that it Sits between syntactic and logical form.

387. How many types of quantification are available inartificial intelligence?

a) 1

b) 2

c) 3

d) 4

Answer: b

Explanation: There are two types ofquantification available. They are universal and existential.

388. What kind of interpretation isdone by adding context-dependant information?

a) Semantic

b) Syntactic

c) Pragmatic

d) None of the mentioned

Answer: c

Explanation: None.

389. How can states of units beupdated in hopfield model?

a) synchronously

b) asynchronously

c) synchronously and asynchronously

d) none of the mentioned

Answer: c

Explanation: States of units be updated synchronously and asynchronously in hopfield model.

390. What is synchronous update inhopfield model?

a) all units are updatedsimultaneously

b) a unit is selected at random and itsnew state is computed

c) a predefined unit is selected and itsnew state is computed

d) none of the mentioned

Answer: a

Explanation: In synchronous update,all units are updated simultaneously.

391. What is asynchronous update inhopfield model?
a) all units are updatedsimultaneously
b) a unit is selected at random and itsnew state is computed
c) a predefined unit is selected and itsnew state is computed
d) none of the mentioned
Answer: b
Explanation: In asynchronous update,a unit is selected at random and its new state is computed.

392. Asynchronous update ensures that the next state is atmost unit hamming distance from current state,is that true?
a) yes
b) no
Answer: a
Explanation: Asynchronous update ensures that the next state is at mostunit hamming distance from current state.

393. If pattern is to be stored, thenwhat does stable state should haveupdated value of?
a) current sate
b) next state
c) both current and next state
d) none of the mentioned
Answer: a
Explanation: Stable state should haveupdated value of current sate.

394. For symmetric weights thereexist?
a) basins of attraction correspondingto energy minimum
b) false wells
c) fluctuations in energy landscape
d) none of he mentioned
Answer: a
Explanation: For symmetric weightsthere exist a stable point.

395. If connections are not symmetricthen basins of attraction may correspond to?
a) oscillatory regions
b) stable regions
c) chaotic regions
d) oscillatory or chaotic regions
Answer: d
Explanation: If connections are not symmetric then basins of attractionmay correspond to oscillatory or chaotic regions.

396. For analysis of storage capacitywhat are the conditions imposed on hopfield model?
a) symmetry of weights
b) asynchronous update
c) symmetry of weights andasynchronous update
d) none of the mentioned
Answer: c
Explanation: For analysis of storage capacity, symmetry of weights and asynchronous update conditions are imposed on hopfield model.

397. Reinforcement learning is alsoknown as learning with critic?
a) yes
b) no
Answer: a
Explanation: Since this is evaluative ¬ instructive.

398. How many types of reinforcement learning exist?
a) 2

b) 3

c) 4

d) 5

Answer: b

Explanation: Fixed credit assignment,probablistic credit assignment, temporal credit assignment.

399. Which one of the following is true at any valid state in shift-reduceparsing?

a) At the bottom we find the prefixes

b) None of the mentioned

c) Stack contains only viable prefixes

d) Stack consists of viable prefixes

Answer: c

Explanation: The prefixes on the stackof a shift-reduce parser are called viable prefixes.

400. Match the following.

List-I	List-II
A. Lexical analysis	1. Graph coloring
B. Parsing	2. DFA minimization
C. Register allocation	3. Post-order traversal
D. Expression evaluation	4. Production tree

a) A – 2, B – 3, C – 1, D – 4

b) A – 2, B – 1, C – 4, D – 3

c) A – 2, B – 4, C – 1, D – 3

d) A – 2, B – 3, C – 4, D – 1

Answer: c

Explanation: The entire column an items matches the Column B items ina certain way.

401. Which of the following pairs isthe most powerful?

a) SLR, LALR

b) Canonical LR ,LALR

c) SLR canonical LR

d) LALR canonical LR

Answer: c

Explanation parser algorithm issimple.

402. Consider the following grammar G.

$$S \rightarrow F \mid H$$
$$F \rightarrow p \mid c$$
$$H \rightarrow d \mid c$$

Which one is true?

S1: All strings generated by G can beparsed with help of LL (1).

S2: All strings generated by G can beparsed with help of LR (1).

a) Only S1

b) Only S2

c) Both S1 & S2

d) None of the mentioned

Answer: d

Explanation: There is ambiguity as thestring can be derived in 2 possible ways.

First Leftmost Derivation

$S \rightarrow F$

$F \rightarrow c$

Second Leftmost Derivation

$S \rightarrow H$

$H \rightarrow c$.

403. What is the maximum number of reduce moves that can be taken bya bottom-up parser for a grammar with no epsilon- and unit-production to parse a string with n tokens?

a) n/2

b) n-1

c) 2n-1

d) 2^n

Answer: b

Explanation: The moves are n-1.

404. Which is not a property ofrepresentation of knowledge?

a) Representational Verification

b) Representational Adequacy

c) Inferential Adequacy

d) Inferential Efficiency

Answer: a

Explanation: None.

405. Which is not Familiar Connectives in First Order Logic?

a) and

b) iff

c) or

d) not

Answer: d

Explanation: "not" is coming underpropositional logic and is thereforenot a connective.

406. Inference algorithm is completeonly if_

a) It can derive any sentence

b) It can derive any sentence that isan entailed version

c) It is truth preserving

d) It can derive any sentence that isan entailed version & It is truth preserving

Answer: d

Explanation: None.

407. An inference algorithm that derives only entailed sentences iscalled sound or truth-preserving.

a) True

b) False

Answer: a

Explanation: None.

408. A network with named nodes and labeled arcs that can be used to represent certain natural language grammars to facilitate parsing.

a) Tree Network

b) Star Network

c) Transition Network

d) Complete Network

Answer: c

Explanation: None.

409. Computers normally solve problem by breaking them down intoa series of yes-or-no decisions represented by 1s and 0s. What is thename of the logic that allows computers to assign numerical valuesthat fail somewhere between 0 and 1?
a) Human logic
b) Fuzzy logic
c) Boolean logic
d) Operational logic
Answer: b
Explanation: None.

410. The company that grew out ofresearch at the MIT AI lab is
a) AI corp
b) LMI
c) Symbolics
d) Both LMI & Symbolics
Answer: d
Explanation: None.

411. Which technique is beinginvestigated as an approach toautomatic programming?
a) generative CAI
b) specification by example
c) non-hierarchical planning
d) all of the mentioned
Answer: b
Explanation: None.

412. The primary method that peopleuse to sense their environment is ________________
a) reading
b) writing
c) speaking
d) seeing
Answer: d
Explanation: None.

413. The Newell and Simon programthat proved theorems of Principal Mathematical was
a) Elementary Perceiver
b) General Problem Solver
c) Logic Theorist
d) Boolean Algebra
Answer: c
Explanation: None.

414. Using logic to represent and reason we can represent knowledge about the world with facts and rules.
a) True
b) False
Answer: a
Explanation: None.

415. Uncertainty arises in the wumpus world because the agent'ssensors give only
a) Full & Global information
b) Partial & Global Information
c) Partial & local Information
d) Full & local information
Answer: c
Explanation: The Wumpus world is a grid of squares surrounded by walls, where each square can contain agents and objects. The agent (you) always starts in the lower left corner,a square that will be labeled [1, 1].
The agent's task is to find the gold, return to [1, 1] and climb out of the cave. So uncertainty is there as the agent gives partial and local information only. Global variable arenot goal specific problem solving.

416. A Hybrid Bayesian network contains
a) Both discrete and continuousvariables
b) Only Discrete variables
c) Only Discontinuous variable
d) Both Discrete and Discontinuousvariable
Answer: a
Explanation: To specify a Hybrid network, we have to specify two new kinds of distributions: the conditional distribution for continuous variables given discrete or continuous parents, and the conditional distribution for a discrete variable given continuous parents.

417. How is Fuzzy Logic different from conventional control methods?
a) IF and THEN Approach
b) FOR Approach
c) WHILE Approach
d) DO Approach
Answer: a
Explanation: FL incorporates a simple, rule-based IF X AND Y THEN Z approach to a solving control problem rather than attempting to model a system mathematically.

418. If a hypothesis says it should bepositive, but in fact it is negative, wecall it
a) A consistent hypothesis
b) A false negative hypothesis
c) A false positive hypothesis
d) A specialized hypothesis
Answer: c
Explanation: Consistent hypothesis gowith examples, If the hypothesis says it should be negative but in fact it is positive, it is false negative. If a hypothesis says it should be positive, but in fact it is negative, it is false positive. In a specialized hypothesis we need to have certain restrict or special conditions.

419. The primitives in probabilisticreasoning are random variables.
a) True
b) False
Answer: a
Explanation: The primitives in probabilistic reasoning are randomvariables. Just like primitives in return to [1, 1] and climb out of the cave. So uncertainty is there as the agent gives partial and local information only. Global variable arenot goal specific problem solving.

420. A constructive approach in which no commitment is made unlessit is necessary to do so is
a) Least commitment approach
b) Most commitment approaches
c) Nonlinear planning
d) Opportunistic planning
Answer: a
Explanation: Because we are not sure about the outcome.

421. Which is true for Decision theory?
a) Decision Theory = Probability theory + utility theory
b) Decision Theory = Inference theory + utility theory
c) Decision Theory = Uncertainty +utility theory
d) Decision Theory = Probability theory + preference
Answer: c
Explanation: The Wumpus world is a grid of squares surrounded by walls, where each square can contain agents and objects. The agent (you) always starts in the lower left corner,a square that will be labeled [1, 1].

422. The agent's task is to find the gold,
a) Least commitment approach

b) Most commitment approach

c) Nonlinear planning

d) Opportunistic planning

Answer: a

Explanation: Because we are not sureabout the outcome.

423. How many types of recognitionare there in artificial intelligence?

a) 1

b) 2

c) 3

d) 4

Answer: c

Explanation: The three types of recognition are biometric identification, content-based image retrieval and handwriting recognition.

424. Which provides a framework forstudying object recognition?

a) Learning

b) Unsupervised learning

c) Supervised learning

d) None of the mentioned

Answer: c

Explanation: Supervised learning orpattern classification provides a framework for studying object recognition.

www.ingramcontent.com/pod-product-compliance
Lightning Source LLC
Chambersburg PA
CBHW060115120726
48003CB00009B/2643